Black Child, White Child

Black Child, White Child

The Development of Racial Attitudes

Judith D. R. Porter

Harvard University Press, Cambridge, Massachusetts

To Daniel and Rebecca

"Look back
The color of everyone's shadow is black."

Ann McGovern, *Black Is Beautiful*

Preface

"Our nation is moving towards two societies, one black, one white, separate and unequal." With these words, the Kerner Commission attempted to alert the American people to the grave racial situation in this country. Segregation, prejudice, discrimination, and their effects are not limited to adults, however. The complex of attitudes and behavior surrounding black-white relations reaches down to the youngest age levels. I undertook a study of the genesis of prejudice and its effects with the hope that this knowledge would provide a foundation for changing these attitudes.

In its original form, the material in this book was presented as a doctoral dissertation in sociology for Harvard University. I wish to thank the National Science Foundation for their support during the period in which this research was conducted. I am greatly indebted to Dr. Thomas Pettigrew, the director of the dissertation, for his time and guidance. His constant encouragement throughout my graduate and professional career are much appreciated.

I am also indebted to Dr. Robin Williams of Cornell University, who was the advisor of the master's dissertation which became the pre-test for this study. The late Dr. Gordon Allport's helpful comments were also much appreciated.

I would like to express gratitude to J. Michael Ross for his assistance in data analysis and for his numerous helpful suggestions on the research. I am also indebted to Sarajane Heidt and Martin Wenglinsky for their critical reading of this manuscript.

Many other persons were also helpful during the course of this study. My interviewers deserve thanks for the hours they spent in collection of the data. I would also like to thank the many teachers, nursery school directors, and especially the children, whose cooperation made this research possible. I am also grateful to Marlene Clawar for typing the manuscript.

Finally, I would like to express my sincerest thanks to my husband, Gerald, for the support and encouragement he has given me throughout the preparation of this work. At every stage of the research, from building doll houses to processing data, his help has been invaluable.

Judith Porter

Bryn Mawr College
June 1970

Contents

Appendices

Tables

Figures

Black Child, White Child

"I don't like colored people." "He's lazy because he's colored." Racial attitudes like these are far from uncommon in American society. The only factor that distinguishes the above statements is that they were made by preschool-age children, the former comment by a five-year-old white and the latter by a four-year-old black.[1] The general public might be surprised to find that expressions of this type come from such young children, but numerous studies do in fact suggest that racial attitudes are learned during the preschool years.

Although widely accepted by social scientists now, this conclusion has not always predominated. Previously, sociologists considered that racial attitudes, based on "consciousness of kind," were innate rather than learned. In 1896 Giddings suggested that "our conduct towards those whom we feel to be most like ourselves is instinctively and rationally different from our conduct towards others whom we believe to be less like ourselves." W. I. Thomas in 1904 also stated that "race prejudice is an instinct originating in the tribal stage of society," but he felt that this instinct could be modified.[2] At the opposite end of the spectrum, in the Yale child development studies of 1946, Drs. Arnold Gesell and Frances Ilg suggest that although racial attitudes are learned, "prior to the teens, children tend to be catholic and cosmopolitan in their interracial contacts." They also imply that there is little interest in or comment about race until after ten years.[3]

Prior to 1950, there were a few empirical studies which indicated that both of these positions were incorrect. However, it was not until the Supreme Court desegregation proceedings of the early 1950's that interest in the genesis and development of racial attitudes was reactivated. Kenneth and Mamie Clark's studies of Negro children were cited in a footnote to the Supreme Court desegregation decision of 1954 and began to receive widespread attention. Mary Ellen Goodman's *Race Awareness in Young Children*, and numerous articles by others, indicated that both black and white children as young as three or four years are learning of the existence of racial differences and may even have a high degree of affect connected with racial matters. The above research has also suggested that these racial attitudes have negative effects on the self-esteem of black children.

These general conclusions are by now accepted by most social scientists. But there are many specific questions still to be answered. One area which has been inadequately investigated concerns the effect of sociocultural variables on developing racial preferences. We have no clear picture of the influence of social class, age, sex, contact with the opposite race, and shade of skin color on the formation of racial attitudes in young children. We also need more information on the influence of these incipient attitudes on actual interaction patterns with children of the opposite race. In addition, we have no comprehensive understanding of the effect of these racial preferences on the child's self-esteem; two of the important dimensions of self-esteem which must be investigated here are the child's feelings about himself as a member of a racial group and his basic feelings of personal worth. Because of widespread negative stereotypes about blacks in American society, it is particularly crucial to study the interrelationship of these two components of self-concept for black children. However, existing research presents an incomplete picture of how these dimensions vary among subgroups of the black community.

Although scattered data do exist on all of these issues, studies in this area have been characterized by inadequate methods and poor controls, and the results have on the whole been contradictory and confusing. One of the major reasons why existing research has not provided more clarification of these questions is the problem of the measurement of children's racial attitudes. In a sample of preschool children, many youngsters may be either unwilling or unable to speak adequately because of their age. Poor verbalization becomes a particularly important factor to consider when a population of young lower-class children is tested. Thus, the method of data collection cannot rely heavily on verbal production. Of course, nonverbal techniques can be developed, but then interpretation of results often becomes difficult. Many of the techniques used to measure racial preferences involve simple physical responses, like choosing or pointing on a doll-play test.

A response of this type may be interpreted in racial terms by the investigator but may mean something quite different to the child; if the subject will not or cannot provide verbal clues concerning the reason for his choice, the investigator is left in a quandary. Of course, verbal cues may not always be accurate indicators of real feelings, but if the investigator is able to utilize verbal probes, he may at least collect additional evidence upon which to make inferences.

Although the problems raised by poor verbalization are common to the testing of young children generally, measurement of racial attitudes is especially confusing because the investigator often does not know whether the child is even aware of race as a social category. Responses thus cannot be interpreted as true racial attitudes until racial awareness is first investigated, a difficult endeavor in itself. Determining the effect of these attitudes on self-esteem raises even further problems of interpretation and measurement.

In addition to these basic difficulties, many of the earlier and best-known studies in this area were done prior to the development of current sophistication in experimental design. Interpretation of this material is hampered by lack of adequate control groups; for instance, social class is a factor which is rarely held constant in this research, and this is one variable that can theoretically be expected to affect responses greatly among both black and white children.

If these obstacles can be circumvented to some extent, research on the formation of racial attitudes and their effect on self-esteem and interaction can provide valuable information for both theory and pragmatic application. These data can add to existing literature on the sociological correlates of attitudes and can also elucidate the relationship between attitudes and actual behavior. Theories concerning the effects of racism on black personality would also benefit from this type of study.

Research in this field is highly relevant to public policy. The federal government has already shown interest in the effect of social factors on the growth and development of preschool-age children. President Nixon has even stated that "there is no single ideal to which this administration is more committed than to the enriching of a child's first five years of life."[4] Federal and local education programs for this age group already exist, and new ones are being planned. Data on the genesis of racial preferences and their effect on personality can provide information which has extreme importance for these types of programs; for instance, the curriculum of Project Headstart and questions concerning the advisability of school integration for young children are two areas to which these results would be applicable. The President has recently proposed day care centers for children of working welfare mothers. If these centers are indeed to be devoted to "the development of vigorous young minds and bodies,"[5] as the President suggests, information about racial attitude development and its effects are some of the factors that should be taken into consideration in program planning.

This book reports the results of a study of two interconnected problems. One emphasizes the effect of sociocultural factors on the formation and content of preschool-age children's racial preferences. Specifically, I present empirical evidence on variations in attitudes due to age, sex, social class, intergroup contact, and shade of skin color (for Negroes). In addition to a discussion of the formation and content of attitudes for children of both races, the related issue of possible effects of these preferences on the Negro child's self-esteem is explored. This second problem, closely connected to the first, arises from the fact that the attitudes that the black child internalizes and the objective factors to which he is exposed define him as the occupant of a negatively evaluated social status. Consequently, for Negroes I also studied the influence of racial evaluations on various components of the self-concept, and I saw that this effect varies among subgroups of the black population.

The research presented in this book was done in the Boston, Massachusetts, area during the twelve-month period of 1965. This raises the question whether data collected in the middle sixties before the advent of "black power" are still relevant to the current racial situation. This issue is particularly salient for the black population. It is here that the greatest changes may be expected to have occurred. On the basis of other evidence, I believe that by and large my findings are still applicable to the present scene. A study similar to mine was conducted in the summer of 1967 in Newark, New Jersey.[6] This particular summer was characterized by rioting in numerous cities, and by this time the new black cultural and political movements in the North were more clearly established than they were in 1965. However, the results of the study were generally similar to my data for black children as well as for whites. In addition, it seems to be black youth in colleges and on ghetto streets who are at present the most militant.[7] The children of this generation are the ones who should show the greatest effects of the movement toward black power and black pride, but there is not now a significantly large enough population of these children who are old enough to be tested.

For these reasons and others to be discussed later, I feel that it is as yet too early for really large-scale changes to have occurred in my findings for either race; however, it does appear that some important new trends may be developing. After presentation of my results, I suggest hypotheses concerning the possible nature of these trends and suggest how they might be studied. It is important to remember, however, that any changes which have already occurred can be understood largely as a reaction to the situation described here.

The book is divided into four sections. Section one contains a description of the mechanisms of racial attitude transmission and includes a critical review of previous research. In Section two, the experimental design is presented; I then deal with the influence of several important variables on the formation of racial attitudes. In Section three, the effects of these attitudes on self-esteem and interaction are described. I conclude in Section four by discussing the implications of my findings for theory, for research, and for public policy.

One The Acquisition of Racial Attitudes

1 Mechanisms of Racial Attitude Transmission

Most of this book is concerned with how racial attitudes actually differ among subgroups of children. The way these developing preferences affect the youngster's self-esteem and interaction patterns is also discussed. But before beginning, it is necessary to delineate the mechanisms by which these racial feelings are actually transmitted to the young child. This process of transmission involves both significant others in the child's environment and his cognitive and emotional development. Thus the emphasis in this chapter is on the general means by which children become aware both of racial categories and of the cultural evaluations attached to them. Following presentation of some important definitions and underlying assumptions, mechanisms which transmit racial knowledge and attitudes are described.

The Nature of Prejudice

David Krech and Richard Crutchfield[1] propose a definition of attitudes which stresses the interrelationship of several important components. They describe attitudes as systems which include beliefs about an object, feelings towards them, and dispositions to respond to them. Racial prejudice is a particular type of attitude. It concerns racial or ethnic groups and is "based upon a faulty and inflexible generalization. It may be felt or expressed. It may be directed toward a (racial or ethnic) group as a whole or toward an individual because he is a member of that group."[2] No one can avoid the processes of prejudging or generalizing, of course, since the human mind must think with the aid of concepts or categories whose content resembles an oversimplification of the world of experience. But racial prejudices add to these ethnic categorizations an additional component of rigidity, error, and hostility.

There are different ways of analyzing the causes of these racially prejudiced attitudes. I have divided the causes into three major categories, each dealing with a slightly different facet of the problem. This approach is influenced by elements of Talcott Parsons' earlier work, in which he divides human action into three parts: culture, social structure, and personality. Culture is a shared set of symbols which provides both ways of orienting to others and the standards which are applied in evaluative processes. The social structure is organized around the problems inherent in or arising from the social interaction of many individuals. And the third component, personality, is the set of orientations and motivations of one individual actor. Although these three dimensions are conceptually distinct, they are still interrelated. Cultural patterns are institutionalized in the social structure and help organize the behavior of adult members of society. These cultural standards are also internalized in personality through the process of socialization.[3] This division into culture, social structure, and personality provides a useful analytical device for understanding the nature of prejudice.

The cultural explanation of prejudice, stressing the presence of racial attitudes in the cultural tradition, regards the individual as a passive entity who absorbs these common evaluations from the environment. The individual learns to dislike certain groups of people in the same manner that he learns other prevalent cultural norms and values. This "atmosphere" theory of prejudice is in part accurate. The Kerner Commission Report[4] directly pinpoints the widespread existence of "white racism" in American culture, and empirical studies substantiate this conclusion. Numerous investigations, for instance, find general agreement on social distance ratings indicating that the majority of whites are likely to reject close interracial contacts.[5] Stereotypes concerning the innate inferiority of blacks are decreasing,[6] but beliefs concerning low motivation and the presence of immorality among Negroes are still held by a substantial proportion of the white population.[7] Children are exposed to these common sets of attitudes, and investigators have demonstrated that the content of racial preferences is generally similar among young children in different sections of the country.[8] The similarity and duration of these racial attitudes are possible partly because there are mechanisms primarily devoted to their maintenance. These mechanisms range from processes of inculcation within the family to incorporation within the mass media.

Thus the cultural explanation of prejudice tells us the content of racial attitudes, that is, where, how, and against whom the individual is prejudiced. The social structural approach focuses on the structural strains that create differences among subgroups of the population in the extent and intensity with which those attitudes are held; for instance, fear of status deprivation can be a powerful force perpetuating racial conflict. A number of investigators have suggested that competition between two racial groups for jobs or prestige engenders hostility toward the competitor. It also has been demonstrated that lack of education is related to a simplistic and undifferentiated manner of characterizing other social categories. Interracial competition for employment and prestige is most severe and education most limited at the lower socioeconomic levels; therefore, one should expect the lower class to have more negative attitudes toward the opposite race than their middle-class counterparts. This hypothesis has been empirically substantiated and refined for whites by a number of investigations;[9] and other studies have also indicated that lower-class blacks hold more stereotypic conceptions of whites than does the Negro middle class.[10] Contact with the opposite race seems to be another important structural variable to consider in the prediction of prejudice. Although the relation is highly complex, equal status contact which minimizes conflict and stresses common goals is related to a reduction of negative stereotypes.[11]

The cultural and social-structural explanations of prejudice shed light both on the content of attitudes and on variations in commitment to them within subgroups of the population, but they do not demonstrate why attitudes differ in intensity among individuals within the same social groups. The personality approach clarifies this problem, since, for the crippled ego, prejudice may develop as an incident in total protective adjustment. *The Authoritarian Personality*[12] is the best-known study of this issue. This study does have many theoretical and methodological defects, but it indicates that a generalized ethnocentrism based on pervasive and rigid ingroup-outgroup distinctions is characteristic of at least some individuals with psychological difficulties.

Gordon Allport has suggested that this process pertains to children as well as to adults. By the principle of subsidiation[13] the child may acquire ethnic attitudes which conform to his self-image and fill his needs. If, because of socialization, his self-image is characterized by guilt, fear, or anxiety, prejudice may develop to support his life style. D. B. Harris, H. G. Gough, and W. E. Martin indicate that homes that are oppressive, harsh, or critical may tend to produce prejudiced children.[14] Bernard Kutner[15] has demonstrated that the authoritarian personality, manifesting both prejudice and a characteristic cognitive style of dichotomization and rigidity, may be present as early as age seven. Although few studies have investigated the relationship between authoritarianism and racial attitudes in Negro children, the development of prejudice to support the individual's life style should not be precluded in this group. Thus, for example, Virginia Axline,[16] Richard Trent,[17] and Eugene Brody[18] have indicated that excessive preoccupation with their skin color and rejection of racial status may be an especially characteristic feature of Negro children who are severely emotionally disturbed.

These three interrelated causes of prejudice (cultural, structural, and personality) are all necessary for an understanding of the genesis and development of children's racial attitudes. The prevalence of prejudice in the cultural system suggests that the white child cannot help but be exposed to racial evaluations of blacks which are unfavorable. And the black child is also cognizant of these negative feelings about his race, even if he has little contact with whites. Pettigrew suggests that "the ubiquity of racial prejudice in the United States guarantees that virtually every Negro American faces at some level the impersonal effects of discrimination . . . The socially stigmatized role of 'Negro' is the critical feature of having a dark skin in the United States."[19]

This position is strongly supported by recent data. Seven out of ten blacks believe that whites are either unsympathetic or indifferent to Negro advance,[20] and only a handful of blacks think that whites have a high opinion of them.[21] Also, since 97 percent of lower-income northern blacks have television,[22] it is clear that even ghetto children are not isolated from the wider social system of which anti-black prejudices are a part. The black child may, of course, be exposed to anti-white feelings and/or pro-black feelings within the black community at the same time, so he may internalize several conflicting sets of attitudes.

All children, then, become aware at some point of the existence within the dominant cultural system of racial prejudice which is directed against either their own or other groups. However, the extent and intensity of the child's attitudes and the nature of his response vary with social-structural features of his environment and with his personality system.[23] With this basic framework in mind, we now investigate in greater detail the mechanisms by which these racial attitudes are conveyed from the cultural system to the child.

Development of Racial Awareness

First, we must consider how a child becomes aware that racial differences exist. We define race as a social category based on biological characteristics like skin color. When we speak of awareness, we mean that the young child is learning both that differences among categories exist and that people may be classified into these divisions on the basis of certain perceptual cues. Mary Ellen Goodman[24] suggests several major variables which influence the age at which these racial differences are realized. The reaction of others to the child's personal appearance is an important variable, since race may be brought either directly or indirectly to the child's attention by this means. Remarks about skin color, hair, and facial features alert the youngster to the fact that there are others who look different. Cognitive development is also a highly important variable. The child's perceptual keenness and growth of logic determine when differences are noted and given significance.

Awareness also depends on the opportunity to observe racial differences through actual interracial interaction or through sources of indirect contact like television. Contact in an integrated play group or school can be an effective mechanism promoting awareness. Opportunity to observe the opposite race in new and unfamiliar settings (such as an integrated nursery school) may heighten cognizance, because the newness of a situation may itself be a stimulus to seeing and registering what was seen before and not noticed.

In these ways, the child learns of the existence of racial categories, and at the same time he becomes aware of the evaluations attached to them. The relationship between the genesis of racial awareness and attitudes is a complex one, for a youngster may even exhibit cultural preferences before he has a really clear knowledge of how people are classified into racial groups. We now investigate how these incipient attitudes are acquired.

Genesis of Racial Attitudes

One of the most important agents of attitude transmission is the family. The child may accept the parents' norms, values, and behavior patterns as his own through such processes as identification; since he is not born with social values and attitudes, topics beyond his comprehension leave him no alternative but to internalize the values of others. These racial attitudes may be transmitted directly and explicitly by the parents. Horowitz[25] and Goodman, however, had difficulty in investigating the extent of direct parental instruction, since the parents were either unwilling to admit overt teaching of prejudice or unaware of having done so. Although Horowitz dealt only with parental instruction of white children, other studies suggest that this variable is also important in black families.[26]

Another way in which cultural implications can be transmitted by the family is in overheard conversations between parents. Adults often discuss matters pertaining to racial issues with one another, assuming that the child playing nearby has neither the interest nor the intellectual capacity to follow their conversation. But young children can and do listen to such discussions, and studies have shown the particular potency of such overheard conversations for attitude change.

Attitudes which must develop to accompany human behavior may be implied by subtle behavioral cues, and it is probably in this fashion rather than by direct instruction that such attitudes are primarily learned. Erik Erikson suggests that "minute displays of emotion such as affection, pride, anger, guilt, anxiety . . . (rather than the words used, the meanings intended, or the philosophy implied), transmit to the child the outlines of what really counts in his world."[27] So by the time a child is explicitly told for the first time that blacks are inferior, he may already be convinced of the fact. Lillian Smith graphically describes this process in

Killers of the Dream: "The Negro . . . was [not often] discussed at length in our home. We were given no formal instructions in these difficult matters, but we learned our lessons well . . . we learned far more from acts than from words, more from a raised eyebrow, a joke, a shocked voice, a withdrawing movement of the body, a long silence, than from long sentences."[28] Miss Smith is a southerner, but similar processes are operative in northern settings. The white mother who presses down the locks on her car doors as she drives through a ghetto area is indeed providing highly effective instruction about race.

Black families also transmit attitudes by these behavioral cues: "It was possible to define a conscious message about color deliberately offered by the mother to the son, [but] it was also possible to define another message transmitted through action, attitudes and feelings rather than words. The most frequently encountered conscious message was to the effect that 'People are all the same inside' . . . The implied, simultaneously transmitted unconscious message, mediated through affective and behavioral cues, was essentially, 'While I tell you that people are the same inside, I expect you to behave as though this is not true, and in fact I don't believe it myself.' "[29] Attitudes toward whites and feelings of racial acceptance as well as self-hatred can of course be transmitted by similar behavioral processes.

Helen Trager and Marion Yarrow, and Charles Bird[30] indicate that there is not a one-to-one correspondence between the attitudes of children and their parents. One possible cause of this difference is the child's play group, for even a young child may pick up new attitudes from his peers. Goodman reports that the real implication of race is strikingly pointed out to many children when they first enter school, since members of his own or other racial groups may make positive or negative comments about the child's appearance or racial membership. In integrated schools, interracial contact may have either positive or negative effects on the child's developing attitudes. The result depends not only on the type of contact situation itself[31] but also on the teacher's own attitudes and how she handles racial incidents. Let us say that the teacher ignores incidents of racial name-calling. Any negative attitudes the child already has toward blacks will be reinforced. But even if a youngster is not fully aware of race, racial epithets he hears from his classmates may have an effect prior to the learning of the referent. Because of linguistic precedence in learning, a negative feeling toward the term "nigger" may precede understanding of the fact; thus, the teacher must not only firmly express disapproval of racial name-calling but must also try to offset negative incidents of this type by creating positive racial feelings and an atmosphere of interracial understanding. (In other chapters the issue of integration is discussed at greater length.)

Even in segregated school settings, contact with children from different home backgrounds may prompt learning of racial attitudes, although probably less stimulus for racial comments is provided in this type of environment than in an integrated school. Reaction of black children to one another's appearance or occasional comments overheard in an all-white school are effective transmission mechanisms for racial feelings.

Admiration of personal appearance, whether by play group, parents, or others, is an important enough mechanism of attitude transmission to be considered separately. The fair-skinned, blonde, blue-eyed child is admired. She may eventually infer that other skin and hair colors are less acceptable. Particularly for a black child, admiration of personal appearance may be an extremely crucial variable to consider in judging the image he has of the Negro group. For instance, his appearance may be judged partly by white standards, and in some situations, the more he approaches white standards of attractiveness, the more he may be envied by darker Negroes.[32] This type of evaluation may now be changing because of the recent stress on "black is beautiful." But whether he is the recipient of admiration or of pity, blacks will soon teach the Negro child how important his shade of skin color is.

Other important mechanisms of attitude transmission also affect a youngster's developing attitudes. Value-laden words are a source of potential prejudice, since in this culture "white" generally has more positive connotations than "black." Coles has expressed this fact vividly: "Words like 'dark' and 'black' or 'light' and 'white' have a number of connotations—biological, social, psychological, and symbolic. The night, with its sleep and dreams, is dark; and there are the long, cold nights in winter, not to mention the longest night of all, death. Blindness, and its solitude, is continual darkness. The clouds darken the sky, keep away the sun, bring thunder and lightning. Dirt is dark, and summons in hygienic middle-class minds all sorts of fears — germs and illness, contamination. Man's waste products are dark . . . The devil is dressed in black; and the evil of our sins is dark, a stain upon our good conscience."[33] These connotations are absorbed by the child, particularly the relationship of darkness and dirt. Their similarity was frequently pointed out by Goodman's nursery school subjects and by many of the children in my study; thus, in a culture where cleanliness is so heavily stressed, negative affect becomes attached to the color brown and can generalize to brown skin color as well.

In a study of kindergarten children, Trager[34] has convincingly demonstrated that another important factor in the creation of incipient prejudice is exposure to stereotypic reading materials. Overt stereotypes of blacks, such as in *Little Black Sambo,* now appear more rarely in children's books than they did in the past, but more subtle transmission of preferences still occurs. One popular book aimed at teaching color differences to preschool-age children contains the following discussion:

Nick was a boy who liked colors. He liked almost every color, except he didn't know if he liked black. It was so dark, like night. But . . . he liked the sooty black furnace . . . And he liked the pictures he could draw with black ink. But when he was drawing a house he spilled ink all over the paper. Then he didn't like black so much. "You have to be careful with black," he said.
Nick thought white was a good color. Clouds were white, and so were lambs and clothes on the line and swans in a pond. Nick went outside and built a snowman. "There are lots of white things in the world," Nick said, "especially when it snows."[35]

Although the color brown is described in this book as having pleasant associations (chocolate, nuts), the white-black contrast is striking. Black is night and dirt and something of which to be wary. White is highly positive, connoting pretty things and fun. As already indicated, color connotations of this type do affect developing racial attitudes.

A youngster who sees only white faces confronting him from the pages of children's books may also make inferences about race, since whiteness as the proper model for identification is reinforced by this means. Black children are beginning to appear in juvenile literature,[36] but in most books aimed at preschoolers the cast of characters remains totally white.

The mass media are another very potent means of attitude transmission, since Suzanne Keller[37] estimates that three-quarters of lower-class, six-year-old children spend at least two and often as many as five hours daily watching television. Stereotypic portrayals like "Amos 'n Andy" are disappearing, and several popular television shows even have black actors in central roles, although the characters portrayed are usually strongly middle class and far removed from the average ghetto experience. Negroes also appear more frequently in television commercials, and programs on interracial relations, black culture, and black problems are no longer a rarity. The recent public television series "Sesame Street," aimed at the cognitive development of preschoolers, is an outstanding example of a creative approach in the area of race. Although the major characters are black, the cast is totally integrated, and acceptance of the importance of all races is an implicit theme. This greater visibility of blacks in nonstereotypic roles and the more sympathetic treatment accorded issues concerning blacks may be expected to exert a favorable influence on attitude development. However, the majority of television advertisements are dominated by whites enjoying the fruits of affluence. Black representation on popular television shows is still enough of a novelty to receive heavy publicity. These factors may bring the exemption mechanism into play, at least for the parents, who may transmit this to the child. In other words, the television personality may be regarded as an exception, lacking stereotyped characteristics attributed to all other blacks. This type of exemption may neutralize the possible positive effects of favorable black portrayals.

There is an additional, frequently overlooked, influence that the mass media exert on attitude formation. The daily news on television or in newspapers provides a powerful stimulus for parental conversation about racial issues, thus affecting children's attitudes through indirect instruction. The white parent may express anger at news about black militancy, or he may comment about government action in the area of race. And of course the black parent may also comment about these matters. The child can overhear and learn in the manner already described.

The data of this study do not provide much clarification of the way in which mass media news coverage and parental comments interact to shape attitudes. The year the study was done, 1965, was characterized by a shift in focus from the largely nonviolence-oriented, integrated demonstrations in the South to the exploding ghettos of the North and West. The mass media gave much publicity to such important events as the passage of the voting rights act, the assassination of Malcolm X, the Selma-Montgomery march, the murder of Viola Liuzzo, Martin Luther King's civil rights drive in Chicago, and particularly the Watts uprising. In addition, in the Boston area, where my data were collected, heavy coverage was given to school integration controversies and to the murder of a local minister, James Reeb, who was killed doing civil rights work in the South. It is interesting that almost none of the children in our sample remarked directly about these prominently featured events. This is due in large part to the fact that these youngsters were too young to understand the significance of these occasions. This does not preclude the possibility that current events provided a stimulus for expression of parental racial feelings. This racial affect itself can be internalized even by children who have no comprehension of the specific event that prompted it.[38]

Robert Coles[39] has remarked that children he has studied not only are interested in the race of television performers but notice also the race of public personnel like bus drivers and policemen. His sample was older than the age group discussed here, but Trager's data[40] clearly demonstrate that even young children are sensitive to the racial occupancy of social roles; for instance, a child may observe blacks only in such roles as maid, janitor, or laborer. Particularly if low esteem for these statuses is made obvious by parental comment or behavior, negative feelings toward blacks may be developed or reinforced for children of either race. Trager's study also shows that children are aware of other factors like the relationship between race and poor housing and that there is a tendency for white children who ascribe inferior roles to Negroes to be hostile or rejecting toward them on the attitude test. The child's attitudes are thus definitely influenced by the social situation he sees around him, and these attitudes in turn influence his perception of his environment.

Racial attitudes are transmitted, then, by a variety of mechanisms, but this does not necessarily mean that a clear awareness of racial differences precedes this process of attitude internalization. Allport suggests that the learning of prejudice is a three-stage process.[41] The first stage is pre-generalized learning, in which the child does not quite understand what a Negro is or what his attitudes toward Negroes should be. But he may already have feelings connected to color; for instance, he may think that white is nice or good and brown is not; and white and brown individuals may be evaluated in this fashion. He may also know that the term "nigger" connotes bad things; however, he is not quite sure exactly to whom this term refers. Gradually the child begins to realize that "brown" and "white" are attached to clearly defined racial categories, and any racial names he has heard also begin to acquire a clear social referent. These early feelings or incipient attitudes in the pre-generalized learning stage form the basis of real attitudes about racial categories, and environmental stimuli may continue to reinforce this connection between white and good, and brown and bad.

The second stage is total verbal rejection of the unfavored status. This occurs after the child has become clearly aware of the existence of racial categories and has internalized more well-defined cultural evaluations of them. He may then express totally negative opinions about members of his own or the opposite race. Differentiation characterizes the final stage of attitude development, when prejudice becomes less "totalized" in order to make it more rational and acceptable to the individual. The child then begins to exempt certain individuals from stereotypes applied to the whole racial group and also to rationalize prejudices. Allport's scheme is somewhat simplistic, as I will argue later, but it indicates that affect may actually precede racial awareness. Once awareness develops, however, it provides the necessary stimulus for the sharpening and focusing of fully developed attitudes.

Thus, it appears that the first five years of life are important, though not conclusive for the development of racial attitudes. A directional set is given to the mind during the preschool years by the reaction of parents in terms of direct instruction, indirect instruction, or behavioral cues; the comments of peers; exposure to stereotypes in mass media and literature; spontaneous color associations; and observation of role occupancy. The processes of selective perception, reinforcement, subsidiation to self-image, and cognitive closure help give these attitudes their final form as the child grows older.[42] Although the mechanisms which transmit attitudes are similar for all children, the extent of these feelings and the reaction to them is affected by the child's psychological and sociological environment and his racial membership. The remainder of the book discusses the sociocultural factors creating variations in these incipient attitudes and their effects on the child's self-esteem.

During the last three decades, a body of literature has developed on the racial preferences of preschool-age children and the effect of these preferences on personality. The studies of Kenneth and Mamie Clark contain some of the earliest and best known data in this area. Many other investigations have since elaborated on the Clarks' findings; however, interpretation of much of this research is difficult because of problems in experimental design. This chapter reviews the empirical findings of other studies, dealing first with results on the formation of racial awareness and then with factors affecting the development of racial attitudes. Finally, discussion of the literature on racial self-identification provides clues about the possible effects of these incipient attitudes on self-esteem.

Studies of Racial Awareness in Children

"Racial awareness" is defined by most investigators as knowledge of both the visible difference between racial categories and the perceptual cues by which one classifies people into these divisions. It is difficult to fully interpret data purporting to measure either racial attitudes or racial self-esteem unless one has a knowledge of the level of awareness of the subjects in the group under consideration. For this reason studies of the effect of age, sex, social class, and skin color on racial cognizance during the preschool years are reviewed here in detail.

Many studies of awareness have been concerned with the age at which the child realizes that certain physical differences have social meaning. Awareness of race increases with age. As a child grows older, his perceptual keenness develops, he becomes more aware of cues, and he can more easily verbalize what he notices. His sphere of contact is also increased, since he interacts with others in play groups and school; hence, he is more apt both to notice differences and to have differences brought to his attention.

Although the empirical findings on the age at which awareness occurs remain unclear, they do suggest that most children become cognizant of race during the preschool years. Bruno Lasker, in *Race Attitudes in Children,* published in 1929, was the first serious investigator to deal directly with this problem. He felt that children up to the age of eight are often ignorant of racial differences.[1] But his conclusions are questionable: he studied not the children themselves but adults' reminiscenses of childhood experiences and teachers' observations of elementary school subjects. One of the first actual empirical studies of nursery school children was done in the 1930's. In this investigation, Ruth Horowitz reported that racial awareness appears as early as nursery school age, but her small sample of twenty-four did not allow her to make more specific deductions.[2]

Clark and Clark, using Horowitz's line drawings of children and their own doll-play techniques, demonstrated that for some Negro children basic knowledge of racial differences may begin even as early as age three.[3] Furthermore, they found that this knowledge develops more definitely from year to year and reaches a point of stability at the age of seven. The Clarks' doll-play study remedied a defect found in both their earlier work and the Ruth Horowitz investigations, since they specifically asked the child to identify the "Negro," "colored," and "white" doll rather than drawing inferences about level of awareness from the youngster's correctness of racial self-classification. Racial self-identification is a poor measure of awareness for black children. Self-classification taps affect connected to race as well as racial cognizance, and Negro children who are highly aware of racial differences may identify as white because they dislike their racial status.

Less is known for white children about the age at which awareness occurs. Using a variety of techniques, Mary Ellen Goodman was able to divide her sample of four-year-olds into low, medium, and high awareness groups. Yet, since all her subjects were the same age, she is unable to say anything about the growth of sophistication in racial knowledge over the entire preschool period.[4] Harold and Nancy Stevenson, studying a group of ten children two and a half to three and a half years old, in Austin, Texas, indicated that these children occasionally demonstrated awareness of race, though less often than did Goodman's four-year-old subjects.[5]

Kenneth Morland is one of the few investigators who has attempted a comprehensive study using the same instrument (in this case, a set of pictures of Negroes and whites) on a group of white children ranging in age from three to five.[6] He finds that white children may be cognizant of racial differences as early as age three, although awareness seems to have its fastest development during the child's fourth year. Since his sample consists of children in a nursery school in Virginia, one must be cautious about generalizing his results to a group of three-year-old northern children for whom race may have less salience. When Morland did his study, racial issues were more a matter of concern for white southerners than for northern whites. In a later article Morland's data do in fact suggest that northern white children tend to have somewhat less racial recognition ability than southern children do.[7]

Some of the studies on the relationship of awareness and age treat awareness as though it were unidimensional. But this assumption is not accurate for young children. Even before he is cognizant of racial terms, a child may be aware that some people are brown and some white, and he may have vague evaluations of these differences as well. Thus, it is imperative to treat "awareness" as a multidimensional concept which includes at least the ability to classify by color and the knowledge of racial terms. One study does focus specifically on the ages at which various components of racial cognizance develop. Graham Vaughan has investigated the development of the concept "Maori" among white children in New Zealand, and he finds that ability to classify the self racially appears before ability to discriminate which of several figures in a group is racially different. Verbal classifications are the last component of awareness to be mastered. By age four, the majority of whites could correctly classify themselves with a white child in a picture; by age six, the majority could discriminate between racial groups in pictures, and by ages seven to ten varying degrees of sophistication in verbal conceptualization were evidenced.[8] It is not clear that Vaughan's data on the extent of awareness of these various components at each age level can be generalized to the United States, since race is a more prominent issue here than it is in New Zealand, but his study does clearly indicate that the development of racial cognizance is more complex than some other investigations have supposed.

Existing studies indicate that nursery school children may often be aware of racial differences. Yet a number of points remain to be clarified in the age-awareness relationship. Several investigators have measured awareness by correctness of self-identification (e.g., Horowitz). This is an inadequate technique, because self-classification measures emotional as well as cognitive factors. Another favorite method is asking the children to match similar families of dolls or puzzle parts representing people (e.g., Goodman). This approach, though, fails to distinguish between purely intellectual color matching and actual awareness of race as a social category. A child may be able to put brown and white dolls into two separate piles on the basis of color differences alone, without any realization that this categorization has social meaning. Although some studies do have direct measures of awareness (e.g., knowledge of racial terms) there are few studies which divide racial cognizance into several dimensions in order to investigate the way knowledge of these components changes as the child grows older. In Chapter 4, data are presented on black and white children which both disentangle the race-color relationship and measure the variance of the separate dimensions of awareness with age.

Although the connection between age and awareness is still not clarified, the association between sex and level of cognizance is even more obscure. Girls should be more aware of race than boys are, since personal appearance is stressed for girls more than it is for boys. If girls are highly conscious of appearance, there is reason to expect the existence of a sexual difference in sophistication of recognition of racial categories. Goodman says more girls than boys are in her high awareness group. Although Morland finds no difference in awareness by sex, his sample is composed of a group of southern children.[9] This may only mean that if race is a matter of extreme importance in the child's environment and is frequently discussed in the home, the sexes are equally cognizant at an early age. Chapter 6 shows that the relationship between sex and awareness is more complex than other investigators have supposed.

Another area that has been studied is the existence of racial differences in awareness. Black children should be more aware of race than whites are because race is a more highly salient matter for them. Although

Lasker suggested that Negro children have a greater realization of racial differences than white children do, Ruth Horowitz was the first to demonstrate this process empirically.[10] In Goodman's sample, 40 percent of the black and 24 percent of the white children show high awareness;[11] even in her low awareness group, Negroes sense that color is a key characteristic and has something to do with themselves. Morland finds that northern blacks tend to have slightly (though not significantly) greater racial recognition ability than northern whites,[12] but both he[13] and Stevenson and Stewart find that southern whites are more cognizant of race than are their black counterparts. Morland claims that since many southern white children are in constant contact with Negro domestics in the home, they have a greater chance to notice racial differences than do southern Negro youngsters. Yet the fact that both Stevenson and Morland used white interviewers may have affected the validity of their results in a segregated southern Negro school. The problem of bias because of the interviewer's race is of particular importance in a segregated environment. Irwin Katz suggests that under conditions of threat, the use of a white experimenter has a demonstrable effect on the responses of black subjects. A white who asks black children in a segregated southern school about their racial preferences is surely creating a threat situation.[14] This problem of bias is discussed in Chapter 3, but it should be kept in mind in interpreting the following results. Chapter 4 verifies the proposition that black children are more concerned and preoccupied with color differences than their white peers are.

The relationship between social class and awareness also has not been fully investigated. Catherine Landreth concludes that white children whose parents are engaged in the professions perceive skin color in cognitive terms, while those whose parents are in semiskilled occupations perceive skin color in affective terms.[15] In a Virginia community, Morland[16] found no difference in awareness among whites by social class, but again the high salience of race may cancel out socioeconomic differences in the South for reasons already discussed.

There have been few studies of the relationship between social class and awareness for the Negro child. One of the Clarks' studies does suggest indirectly that a class factor may be related to awareness for Negroes. Using knowledge of the terms "Negro," "colored," and "white" as a measure of racial cognizance, the Clarks found that although the relationship is not statistically significant, the darker Negro children seemed to have a slightly more definite knowledge of racial differences.[17] Does a dark-skinned child actually notice more differences between himself and the majority of his playmates than a lighter-skinned or medium-skinned Negro child does? The factors which operate to explain the relationship are unclear.

This trend may be explained by factors other than skin color alone. The Clarks have not controlled for socioeconomic status. In the North, and particularly in the South, the lower socioeconomic statuses contain a larger proportion of dark Negroes.[18] It is possible that the lower-class parent may give the child direct instruction on how to act with whites, and lower-class parents are more likely to let the child play on the street without supervision and less likely to choose his friends for him.[19] Therefore, a youngster can increase his realization of differences by direct or indirect instruction. In Chapter 5 we show that working-class and lower-class children of both races do in fact seem more cognizant of color differences than middle-class youngsters are.

The connection between social class and the realization of racial differences has not been fully investigated in other studies, but a problem about which even less is known is the relationship between awareness and amount of interracial contact for both white and Negro children.[20] Contact and racial cognizance should be highly related; children in desegregated schools are more likely to be sensitized to the existence of racial groups. This proposition is demonstrated in Chapter 5.

Previous investigations of the development of racial concept formation indicate only that awareness of racial differences occurs between the ages of three and five. It is difficult to draw more specific conclusions from existing evidence, although there is some indication that the fourth year of a child's life is crucial as far as development of racial awareness is concerned. Also, Negro children may be cognizant of racial differences earlier than are whites. But these points must be clarified, because data on racial awareness are of crucial importance for interpreting evidence on attitude formation and its effects.

Studies of Children's Racial Attitudes

A large body of research has dealt with the development of racial attitudes in children. These studies are confusing, however, since many of them do not investigate the presence of racial awareness as well. Thus it is unclear what the instruments are measuring; for instance, in those studies where choice of dolls is used as an indicator of attitudes on racial preference questions, white doll selection may just measure response-set for a type of toy the child owns.

Despite the fact that its meaning is unclear, the outstanding finding in existing investigations of racial attitudes is that children of both races tend to exhibit preference for white. The Clarks' doll-play study demonstrated that, at each age from three to seven, a majority of the Negro children prefer the white and reject the brown doll; however, this preference decreases gradually from five to seven years.[21] Horowitz, Trager, Goodman, Morland, R. B. Ammons, Asher and Allen, and others have further documented white preference by children of both races.[22] According to Doris Springer, Oriental children in Hawaii also tend to select whites as playmates.[23] In Chapter 4 we will see that a high rate of white doll choice in fact is indicative of at least incipient racial attitudes for the majority of preschool youngsters of both races. These attitudes are not uniform for all children, however. They seem to vary with age, social class, contact, region, and shade of skin color.

The relationship between age and preference has been studied by several investigators. In the last chapter, Allport's three-stage pattern in the development of attitudes was discussed. In the first stage, called "pregeneralized learning," the child has not yet generalized after the fashion of adults. He has vague preferences but does not quite understand what Negroes are and what his attitudes toward them should be. The second stage is a total verbal rejection in which whites are assigned all the virtues and Negroes, none. The third stage is differentiation, where prejudice begins to grow less total and approximates an adult attitude. Blake and Dennis provide evidence that the second stage of rejection is present by the fourth grade and the third stage of differentiation begins at the tenth or eleventh grade for white children.[24] However, Goodman suggests that negative attitudes about Negroes are found in some white children even by age four. This disagreement is clarified by Morland's study of southern white subjects between the ages of three and five. On a question where they were forced to choose between a Negro and a white as a playmate, the older children tended to select whites more frequently than did their younger counterparts, with the big jump in white preference occurring between ages three and four. This white preference was evidenced even among children of low awareness. But, in addition, Morland asked his subjects only if they would like to play with the Negro child in a picture and did not force a choice between two racial alternatives. The older subjects here were also less likely to accept Negroes as playmates, but, even among five-year-olds, less than one-third refused to accept a Negro child when no choice between races was required. On the alternative where selection between races was forced, however, three-quarters of the five-year-old subjects selected the white doll.[25] These data suggest that by the age of five, white preference may be highly established even if racial awareness is low. For the majority of children, positive attitudes toward whites do not involve a corresponding rejection of blacks, but further investigation is needed of variables which differentiate the majority from the minority of children who are hostile toward the opposite race. (Such data are provided in Chapter 6.)

Results are also available on the relationship between racial preference and age for Negroes. The Clarks suggest that by age four, many Negro children show clear preference for white dolls.[26] The possibility of ambivalent and retaliatory responses to their racial membership is indicated in Trager's study of a group of six- and seven-year-old black youngsters. She provided her subjects with Negro and white dolls and a large selection of clothes, ranging from shabby work clothes to attractively styled "dress-up" outfits. The child was asked to dress both dolls and describe the activities in which they might be engaged. Seventy-eight percent of the Negro children gave the Negro doll the prettier clothes, but only 43 percent of them assigned it more desirable activities. Some of the Negro subjects tried to avoid the connection of low status and race by giving the doll of their own race activities which did not involve a comparison of social status. Trager concluded that ambivalence toward own and opposite race was present in this age group and that Negro children's assignment of poor clothes to the white doll could be interpreted as a defensive reaction.[27] All of these findings on age and attitudes suggest that Allport's three-stage paradigm is overly simple. The data in Chapter 5 do in fact demonstrate that each of his stages occurs at an earlier age and is more complex than has previously been supposed.

The relationship of attitudes to region, social class, and contact are other areas where further investigation is needed. Horowitz gives evidence that white children in urban and rural Georgia, urban Tennessee, and New York City have negative attitudes toward Negroes. Goodman, Trager and Yarrow, and Stevenson and Stewart have demonstrated that in Boston, Philadelphia, and a Texas town, white preschool children prefer white to brown; however, southern white children do tend to exhibit a slightly greater degree of white preference and black rejection than their northern peers.[28]

The connection between social class and racial attitudes for white children has also not been clarified. A large body of sociological evidence shows that white working-class adults have more negative attitudes toward blacks than middle-class adults do, so we should also expect to find this difference among children. But Charles Bird, and Asher and Allen indicate that there are no differences between middle- and working-class white youngsters in racial attitudes and social distance scores.[29] Morland does find more white preference among lower-class white youngsters in one study,[30] but other data of his indicate that lower-class whites seem to accept Negroes as playmates more often than middle-class whites do.[31] The interpretation of these latter data in terms of prejudice is problematic, since middle-class children generally exhibited a more cautious attitude toward acceptance of any child, including a white child, as a playmate. In Chapter 6 we find that working-class white children in fact dislike blacks more than do their middle-class peers.

The evidence on effects of interracial contact for whites is even slimmer than the literature for social class differences in attitudes. Evelyn Helgerson has found that on a projective test two-to-six-year-old whites in an integrated school choose white playmates more frequently than do those in an all-white school.[32] But far more data are needed on the effects of integration upon racial attitudes, since this question is important for public policy. The results in Chapter 5 show that the effect of contact on white attitudes is in fact highly complex.

The relationship between attitudes and region, contact, and social class is more difficult to interpret for Negroes than it is for white children. Inadequate controls make it difficult to analyze the existing data on the effects of each of these variables on racial evaluations. In Helgerson's test, black children in an integrated school choose a white playmate more frequently than they do in a segregated school;[33] and Springer isolates the same tendency in Oriental children in homogeneous and heterogeneous schools in Hawaii. In one of their series of investigations, the Clarks find that Negro children in an integrated northern school react to their test with more intense emotion than do their segregated southern subjects. Also, 70 percent of segregated southern children colored their preferences brown while only 36 percent of northern integrated children did so.[34]

The Clarks' studies introduce a perplexing note into the entire issue. Their doll-play research reveals that although all groups of Negro children prefer white, the dark- and medium-skinned subjects have more tendency than their lighter counterparts to prefer the Negro doll. But a majority of the Clarks' dark subjects attend segregated southern schools, and the vast majority of the light children in this study are in the North and attend integrated schools. We are thus left with the problem of explaining the preference of some groups of Negro children for the Negro doll. Is amount of contact with white children, the section of the country, or the child's color the crucial variable in explanation of racial preference choices? The Clarks suggest that, holding color constant, segregated southern subjects still exhibit less rejection of the brown doll than northern integrated subjects do; but since they do not actually present these data, we do not know how much of the variance in preference on the doll-play technique is explained by skin color and how much by region and/or by contact.[35]

A fourth possibility also exists. Since skin color is to some extent a correlate of social class among Negroes, does the higher rate of preference for the brown doll among darker-skinned children point to a lower-class phenomenon as the explanation of these results? Although they do not control for skin color or contact, Asher and Allen find that lower-class black children do exhibit less white preference than their middle-class counterparts.[36] But the Clarks ignore the fact of social class altogether; in one study they even take their subjects from WPA nursery schools and private nurseries and do not analyze the results separately.[37]

Results from the Clarks' coloring test introduce a further note of confusion. These data to some extent contradict the skin-color results found by the doll-play technique; in the coloring test, the very dark subjects are *less* likely than their light and medium counterparts to prefer brown. But other data suggest that this overall low own-race preference among dark children may be due to responses of the dark youngsters in northern integrated schools.[38] Thus, a complex relation between shade of skin color, contact, and/or region is suggested by the coloring test but not by the doll-play technique. It is obvious that since social class, contact, region, and shade of skin color are highly interrelated, the effect of each variable can only be estimated by strictly controlling for the other three. Statistical techniques to uncover possible interaction effects should also be utilized.

Each of these four variables probably makes some difference in explanation of the racial preferences the Clarks find for subgroups of Negro children. A child in an integrated school may be exposed to the hostility of his classmates, and his attention may be constantly attracted to his skin color. The status differential between Negro and white is thus sharpened, and the Negro child may exhibit preference for the favored status. Not only this factor but the possibility that his doll-play choices are reflecting reality (he is actually playing with white children in school) also must be taken into consideration. A child in a segregated school may not be exposed to this negative affect, and the fact that he is playing mainly with Negro children may make him more liable to choose the Negro doll. The southern or lower-class child may accept the fact of his racial status and thus choose the brown doll more frequently than does the northern or middle-class Negro child, who may experience more conflict about his racial membership. The light-skinned child may also experience more conflict, since he is likely to compare himself with whites,[39] but a very dark child in an integrated school may be made the target of unfavorable remarks by white children and also exhibit high rejection of the black doll. In Chapter 5 the class-color-contact interplay is disentangled, but additional data are still needed on the effect of region of the country, controlling for these other three variables.

The fact that the Clarks do not provide this type of statistical analysis or controls must be viewed in relation to the level of methodological understanding of the era in which the studies were done. The Clark studies are similar to the research of most psychologists at that time in their lack of sociological sophistication. But even though the work was done almost three decades ago and does have methodological problems, it remains one of the most comprehensive and important bodies of data available in this area.

The material just reviewed suggests that a national pattern of white preference is evident. Although these preferences vary with age and other environmental influences for children of both races, the existing work in this field does not systematically investigate these effects. Also, the question of whether choice of a white doll measures at least incipient racial attitudes for the majority of preschool youngsters is not fully clarified by this research.

Studies of Racial Self-Identification in Children

Many investigations have shown interest in the effect of prejudice on the self-esteem of black children. The black child is exposed both to negative attitudes about his race and to objective factors like discrimination or low social position. Thus he must learn to adapt to these pressures in some way. Racial evaluations affect him more directly and personally than they do the white child, who is not forced to cope with the problem of being stigmatized because of his skin color.

The self-esteem of even preschool-age black children is adversely affected by prejudice and discrimination, and some reject themselves on racial grounds as a result. Racial self-rejection is most frequently measured by asking the child to identify himself with a picture or doll of the appropriate race. This process of self-classification involves at least two components: the perception by a child that he belongs in a particular racial category and his willingness to admit this fact. Available work has shown that the child may have knowledge of racial differences and yet not overtly admit his racial membership. This finding suggests that the social meaning of racial differences plays a large part in determining how a young child will apply these differences to himself. But the status of self-identification as a measure of personal rejection on racial grounds is still unclear. Some investigators claim that self-classification is based on purely perceptual grounds for both Negroes and whites, and others have interpreted self-identification results for black children in terms of self-esteem. We now review the self-identification literature in order to see where further clarification is needed.

The most consistent agreement among the whole range of studies on racial self-identification concerns the tendency of many Negro children to identify themselves as white. Clark and Clark discovered that approximately nine out of ten Negro children (from three to seven years old) are aware of racial differences as indicated by their correct choice of "white" and "colored" dolls on request, but only six out of ten make socially correct self-classifications with the brown doll.[40] Helen Trager and Marion Yarrow, Stevenson and Stewart, Morland, and Goodman have also found that many black children tend to incorrectly identify themselves. The only contradictory data are provided in a study by Greenwald and Oppenheim. Instead of using only a black and a white doll, they add a "mulatto" as well. Under this condition, only 13 percent of black children identify with the white doll. Thus, they argue that the results of other studies on black misidentification are artifacts of the procedure. But in their study, although 38 percent of the Negro children identify with the mulatto doll, so do 25 percent of the whites. This suggests that many children may not have been able to discriminate effectively between the mulatto and the light doll, particularly since some of these subjects were only three years of age.[41]

It is necessary, of course, to utilize a white control group in interpreting the existing data on misidentification by black children. Goodman seems to find that white children classify themselves more accurately, but Ruth Horowitz found that white boys, when they had to choose the picture most resembling themselves, classified themselves less accurately than did Negroes.[42] However, since the children Horowitz studied are slightly younger on the average than those Goodman studied, this may mean that whites realize racial differences later than Negroes do because race is less salient for them. Morland suggests that, as whites become cognizant of racial differences, they tend to classify themselves more correctly. For blacks, however, the opposite relationship seems to hold: for black children up to age six, the percentage of children identifying with their own race tends to decrease as racial recognition ability increases.[43]

These data have been interpreted in various ways. In their early papers, the Clarks do not give sufficient emphasis to the fact that young children internalize attitudes about race.[44] Because of this, they have difficulty in interpreting some of their research, and they sometimes interpret puzzling test scores in part by blaming the insensitivity of their measuring instruments.[45] Both Goodman and Ruth Horowitz, however, suggest that a wish-fulfillment mechanism is operative for some black children. Since the image that the black child often sees of himself is an unfavorable one, incorrect self-classification may be a reaction to this interpretation. More recently Clark, too, has adopted the wish-fulfillment hypothesis: "the child . . . knows that he must be identified with something that is being rejected, and something that he, himself, rejects. . . . Many Negro children attempt to resolve this profound conflict either through wishful thinking or by seeking some form of escape from a situation which focuses this conflict for them"[46] In Chapter 6 we see that the self-identification index is actually a measure of racial self-concept for black children.

Other variables, such as class, color, contact, and sex, must be taken into account in any study of self-identification, since the pattern of self-classification is not uniform for all children in each racial group. There is little work available on differences between whites, although Morland's data suggest that southern whites tend to identify slightly (though not significantly) more correctly than do northern whites.[47] Morland also finds that there is no social class difference in self-identification among southern white children.[48] New findings on the self-identification patterns of white youngsters by class, contact, and sex are presented in Chapter 6.

There is more literature available on variations among subgroups on self-identification for blacks than for whites, and most of this research has been done by the Clarks. One area they have investigated is the relationship between self-classification and age. With black subjects from ages three to seven, the Clarks' doll-play technique demonstrates that by age seven the vast majority of black youngsters begin to classify themselves correctly.[49] A young black child may not realize that there are racial differences and classify himself randomly, or he may realize differences but not be able to separate fantasy and reality fully. Some children may have a vague sense that dark color is bad, and because they want to be good, they may have a tendency to classify themselves as "good" or "white." At a later age, the child's sense of reality is more fully developed; he not only is more aware of race but because of outside pressure must also face the fact of his true racial identity.

The Clarks did not thoroughly investigate the relationship between sex, age at realization, and correct self-classification. Their studies suggest that the self-classification of three-to-five-year-old Negro girls approximates chance, while the boys' self-classification shows a statistically significant increase in correctness in the same age range.[50] Yet this interpretation may not be valid, because they presented only line drawings of boys and asked girls to classify their cousins or brothers. If a girl does not have a male sibling or cousin, she may have difficulty in answering this question. Also, young girls may be more conscious of their own appearance than of the appearance of their relatives. The Clarks do not itemize most of their other results by sex, so it is impossible to deduce the amount of variation in group scores in the line-drawing studies due to improper measurement of girls' attitudes. Chapter 6 shows that sex does in fact have a major effect on self-identification. Black girls tend to have a particularly high rate of misclassification.

Another relationship the Clarks consider is the connection between shade of skin color and identification of the self. They suggest that the dark and medium Negro children classify themselves more correctly than do their lighter counterparts.[51] The relationship between color and self-classification may be a function of the fact that the dark child is less able to deny his skin color in fantasy because it is so obviously different from white.[52] It has already been indicated that dark children are slightly more aware of racial differences; however, since awareness of differences does not predicate correct self-classification, this relationship must be investigated further. The Clarks first hypothesized that most children identify themselves on the basis of physical characteristics rather than socially defined racial differences, but an analysis of their data offers several objections to this interpretation. If self-classification is based solely on the physical fact of color, why do from one-fifth to one-third of the light children consistently classify themselves with the brown doll or with the Negro boy in a drawing? Why do approximately 20 to 40 percent of the very dark children classify themselves as white?[53] In their early papers the Clarks seem to assume that self-identification on the basis of observed skin color precedes consciousness of self in terms of racial differences. But their later paper suggests that awareness of racial differences often precedes correct self-classification.[54] Skin color may exert an independent effect on self-identification either because the light child is identifying on a purely perceptual basis with the doll he most resembles or because he knows his racial membership but wants to be white. However, there is still quite a bit of unexplained variance. Also, since color is confounded with several other variables, the effect due to shade of skin color alone may be weaker than the Clarks predict.[55]

Since in the Clarks' doll-play studies more of their dark subjects are in the South, there is a possibility that part of the skin-color results in this test are actually due to regional variation. The southern child might be forced by more pressure from inside and outside his group to identify himself correctly. Although there is no statistically significant relationship between correct self-classification and section of the country, slightly more southern than northern Negro children seem to correctly classify themselves.[56] Does section of the country explain either the deviant cases or some part of the relationship between self-identification and color itself?

In the Clarks' later papers, all of the southern subjects are in segregated schools and all of their northern counterparts are integrated, so contact becomes another variable which may exert an independent effect on the explanation of these skin-color results in the doll-play test. And one of the Clarks' early papers, where they do exert some controls for region of the country, does show that in segregated environments there are more self-identifications with a brown than with a white boy. Yet in an integrated environment in the same study, there are equal choices of brown and white as a self-identification figure. When just medium and dark children in both types of environments are considered, the self-identification results are the same as the ones above.[57]

Since color and socioeconomic status are probably related in the Clarks' sample, the latter may also be an important variable to consider. The parent in higher social classes may actively strive for upward mobility and thus emphasize the importance of light skin color, admire the child for his lightness, and speak in a derogatory fashion about darker Negroes. This may cause the child to place greater value on lightness. If there is more acceptance of color in the lower class, there may be more correct self-identification. Some of the light-skinned children who classified themselves as Negro may have been from the lower class. Color, area, contact, and class may all be interrelated in the Clark studies. Unless careful controls are utilized, we cannot uncover the influence on self-classification of each variable by itself or in interaction with the others. In Chapter 6, these class-contact-color effects are separated out, but additional research with proper controls is needed on the influence of region of the country on accuracy of self-identification.

Studies in the area of racial self-identification show that white children identify themselves more accurately than do Negro children. Aside from this finding, the studies present a confusing picture. There is no clear set of assumptions about what self-identification measures, and the studies are poorly controlled. We know little about the relationship between age, sex, social class, and self-identification for the white child. It is not clear from existing studies exactly what overt self-classification is measuring for black children. Does correct self-identification signify perception of membership in a purely biological category or in a socially defined category based on biological characteristics? Does incorrect self-classification accompanied by knowledge of skin-color differences mean actual lack of awareness of one's own racial membership? Or does it mean awareness of one's race but an unwillingness to face this fact and define the self as belonging to an undesirable group? In order to solve the problem of the effect of racial attitudes on the self-esteem of the Negro child, one must carefully test awareness and attitudes as well as self-classification. In the following sections data on awareness and preferences are presented, the meaning of self-identification is assessed, and variations between subgroups of black and white children are examined on this index.

Two Sociological Correlates of Racial
Attitude Formation

Difficulties in the interpretation of previous research on racial attitudes and their effects suggest the need for a new technique of investigation. This method should be sensitive enough to uncover the meaning of preference choices but uncomplicated enough to be used with young children. A procedure was developed which was intended to fulfill these criteria. In this chapter, the technique used in this study to measure racial preferences and their effects is discussed.

The method was based loosely on a projective test called the "Movie-Story Game," developed in 1947 by Mary Collins Evans, Isidore Chein, and Russell Hogrefe, for use with elementary school children. In the Evans-Chein-Hogrefe test, the child was presented with twenty-two white and Negro dolls and two stage-sets. The ostensible purpose of the experimental session was to elicit information concerning the kind of stories children enjoy in movies. An identification figure of the same race and sex as the subject was presented as the leading character in two situations, one concerning a day in school and the other a birthday party. At several points in each story, the investigator asked the child to help construct the plot by choosing appropriate dolls. The two stories were almost identical except for differences in setting and were designed to elicit racial attitudes held by the child without arousing his suspicion of the test's purpose.

This technique was found to be extremely successful in several studies, but the test's length and assumption of at least some racial sophistication on the part of the subject made it unsuitable for use with children below the age of seven. The Movie-Story Game does provide, however, an excellent framework which can be adapted for use with a preschool group. Since Goodman's social episodes technique was a more naive version of the Evans-Chein-Hogrefe material, her hypothetical situations were used as a guideline in revising the content of that original material for use with a younger sample.

A new procedure based on these methods was developed and proved in a pre-test on a sample of 130 children to be a highly adequate measure of incipient racial attitudes.[1] The immediate advantages soon became apparent. Since the child was presented with a variety of novel and stimulating toys, the attention of even the youngest subject could be engaged and held for a rather long time by his active part in the story-telling situation. Children who were not too facile with words could designate their choice of doll by merely pointing, while more verbal children had the chance to express themselves with greater sophistication. Because of its initial success, the new technique (with several minor revisions suggested by the pre-test results)[2] was used as the measure of racial preference in this study.

The TV-Story Game

Three interviewers (two whites and a Negro) administered the test to the present sample. All three were trained in social science[3] and had extensive experience with young children. The investigator would visit each nursery school for several days, if possible, before commencing with the experimental session. By this time, most of the children had accepted her as a familiar figure and were eager to see the toys. Each child was approached individually and asked if he would like to play a game. Upon entering the testing room, he was invited to sit on the floor with the experimenter. A furnished schoolroom stage-set was directly in front of the subject, and a living room stage-set was next to it, turned with its back to the child so that he was unable to see the inside. The dolls were hidden behind the living room. The situation that was presented to each subject is described below.

The Story Situation

Do you like to watch TV? What program do you like best? Do you know what we're going to do now? We're going to make up a story for a TV show about kids. We're going to use dolls and doll houses to help tell our story.

We're going to pretend that this is a school, just like the school you go to. First, we're going to make up a story about a boy named Johnny who goes to this school.[4] Now Johnny is a boy who looks *just like you*. Which one of these dolls will be Johnny in our story? (Experimenter presents

Negro and white dolls of same sex as the child.) All right, now you hold Johnny (rejected doll is removed from view). Johnny is the first one in nursery school this morning and he's waiting for someone to come and play with him. The first two boys come to school. One of these boys is Johnny's friend that he plays with all the time. Which one of these is Johnny's friend that he plays with?[5] Why do you think this one is Johnny's friend? Now you hold Johnny's friend. They start playing with dolls (toy trucks) and then the next two kids come to school. Johnny's friend says, "One of these kids is very nice. Let's ask him to play." Which one of these kids does he think is the very nice one? Why do you think that one is very nice? They ask him to come over and all three of them play. What do you think they're doing? Then two more kids come into school. Johnny says, "Let's ask them to play, too." But his friend says, "Nah, I don't like one of these kids. He's so lazy and stupid!" Which one of these kids does his friend think is lazy and stupid? Why do you think this one is lazy and stupid? What does Johnny say to his friend? Then all of them start playing together. What do you think they're doing? What do kids really do in your school?

Then it's time to go home for lunch, and Johnny decides to take one of the kids in his class home for lunch with him. Which one does he take home? Would Mommy like him to take the other one home, too? (Experimenter presents rejected doll.)

Why don't we tell a different story now? Will you help me take the chairs out of the school first? O.K., now we're going to tell a story about a house (school is turned backward and house is turned so that it faces child), and about a boy named Bobby who lives in this house. Now Bobby is a boy who looks *just exactly like you*. Which of these will be Bobby in our story? All right, now, you hold Bobby. Which one of these women is Bobby's mother? All right, you can hold her, too. Today is Bobby's birthday, and his mother says that he can have a party and invite all his friends.[6] So Bobby goes and tells all his friends to come. The first two girls come to the party. Mommy doesn't know them, so she meets them. Then she turns to Bobby and says, "One of these girls looks so clean and neat." Bobby says, "Which one, Mommy?" What does Mommy say? Which girl looks clean and neat? Then some more children come to the party. What do you think they will do at the party? Will they play games?

Then it's time to eat, so Mommy brings out some lollipops. She has a lollipop for each child, but then she gets to these two children and finds she has only one lollipop left. She says, "Bobby, which one should I give the lollipop to?" What does Bobby say? Which one gets the lollipop? Why does this one get the lollipop? What else do they eat at the party? Then they open presents. (If the class is integrated, another question is added: "Who in your class would you invite if you were really giving a party?") Then Bobby opens his presents and then it's time to play. Some of the boys go outside and some of the girls play inside. (Boys are removed from set and two Negro and two white dolls are lined up in the order N, w, N, w.) Which ones of these girls look like Negro children? Can you show me? (If the child points to only one correct doll, the experimenter asks, "Does anyone else look like a Negro child?") Then the girls go out to play and the boys come inside. (Girls are removed and four boys are lined up in the order N, w, N, w.) Which ones of these dolls look like colored children? Can you show me? Which ones look like white children?

O.K., would you like to make up your own TV show all by youself? You can use both the house and school and any of the dolls you want. They stand up and you can sit them down on the furniture. (House and school are turned toward the child. All dolls are placed in a pile in front of him.)

Child is allowed to play. As the subject's attention begins to wander, the investigator picks up a doll of the subject's own race and sex and asks, "Who is his mother?" After the child picks a doll from the pile he is asked to pick its brothers and sisters to complete the family. The same process is repeated with the opposite race doll. The child is then presented with four dolls of the same sex as he is. The dolls can be matched by either race or dress, since the dolls which are dressed alike are of opposite races (i.e., white and Negro girls with red dresses and white and Negro girls with blue dresses). After the subject is asked to select the two dolls that look most alike, he is given the opportunity to match by either race or sex. Four dolls dressed completely differently are lined up (white boy and girl and Negro boy and girl) and he is again asked to choose the two which are most similar. The test is then terminated and the subject is taken back into the classroom.

The structured part of the test takes from ten to fifteen minutes to administer, and the unstructured part lasts as long as the child remains interested. Because of the variety of equipment, stories, participation by the child, and change of sets in midstream, even the three-year-olds were interested and involved throughout the entire test, and many requested the opportunity to return and play again.

The Equipment

The equipment was built and/or purchased to suit the specifications of the test. The basic material consists of eighteen four-and-one-half inch dolls dressed like nursery school children. The dolls are flexible and can be made to stand and sit easily by even a very young child. Because they are quite expensive and not easily purchased through regular commercial channels, the contaminating effect of response set for a familiar toy is minimized.

Since small, realistic Negro dolls of the type desired were unavailable at the inception of the study, it was necessary to transform a set of white dolls into Negroes by the application of paint and dye. A medium brown shade of dye was used, because an intermediate color makes identification possible for both light- and dark-skinned Negro children. The dolls have hair of the coarse-curl variety which, when dyed black, is a reasonable approximation of Negro hair texture. Since the dolls are small, the facial features are not too distinct and do not appear out of context with the skin color and hair texture. The finished product resembles a Negro child more closely than do most commercially available approximations.

After the pre-test and half of the final sample were tested, it was necessary to replace the toys because they had become damaged by excessive handling. The original dolls were no longer on the market and could not be reordered; therefore, a second set of dolls very closely resembling the first was made specifically for the study by a local toy manufacturer. A reliability check with two matched groups of twenty subjects each re-

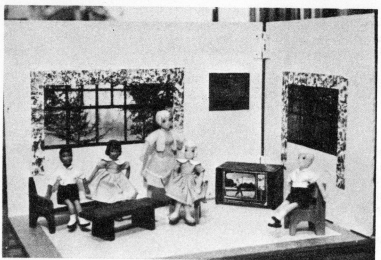

1. Equipment for the TV-Story Game.

vealed no significant difference in response caused by substitution of a
new set of dolls.

Nine of the dolls are white and nine brown. Each racial set is composed
of one woman, four boys, and four girls. Each white doll has an exact
Negro match in sex and dress; however, no two dolls of the same race and
sex have similar clothing, since it was felt that there would be less chance
of contamination if completely different sets of dolls were presented for
each question. All of the white dolls have blond hair, while the Negro
dolls' hair is black. Because of the age of the subjects and the size of
the dolls, Clark seemed to feel that it was advisable to use blond-haired
white dolls in order to maximize the differential in skin color.

The rest of the equipment consists of two stage sets representing a
house and a school, containing furniture built to scale for the dolls. Both
sets are constructed from wood, and two sides are left completely open,
giving the child additional play space. The insides of the sets are deco-
rated to represent a living room and a nursery school. The school is furnished with benches, double desks, a work table, chairs, and blackboards.
The living room contains a couch, a bench or coffee table, a television
set, and chairs.[7]

How the Variables Were Defined

To facilitate presentation of the data from the structured questionnaire, the operational definitions of the dependent variables are summarized below.

1. Awareness: knowledge of the social definition of racial differences
and of the perceptual cues by which one classifies people into these divisions. Match mother and child, match brown and white families, dress
v. color and sex v. color salience, identify "Negro," "colored," "white"
dolls.

2. Self-identification: perception of membership in a racial category
and willingness to state this fact. Two chances, one at beginning of each
story, to choose "the boy [girl] that looks just exactly like you." To be

scored correct, child has to choose correctly both times. Incorrect means at least one incorrect choice.

   3. Attitudes

      a. Stereotypes:

         1. Negative black stereotypes – "lazy and stupid." At least 75 percent of Blake and Dennis' tenth and eleventh grade group chose "lazy" as a Negro stereotype and at least 86 percent of them chose "ignorant."[8] (The Brink and Harris poll shows that 66 percent of whites indicated that Negroes were less ambitious and 39 percent said that Negroes were ignorant.[9])

         2. Positive white stereotypes – "neat and clean." At least 60 percent of Blake and Dennis' fourth and fifth grade groups and 97 percent of the high school group chose "neat" as a white stereotype. "Clean" was chosen by 95 percent of the Blake and Dennis high school group and 70 percent of the fourth and fifth grade group. (Ambition stereotypes are used for Negroes and appearance stereotypes for whites, since questions in the reverse order raise problems of validity. Using "dirty" as a negative Negro stereotype makes it difficult at this age level to differentiate stereotypic responses from responses based on a simple connection between brown and dirt.)

      b. Preference – "Which one gets the lollipop?" (used by Goodman); "Which one is nice?" (used by Clark, Goodman).

      c. Social Distance: "Which one does he play with?" (used by Goodman, Clark, Eugene Horowitz); "Which one does he invite home for lunch?" (used by Goodman, Eugene Horowitz). Brink and Harris show that 41 percent of white parents object to their child bringing a Negro home for dinner.[10] "Would Mommy like him to bring this one [rejected doll] home for lunch, too?"

There are several problems with the test. Because the subjects are quite young, the situation must be highly structured; the presence of numerous alternatives might be confusing to the child. It is thus difficult to tell whether choice of a white doll indicates rejection of Negroes, preference for whites, or both. Also, we have already suggested that these alternatives are by no means the only ones available, since a child may feel positively or negatively toward both races. The situation is one of forced choice, and selection of a white doll may only indicate that the child has no definite and deeply felt opinions but is slightly more favorable toward whites. I have thus added the unstructured material (probing for comments, free play) as an aid in interpreting the results, since this type of approach can be useful in uncovering subtleties of response to own and opposite race. Analysis of these unstructured data can often demonstrate exactly what rate of choice of a white doll means for different groups of youngsters. If children not only select the white doll but also make comments that white is good and black is not, a pattern of at least incipient racial attitudes is indicated.

Measurement Problems: Reliability, Validity, Bias

The split-half reliability of the original "Movie-Story Game" is .75, but this method of computing reliability is inappropriate for my version of the test. Since attitudes are partially a function of awareness in this age group, a low correlation between the two halves of the test may mean only that awareness increases as the test progresses. Reliability can also be determined by seeing if different instruments used on the same individual at the same time yield consistent results. This equivalence procedure was used in the pre-test. White children in desegregated schools were asked to name those in their class whom they would really invite to a party. Strong white preference was exhibited both on this sociometric technique and on the racial doll choice pattern. Because of the age of the children, the conventional methods of measuring validity seemed inappropriate. In the initial pre-test, all the major hypotheses were supported by this technique,[11] and so it was assumed to have face validity.

One control is absolutely necessary in this type of research, since a number of investigators have demonstrated that race of the experimenter may affect the validity of results. Answers of Negroes to the 1942 Memphis poll on the effects of a Japanese invasion were partially determined by the race of the interviewer, and, in later studies in North Carolina and

Boston, Negroes also were less militant when interviewed by white interviewer than when interviewed by a black. Pasamanick and Knobloch, and Richard Trent have found that responses of even young subjects may be affected by bias because of the experimenter's race.[12] This process is complex, however, since according to John Rohrer and Munro Edmundson's data, black and white interviewers can uncover different but supplementary aspects of the subject's personality.[13] The amount of approval and threat present in the experimental situation also seem to be crucial factors to consider. Irwin Katz found that under conditions creating a high expectancy of success, southern black college students performed better with a white than with a black experimenter. When an element of threat is introduced, however, other work by Katz shows that the presence of a white adminstrator can lead to suppressed hostility on the part of a Negro sample.[14]

These results suggest that black interviewers should be used with black children where the experimental situation produces threat. However, I wished to interview part of the black sample myself, despite the fact that I am white, because observation of subtle responses like facial or bodily movements helps clarify the youngsters' feelings about the questions, and interpretation of the data is often aided by such personal observations.

The Katz studies played a large part in determining the sample of black children which was selected for this purpose. It seemed that if race of the interviewer affected the results, it would do so particularly in a segregated Negro school. Here the presence of a white might be viewed as an unusual and hence disturbing factor. The results indicated that this assumption was correct. In an integrated setting, there were no statistically significant differences on any test questions between the responses of black children tested by a black and those tested by a white experimenter. In the segregated environment, however, the race of the experimenter did seem to affect the results on the self- identification question. Controlling for age and class, we find that there was a higher rate of misidentification among those Negro children tested by a white interviewer than there was among those tested by a black. There were three correct and thirteen incorrect identifications with a white interviewer, and eighteen correct and twenty incorrect with a black interviewer ($x^2 =$ 3.82; p≤ .06). This question, though, was the only one influenced by race of the investigator in the segregated school.[15]

Not only these results but the nature of the test itself suggested that a white interviewer could be utilized in an integrated setting. Our measure was indirect, the equipment was unusual and enjoyable, the interviewer attempted to create a relaxed situation, and the children were familiar with the interviewer and felt at ease with her. It was thus expected that the experimental situation would be relatively supportive and nonthreatening. My own impressions seemed to verify that the experience did not unduly provoke anxiety, for the black children in the integrated schools played and spoke freely in my presence, and they made both favorable and unfavorable comments about each race with no apparent self-consciousness. Many of the black children even begged to be allowed to return for another experimental session. For these reasons, it was decided to have a black interviewer work in the segregated schools, and I selected my part of the sample only from integrated settings.

Later studies of Katz's indicate that this procedure was appropriate. His studies of black northern urban boys show that these subjects performed better with a black than with a white experimenter under all conditions. Although he does not explicitly state whether the schools were segregated, his discussion implies that the boys had had little previous contact with white children.[16] It is important to note, however, that the performance of these youngsters was positively affected by approval, regardless of the experimenter's race.

If a technique is less projective than mine or if the children are unfamiliar with the experimenter, I would suggest that only a black interviewer be used in integrated schools. But statistical evidence and the nature of my test seem to indicate that my results in integrated schools were not affected by bias toward the experimenter.

Another form of bias which should be investigated is the presence of idiosyncratic effects due to the individual experimenter. Bias toward the experimenter within race was not expected to be high, because the test was structured, easy to administer, and all the interviewers were accustomed to working with young children. There were no significant differences in response among subjects tested by the two white investigators. This factor was not checked for the lone black interviewer because it was not possible to find another qualified black interviewer who was able to participate.

How the Data Were Scored

To make the data-gathering procedure as reliable as possible, a standard score sheet was provided for the structured test. Also everything the child did and said during the free play period was completely recorded. (The process was facilitated by the fact that the children were young and hence not highly verbal.) Based on responses in the pre-test, a detailed scheme for coding verbal and behavioral discrimination was designed; the protocols were scored according to these categories by two coders at the termination of the data-gathering period. Each subject's verbal and behavioral responses were analyzed independently with no identifying information about the child.[17] Inter-rater reliability was high, since there was 81 percent agreement on the behavioral and 85 percent agreement on the verbal categorizations.

It was also necessary to design an index of skin color for the Negro subjects. Each child was rated on a four-category basis (light, light-medium, medium, and dark-dark medium). Light was defined as close to white or very light tan; light medium as a light brown color; medium as a middle shade of brown; and dark-dark medium as the dark brown to black end of the color continuum.

On a subsample of fifty-seven subjects, two whites concurred 87 percent of the time using this four-category scheme. However, categorization of sixty subjects yielded only 50 percent agreement between a white and black coder. The disagreement was in a consistent direction, however. The black coder was regarded by the whites as dark medium but seemed to regard herself as medium; hence, she tended to rate the very dark children a shade lighter than the whites did.

The difference in color coding between the white and black raters may be due either to a personal subjective bias on the part of the black (that is, she perceived herself as lighter than she actually was) or to the inability of whites to perceive the exact meaning of color differences in the black community. This latter interpretation would imply that the black interviewer was more accurate in her coding. That is, her ratings were closer to the way a cross-section of the black community would rate these same children. But we did not have several black raters, so these questions must remain unanswered.

Another question that cannot be answered is whether the ratings of either black or white coders would agree with the way the child actually perceived himself. Subjective perception of the subject's own color cannot be measured, since the children in this study were too young (see Chapter 10).

An attempt was made to handle these problems of subjective ratings of skin color by collapsing the ratings into two categories (light/light medium and medium/dark-medium). Agreement was increased by this procedure to 80 percent between the black and white raters and to 92 percent between the two whites.[18] It was hoped that these broader classifications would obviate some of the difficulties, since there is less room for disagreement in broad categories than there is if fine distinctions are made.

It was necessary to construct an index of social class. Because of the paucity of background information in the school records and the unwillingness of many teachers to reveal the child's name and address, the only available index of social class was father's (or principal wage-earner's) occupation. The Reiss index of occupations, with an adjustment made for blacks, was used as a means of separating the children into middle and working class.[19] It is important to point out that my "middle class" category has a varied range of occupations. The white middle class tends to cluster at the upper levels of the occupational heirarchy. My sample contains numerous white children whose parents were professionals, either self-employed or connected with industry or universities. There were also many youngsters whose fathers were in high-level managerial positions. The black middle-class sample, however, clusters at the lower middle-class end of the continuum. There were several parents who were lawyers or engineers, but the vast majority of the middle-class black children had parents who were either in lower-level white collar positions (e.g., salesmen, secretaries), lower-level civil service positions, or highly skilled crafts (welder, plumber, machinist).[20] The group on relief (Aid to Dependent Children) was considered as a separate "lower class" category for both races. As a check on this method, father's occupation was also classified by the census code; however, the class data are presented in terms of the Reiss index unless otherwise noted.

A means of classifying schools as segregated or integrated was also necessary. A segregated school was defined as one with 10 percent or fewer students of one race; all others were considered integrated. This particular means of division seemed feasible because of the age of the subjects and the class size; for instance, in a predominantly white school, a proportion of less than 10 percent Negroes would mean that there was one Negro child in the class. If this child were light, many of his schoolmates might not even realize that he belonged to a different racial group.

How the Results Were Analyzed

The data were statistically analyzed by an analysis of variance technique. This method allowed me both to apply proper controls and to uncover possible interaction effects between variables. To facilitate use of an analysis of variance, the items on the structured portion of the questionnaire were combined into indices, and a +.20 correlation between individual items was considered to be sufficient justification for consolidating responses into an overall measure.[21] Such a low figure was selected because several factors tended to depress the correlation between items. Many of the youngest children had little awareness of racial differences and were either choosing randomly or manifested a response-set for the doll in a particular hand. Also, since the child was forced to choose either a white or a Negro doll, some of the relatively nonprejudiced subjects resolved the dilemma by alternating their racial choices.

Table 1   Description of Schools and Children in the Sample

School[a]	Age, years	White, number	Negro, number	Teaching staff	Social class of children	Comments
A	3, 4, 5	15	51	Integrated	Middle, working, ADC	Located in black ghetto. School primarily for children of working mothers. Children referred by welfare agencies attend free, others pay on a sliding scale
B	3, 4, 5	22	14	Integrated	Middle, working, ADC	Payment on sliding scale
C	5	6	9	White	Working, ADC	Located across street from public housing project where most of children live. No charge for attendance
D	5	0	13	Integrated	Middle	Mostly children of professionals, (e.g., engineers), sales, or civil service employees, with some skilled workmen (such as plumbers). Tuition required
E	3 and 4	0	27	Negro	Middle, working	Located in black ghetto. Run by church-payment on sliding scale
F	5	4	8	White	Working, ADC	No tuition

Table 1 Description of Schools and Children in the Sample (continued)

School[a]	Age, years	White, number	Negro, number	Teaching staff	Social class of children	Comments
G	4	1	28	Integrated	Working, ADC	Located in black ghetto. Run specifically for lower-class children. Financial need a criterion for admission
H	4	0	23	Negro	Middle	Located in upper middle-class Negro neighborhood. Mostly children of professionals (e.g., lawyers); civil service, sales, or skilled craft (e.g., welders)
I	4 and 5	19	1	White	Middle, working	Run by religious group for children of all denominations. Payment on sliding scale
J	5	17	0	White	Middle	Summer program run for pre-first-graders by upper middle-class white suburb. Mostly children of professionals working in high-level positions in industry (e.g., research and development, personnel)
K	3 and 4	12	0	White	Middle	Located in upper middle-class white suburb. All children of professionals
L[b]	4 and 5	53	2	White	Working, ADC	Project Headstart center run by Catholic Church. Four classes, both Negroes in same class

Table 1   Description of Schools and Children in the Sample (continued)

School[a]	Age, years	White, number	Negro, number	Teaching staff	Social class of children	Comments
M	4 and 5	6	6	Negro	Working, ADC	Project Headstart center
N	4 and 5	0	14	Integrated	Working, ADC	Project Headstart center
O	4	19	0	White	Middle	Mostly children of church members
P	5	14	3	White	Middle	High tuition, mostly children of professionals, (e.g., architects, college professors, graduate students)

[a]Schools are designated by letter to preserve anonymity.
[b]Since this school is located in an area of high racial prejudice, I thought this group might be atypical, but it did not differ from the rest of the working-class sample.

The six preference items correlated well enough with one another to justify construction of an overall attitude index. These data also indicated that the stereotype, social distance, and affectual dimensions of attitude were not differentiated from each other in this age group. It was necessary to utilize three separate measures of awareness, however, since the items grouped themselves into three clusters which did not correlate highly with one another. The "color terms" index is composed of knowledge of the terms "Negro," "colored," and "white"; the "color match" measure refers to the ability to match families by race; and the "color salience" index includes the race v. sex and the race v. dress salience questions. (The correlation matrices appear in Appendix 2).

Table 2   Sample by Age, Race, Class, and Sex[a]

	White					
	Middle class		Working class		ADC	
Age, years	male	female	male	female	male	female
3	3	9	1	3	3	1
4	14	21	8	11	4	12
5	23	20	12	9	11	10
	Negro					
	Middle class		Working class		ADC	
	male	female	male	female	male	female
3	3	5	6	13	4	7
4	7	18	20	25	14	14
5	10	4	16	7	5	6

[a]The sample here is slightly smaller than the original 387 tested. Some subjects had to be omitted in the final analysis of variance because of blanks either in background information or in the structured portion of the test, and the two lone integrators in schools G and I were also not included because of their atypical situation. The actual statistics were computed on the basis of 359 children.

Table 3   Sample by Class, Race, and Contact[a]

	Whites	
Class	segregated	integrated
Middle	56	34
Working	19	25
ADC	24	17
	Negroes	
	segregated	integrated
Middle	29	18
Working	35	52
ADC	29	21

[a]Of the light Negroes in the sample, 23 were in the middle class, 26 were from the working class, and 17 were from families receiving ADC funds. Of the dark Negroes, 23 were middle class, 61 were working class, and 34 were from ADC families.

Table 4   *Summary of Sample Size*

	Whites	*Negroes*
Class		
Middle	90	47
Working	44	87
ADC	41	50
Sex		
Male	79	85
Female	96	99
Age, years		
3	20	38
4	70	98
5	85	48
Contact[a]		
Segregated	99	93
Integrated	76	91
Color		
Light/light medium		66
Dark/dark medium		118
Total	175	184

[a]White interviewers were used in all sessions with white children and were used in 93 of sessions with Negroes (16 sessions in segregated schools, 77 in integrated schools). Negro interviewers were used in 91 sessions, all with Negroes (76 in segregated schools, 15 in integrated schools).

Sample

The sample was composed of children three to five years old attending kindergartens and nursery schools in the greater Boston area. An attempt was made to test every child in each class, but occasionally this was not possible because a few of the subjects refused to cooperate. Tables 1–4 summarize relevant information about each school and give the sample size by sex, class, contact, age, and race. The data collected from these samples are discussed in Chapters 4 to 6.

Many studies show that young children of both races exhibit preference for white dolls or white figures in pictures. Yet it is not clear that white preference is indicative of actual racial attitudes. This chapter demonstrates that doll choice does have racial connotations for the majority of youngsters. The data show that black children exhibit less preference for Negro dolls than white youngsters do for white dolls. Data on racial awareness help us interpret this difference as due to negative attitudes toward blacks for children of both races. Further explanation of the implications of doll preference are provided by the findings on the relationship between age, attitudes, and awareness. Age results in this study show that for four- and five year-olds of both races and for three-year-old Negroes, white preference has some racial connotation. The choices of the white three-year-old group, however, do not indicate racial evaluations. This finding gives us perspective on new results concerning other sociological correlates of attitude development which are discussed in the following chapter.[1]

Effect of Race on Doll Choice

Other investigations demonstrate that even during the preschool years, children of both races seem to have negative attitudes about blacks and show definite preference for white. But what does choice of a white figure by both black and white children really indicate? Is it measuring a racial attitude; that is, is this choice motivated by feelings about social categories? Or is it, instead, a response-set for a familiar doll or toy, or merely a reflection of the fact that the child may actually be playing with white peers?

Initially, I hypothesized that selection of a white doll would be an indication of incipient racial attitudes for most black children. Racial attitudes affect them directly and personally, and hence they may be at least vaguely aware of the social connotations of race at an early age. A low rate of choice of the brown doll thus should mean rejection of their own race or ambivalence toward it. (By ambivalence I mean that the black child may prefer whites to blacks but still does not totally reject his own group.) The meaning of doll choice for the white youngsters, I thought, would be less clear. I was convinced that although many of the whites were also selecting dolls on the basis of incipient racial attitudes, some white subgroups might be choosing dolls on other bases. The only way to gain understanding of this issue was by the application of several measures. I used an index constructed from the six attitude questions on the structured test, spontaneous verbal and free play material, and data on the three awareness indices to make inferences about the meaning of the difference between black and white children in own-race preference choice.

Consider the statement of a black four-year-old youngster who tells us, "All the brown dolls, the ugly ones, they can't come up [and play]." The preference results indicate that generalized rejection of this type or at least ambivalence is a characteristic reaction of some of the Negro children to dolls of their own color. The white subjects, on the other hand, seem to reject blacks and are positively attracted to their own membership group. Controlling for sex, class, and age,[2] we find that more whites than blacks prefer dolls of their own race on our attitude index. ($p \leqslant .01$, see Table 5).[3] It is important to note, however, that although Negroes have an affinity for dolls of the opposite race, they still choose white dolls less often than white children do. ($F=7.26$, $p \leqslant .01$, see Table 5).

Many other investigators also indicate that light-skinned dolls are preferred by both black and white children,[4] but it is still not clear what this choice means to many of the subjects. If they not only consistently prefer the white doll but also make spontaneous comments suggesting that possible racial factors are influencing their selection, we can begin to offer tentative explanations about the meaning of doll preference on the attitude index. A comparison of comments made about the color of the dolls helps clarify this issue. White children made more positive and less negative comments about their own color than did Negroes. If whites spoke about their own color at all in affect-laden terms, the reference was favorable; however, for blacks there was a slight tendency in the reverse

Table 5   Attitude Means[a] *— Analysis of Variance by Sex, Class, Race, and Age*

1 = High own-race preference
2 = Low own-race preference

Males

	Middle class				Working class		
	3 yrs.	4 yrs.	5 yrs.		3 yrs.	4 yrs.	5 yrs.
White	1.39	1.29	1.31	White	1.50	1.31	1.24
	N=3	N=14	N=23		N=1	N=8	N=12
Negro	1.72	1.67	1.82	Negro	1.53	1.56	1.51
	N=3	N=7	N=10		N=5	N=17	N=15

	ADC lower class		
	3 yrs.	4 yrs.	5 yrs.
White	1.39	1.33	1.26
	N=3	N=4	N=11
Negro	1.83	1.63	1.67
	N=1	N=12	N=5

Females

	Middle class				Working class		
	3 yrs.	4 yrs.	5 yrs.		3 yrs.	4 yrs.	5 yrs.
White	1.46	1.27	1.28	White	1.33	1.19	1.19
	N=8	N=21	N=20		N=3	N=11	N=9
Negro	1.58	1.69	1.58	Negro	1.53	1.58	1.71
	N=4	N=18	N=4		N=11	N=24	N=7

Table 5 *Attitude Means[a] — Analysis of Variance*
by Sex, Class, Race, and Age (continued)

	ADC lower class		
	3 yrs.	4 yrs.	5 yrs.
White	1.17	1.31	1.25
	N=1	N=12	N=10
Negro	1.43	1.63	1.81
	N=7	N=14	N=6

Total race effect, controlling for age, sex, class: White = 1.30 / Negro = 1.64 (p≤.01)

---

[a] Attitudes are presented here in terms of *own-race* preference. To convert to *white* choice for Negroes, subtract each mean from 3.00. "F" for difference in white choice = 7.26, p≤.01.

---

direction (see Table 6).[5] A similar pattern exists for comments about dolls of the opposite race from the child. Whites' reference to the doll of the opposite race is more unfavorable than favorable, but for blacks there is an opposite trend (see Table 6). Comments about cleanliness also exhibit the same pattern of white preference among children of both races.

The equating of darkness and dirt seems to be one means by which the child initially learns to prefer white, since 21 percent of the total number of subjects of both races who spoke made spontaneous comments about the connection between cleanliness and the white dolls or dirt and the brown dolls. For many children, a relationship between brown and dirty generalizes and creates negative feeling for dark skin. A Negro child, for instance, compared the white doll with her own skin and then placed it next to the arm of the white interviewer, saying, "The doll is clean, just like you are." Some white children also make this inference. "Light people are clean," commented one white child, "and dark people look like

Table 6 *Types of Comments Made, by Percent of*
Children Speaking (continued)

Comments	Whites N=159	Negroes[a] N=150
Favorable own-race or own-color	14.5	3.3
Unfavorable own-race or own-color	0	7.3
Neutral own-race or own-color	8	13
Unrelated to race or color	77.5	76.4
Favorable opposite race or color	5.7	9
Unfavorable opposite race or color	18.2	2
Neutral opposite race or color	13	11
Unrelated to race or color	63.1	70

[a] In relation to Chapter 6, it is important to note that of the Negroes making favorable own-race comments, 3 identified correctly and 2 incorrectly. Of those making unfavorable own-race comments, 1 identified correctly and 10 incorrectly. Of those Negroes who made favorable opposite-race comments, 3 identified correctly and 10 incorrectly. Of those who made unfavorable opposite-race comments, 2 identified correctly and 1 incorrectly.

they have dirt all over them." The percentage of children speaking who made comments about dirt is shown in the tabulation below.

Comments*	Whites N = 159	Negroes N = 150
Opposite race (color) dirty and/or own race (color) clean	31.5	4.0
Opposite race (color) clean and/or own race (color) dirty	6.9	8.7

*Of the Negroes who said their own race was dirty, 9 identified incorrectly and 4 correctly. Of those who said the opposite race was dirty, 3 identified incorrectly and 3 correctly.

That many white children internalize positive and that Negroes internalize negative attitudes about their own race or color is further substantiated by the free play data on behavioral discrimination. In an unstructured free play situation, both white and black children tend to reject the brown dolls, as the following percentages show:

*Discrimination**	*Whites* $N = 147$	*Negroes* $N = 186$
Against own race or color	.7	9
Against opposite race or color	17.7	5

* Of those Negroes who behaviorally discriminated against their own race, 15 identified incorrectly and 2 correctly. Of those who discriminated against the opposite race, 3 identified incorrectly and 7 correctly.

All of these data provide additional evidence that children of both races tend to accept whites and show ambivalence or rejection toward blacks. These doll-play choices cannot wholly reflect actual behavior patterns for all of our subjects; even in a segregated school where black youngsters have little chance to interact with white peers, 60 percent of them choose the white doll as a playmate. And when contact differences are controlled, variations between subgroups of children within each race still appear.

Another possible interpretation of preference for the light-skinned dolls should be considered. Perhaps these selections reflect neither attitudes nor the racial composition of the classroom but instead response-set for familiar play equipment. Most of the integrated and all-Negro classrooms, however, do have black dolls. Familiarity with the equipment alone thus cannot fully explain high white preference among the black and at least some of the white youngsters. When we consider some of the spontaneous comments and free play, we have even greater evidence that expressed preference for white by at least part of the black sample has a racial tinge and indicates rejection of minority status or ambivalence toward it:

I'm gonna have a good guy and a bad guy fighting. The good guy [white doll] and the bad guy [Negro doll]. Now I'll pick out the good guys. All the white ones are the good guys. Now I'll pick out all the bad guys [picks out all Negroes]. They fight. [Eventually the white "good guys" overcome the Negro "bad guys."]

Jamie, Negro, five years old

[All the white dolls put in a pile of "nice ones" and all the Negroes in a pile of "mean ones."] All the brown kids have to stay in because they were bad at school. [All white dolls moved to school.] They don't like the brown kids.

Felicia, Negro, four years old

An analysis of the unstructured material shows that the selections of at least part of the white sample also clearly reflect racial attitudes, rather than response-set for a familiar doll:

Negroes do bad things. They broke my brother's pumpkin and stole our toys. That's what Mommy thinks.

Amy, white, five years old

She's all black. She's a colored girl. A long time ago I was over at Grandpa's and my sister said, "colored boys, colored boys" to two colored boys. They almost stabbed her. She shouldn't have said that. They would have stabbed her. My mother told me that.

Robert, white, five years old

Although the following play sequence does not mention race, it may have been an expression of feeling about the school integration controversy which was occurring in Boston at the time of this study:[6]

She [Negro girl] goes to Johnny's school [Johnny is white]. She usually doesn't, but this one [white girl] usually does. She [Negro girl] shouldn't go to Johnny's school. She and her friend [Negro boy] mess up the school. They break the glasses and throw rubbish. They [Negro and white girl] have a fight over which one is Johnny's friend. Johnny comes over and says, "This one [white girl] is my friend."

Johnny and his friend [white boy] go to school, but this girl [Negro girl] came in and punched him. Johnny had a fight with the little girl and throwed her over. The little bad girl [Negro] went home, and she never came back to Johnny's school again.

> Raul, white, five years old
> (integrated school)

Data on racial awareness supplement the measures already discussed and help to clarify the meaning of doll choice on the attitude index. Among groups that are either aware of racial differences or preoccupied by color, there is greater likelihood that choice of a white doll has some racial connotation. I have defined "awareness" as knowledge of social categories based on such biological characteristics as skin color, hair, and facial features. The correlation matrices presented in Appendix 2 suggest that "awareness" seems to be composed of three dimensions. The cognitive components of racial awareness include knowledge of racial names (color terms index) and ability to pair families by color (color match index). If the child can correctly select the two "Negroes" in a row of four dolls when requested to do so, he has a fairly sophisticated conception of how one classifies people into racial categories. The meaning of ability to match families is less clear, since the subject may be pairing dolls on the basis of color alone without realization that color has social implications. The affective dimension (measured by "color salience") may be the most subtle index, for it indicates the emotional importance that color has for the individual. Because the situation is ambiguous (the subject can match dolls by color, dress, or sex), his structuring of the setting reveals the heirarchy of relevance of these factors for him personally.

Controlling for sex, class, and age, there is a racial difference on the color salience measure. In fourteen of the eighteen comparisons, color is more pertinent for the black than for the white child ($F=6.05$, $p \leqslant .025$, see Table 7). The overall mean for the black sample is 1.31, which is far on the color side of the scale. This clearly indicates that color is highly salient as compared to sex or dress for blacks. But the total effect for

Table 7 . *Color Salience Means — Analysis of Variance by*
Sex, Class, Race, and Age

1 = Color more salient than dress and sex
2 = Dress and sex more salient than color

Males

	Middle class				Working class		
	3 yrs.	4 yrs.	5 yrs.		3 yrs.	4 yrs.	5 yrs.
White	1.50	1.25	1.22	White	1.00	1.50	1.46
	N=3	N=14	N=23		N=1	N=8	N=12
Negro	1.33	1.21	1.25	Negro	1.50	1.29	1.21
	N=3	N=7	N=10		N=5	N=17	N=15

ADC lower class

	3 yrs.	4 yrs.	5 yrs.
White	1.50	1.38	1.32
	N=3	N=4	N=11
Negro	1.0	1.42	1.20
	N=1	N=12	N=5

Females

	Middle class				Working class		
	3 yrs.	4 yrs.	5 yrs.		3 yrs.	4 yrs.	5 yrs.
White	1.44	1.58	1.45	White	1.33	1.41	1.72
	N=8	N=21	N=20		N=3	N=11	N=9
Negro	1.37	1.36	1.25	Negro	1.41	1.38	1.36
	N=4	N=18	N=4		N=11	N=24	N=7

Table 7 *Color Salience Means—Analysis of Variance by
Sex, Class, Race, and Age* (continued)

	ADC lower class		
	3 yrs.	4 yrs.	5 yrs.
White	2.0 N=1	1.58 N=12	1.45 N=10
Negro	1.36 N=7	1.32 N=14	1.25 N=6

Total race effect, controlling for class, age, sex: [a]White = 1.45 Negro = 1.31 F=6.05, p≤.025

[a]White = grand mean + mean white.
Negro = grand mean + mean Negro.

whites is 1.45, which shows approximately equal selection of color and dress or sex. Recognition of color differences per se appears early[7] and is probably reasonably uniform for the population tested, so these data suggest that, even if he cannot express it in words, the Negro child is aware that color is a key characteristic which may have something to do with himself.

Analysis of comments provides additional evidence that skin color is more important than other physical features for blacks. Of those 150 Negroes who made spontaneous comments during the test, twice as many referred to color or race (37 percent) as to hair (18 percent). The 159 whites who spoke, however, tended to comment almost equally about the color and hair of the dolls (46 percent and 52 percent respectively).[8] Other studies of older children have also demonstrated that race is far more salient for blacks than it is for whites.[9]

The other awareness indices do not show any significant differences by race.[10] Although Negroes and whites may be equally sophisticated on the cognitive dimension of racial awareness, there is a possibility that these statistical results are misleading. All of the experimenters in this study had the impression that some of the black youngsters were purposefully mismatching or misidentifying the dolls, and this type of response seemed to be unaffected by race of the interviewer. For instance, some children would point to the white dolls when asked to identify "colored" and to the two Negro dolls when "white" was requested. This result is especially interesting when one considers that, during the previous part of the test, some of these same youngsters had used the word "colored" in response to the Negro doll.

We have already indicated that Negro subjects overwhelmingly show preference for white in response to attitude questions. When asked to classify dolls or match racially at the very end of a relatively nonthreatening game, they may suddenly have realized the true purpose of the test and reacted with hostility. The Clarks elicited the same type of inappropriate response from Negro children. When asked to color a picture of a child the color they preferred, fifteen percent of the subjects used a bizarre color like red or green even though they had previously correctly colored a leaf and a mouse. At this point, many of the subjects reacted to the Clarks with anger.[11]

The statistical evidence in my study, then, shows that there is no difference between whites and blacks on the cognitive dimension of awareness, though there is a possibility that these statistics may not be an accurate measure. However, these data do indicate that color is an extremely pertinent factor for the preschool-age Negro, even if he does not have a highly sophisticated knowledge of racial terms.

On the basis of my data I conclude that since color is both highly salient for blacks and more salient for them than it is for whites, the low degree of own-race choices by black children indicates incipient racial attitudes. Even if a black child does not have a sophisticated knowledge of racial differences, he seems to be preoccupied with color and may sense that it is somehow important or personally relevant; his white choices are thus likely to indicate affect that is beginning to be attached to social categories. The preference results for the Negro sample do not indicate whether white doll choice means actual rejection of blacks or ambivalence toward the black child's own race; that is, selection of a white doll on a forced choice question may show only that the child prefers whites to Negroes. It need not also mean hostility toward the brown doll or rejection of it. Analysis of spontaneous comments and free play shows that the preference responses of some black children do actually indicate rejection of their own race. But since many Negro youngsters did not make comments connected to color, and since their choice of a white doll was lower than that of their white peers, we need additional evidence before we can answer the question whether choice of a white doll signifies negative rather than ambivalent response to their own race.

Analysis of the unstructured material on the test suggests that selection of the white doll shows incipient racial attitudes for some of the white children as well. Other white children, however, have a low or average degree of color salience. They may be choosing white dolls on the basis of some nonracial criterion. The fact that many of the white youngsters did not make spontaneous comments about color complicates interpretation of their responses. Does lack of comment mean lack of awareness of race, lack of salience of race or color, or does it indicate, instead, desire to avoid discussion of racial matters?

I conclude only that for many of the blacks and for at least some white children, white preference indicates an incipient racial attitude. The differential between whites and Negroes in own-race choice is accounted for by rejection or ambivalence toward their own race on the part of many of the black children and either positive attitudes toward their own race or racially unrelated factors for the white sample. Although no further conclusion can be drawn from the race data, additional findings on differences within each racial group would help to clarify some of these unanswered problems and explain the meaning of doll choice more fully. Data on age are particularly helpful in this respect, because age is probably one of the major factors influencing the development of racial cognizance.

Influence of Age on Doll Selection

Preschool children are not naive about racial matters: differences in color begin to acquire social meaning for the child at an early age, and he soon realizes that dark-brown Johnny and light-brown Mary belong together in some way. As he grows older, he learns not only how to group people into social categories but also what these classifications mean in terms of social desirability. As we saw in Chapter 2, however, there has been disagreement in the literature about the age at which knowledge of racial differences appears. An answer to this question would clarify some of the problems raised by my data on racial variations in doll preference between black and white children.

Amy, age five, says, "This doll is a Negro." Joey, age three, says, "All these dolls got brown stockings." Joey is beginning to exhibit awareness of color differences. He does not as yet know that people are classified into racial categories on the basis of variations in color, but he does realize that some of the dolls have brown legs. He soon will progress, as Amy has, from noticing differences in complexion to investing these differences with social meaning. Any attempt to measure age at awareness must distinguish between these two extremes of actual knowledge of social categories and ability to differentiate colors.

If a child can match families correctly, he is at least aware of variations in color. My data show that, controlling for race, class, and sex, three- and four-year-old children match families with about the same degree of accuracy. At most levels, however, five-year-olds pair dolls more correctly than their younger counterparts do (F=3.99, p≤.05; see Table 8). This does not mean that three- and four-year-olds are unable to match dolls of the same color. There is a high level of matching ability among even three-and four-year-old children: over seventy percent of children in both the three and the four-year-old groups can correctly match a mother and child of the same color.[12] My data only indicate that five-year-olds have an even greater ability to pair similarly colored dolls than younger children have.

These "color match" results may just mean that children more ac-

Table 8   *Color Match Index — Analysis of Variance by
Sex, Class, Race, and Age*

1 = Correct
2 = Incorrect

Males

	Middle class					Working class		
	3 yrs.	4 yrs.	5 yrs.			3 yrs.	4 yrs.	5 yrs.
White	1.40	1.39	1.28		White	1.0	1.37	1.27
	N=3	N=14	N=23			N=1	N=8	N=12
Negro	1.53	1.34	1.34		Negro	1.36	1.45	1.37
	N=3	N=7	N=10			N=5	N=17	N=15

ADC lower class

	3 yrs.	4 yrs.	5 yrs.
White	1-33	1.40	1.22
	N=3	N=4	N=11
Negro	1.00	1.37	1.28
	N=1	N=12	N=5

Females

	Middle class					Working class		
	3 yrs.	4 yrs.	5 yrs.			3 yrs.	4 yrs.	5 yrs.
White	1.48	1.44	1.25		White	1.40	1.47	1.33
	N=8	N=21	N=20			N=3	N=11	N=9
Negro	1.70	1.39	1.40		Negro	1.36	1.41	1.40
	N=4	N=18	N=4			N=11	N=24	N=7

*Table 8   Color Match Index—Analysis of Variance by
Sex, Class, Race, and Age* (continued)

	ADC lower class		
	3 yrs.	4 yrs.	5 yrs.
White	1.40	1.31	1.22
	N=1	N=12	N=10
Negro	1.37	1.37	1.37
	N=7	N=14	N=6

Total age effect, controlling for race, class, and sex.[a]

3 years old=1.37
4 years old=1.40   F=3.99, p≤.05
5 years old=1.32

[a] Age effect = grand mean + mean for that age.

curately perceive color differences at age five. The color terms index, though, offers proof that this correctness in family matching is due to increased awareness of race as a social category.[13] Most five-year-olds identify the "Negro," "Colored," and "white" dolls with more accuracy than the three- and four-year-olds do (F=18.96, p≤.001, see Table 9).

Other data show that color becomes an affectively laden concept by the fourth year. Analysis of spontaneous comments provides evidence for this. Slightly more neutral than affect-laden (positive or negative) comments are made by three-year-old whites about the color of the dolls. Of the four- and five-year-old white subjects who spoke, however, about twice as many made emotion-laden as neutral references to color (see Table 12). White and brown thus acquire some additional meaning for the four- and five-year-old group in the white sample.

Table 9   Color Terms Index — Analysis of Variance by
Sex, Class, Race, and Age

1 = Correct
2 = Incorrect

Males

Middle class				Working class			
	3 yrs.	4 yrs.	5 yrs.		3 yrs.	4 yrs.	5 yrs.
White	1.44	1.63	1.36	White	1.00	1.67	1.53
	N=3	N=14	N=23		N=1	N=8	N=12
Negro	2.0	1.71	1.47	Negro	1.87	1.71	1.51
	N=3	N=7	N=10		N=5	N=17	N=15

ADC lower class			
	3 yrs.	4 yrs.	5 yrs.
White	1.77	1.63	1.42
	N=3	N=4	N=11
Negro	1.33	1.58	1.60
	N=1	N=12	N=5

Females

Middle class				Working class			
	3 yrs.	4 yrs.	5 yrs.		3 yrs.	4 yrs.	5 yrs.
White	1.75	1.65	1.36	White	1.89	1.85	1.33
	N=8	N=21	N=20		N=3	N=11	N=9
Negro	1.67	1.67	1.41	Negro	1.73	1.67	1.38
	N=4	N=18	N=4		N=11	N=24	N=7

Table 9   *Color Terms Index — Analysis of Variance by*
          Sex, Class, Race, and Age (continued)

	ADC lower class		
	3 yrs.	4 yrs.	5 yrs.
White	2.0	1.61	1.46
	N=1	N=12	N=10
Negro	1.57	1.47	1.38
	N=7	N=14	N=6

Total age effect, controlling for race, sex, and class.[a]

3 years old=1.67
4 years old=1.66   F=18.96, p≤.001
5 years old=1.44

[a] Age effect = grand mean + effect for that age.

If young Negro children mentioned color at all, they tended to do so in a neutral fashion, particularly at age three. They begin to make affect-laden comments at age four, and the number of racially irrelevant comments about the white doll drops from three to four years of age. By age five, black children make more total comments about color than do their younger counterparts. But although the five-year-old black children tend to make more affect-laden than neutral comments about whites, they still make more neutral than emotionally toned comments about their own race. Our color salience measure suggests that color is important for Negro children at all ages, but if they dislike the shade of their skin or are ambivalent toward it, these feelings create tension and conflict which they can resolve by repression. The avoidance of affective reference to their own race in an unstructured situation, therefore, may serve as a defense mechanism for some of the black youngsters.

These data show that three-year-old children of both races are not highly aware of racial differences. They make comments and can match dolls on the basis of color rather than race. Although they have little knowledge of racial terms, children of three do know that "the faces match" or that "this doll has a tan." Of course some three-year-olds did show rather sophisticated racial awareness, but we concentrate here only on group differences by age.

At age four, the score on the color terms index indicates lack of a highly developed cognitive orientation to race, even though children of this age are able to pair dolls by color correctly. However, the comments of the white children suggest that response to color is characterized by an emotional aura which is not so evident at age three. Age four thus seems to exemplify the stage that Allport calls pre-generalized learning. The child does not quite understand what Negroes are, but he has begun to realize that color differences have some type of social meaning: black and white are emotion-laden concepts, and this affect attaches to people as well. This combination of confusion and affect is illustrated by the comment made by white, four-year-old Martin: "She [white doll] is colored, just like we are. We're brown. But the other one's black. I don't like black — it's too much!"

The big jump in conceptual sophistication comes at age five. The preference for white accompanied by a vague awareness of race at age four is transformed for the five-year-old into a clear knowledge that these biological features are connected to social categories. Although cognitive awareness of race appears for both whites and Negroes between the fourth and fifth years, the color salience results presented in our discussion of racial differences indicate that color acquires an importance somewhat earlier for the black than for the white child.

On the basis of these awareness results, we should expect children's preferences to reflect incipient attitudes by age four and real racial attitudes by age five. If we are correct in assuming that social evaluations of race accompany dawning racial cognizance, we should find increases in white doll choice with age for children of both races. The data support this assumption. In general there is an increase in selection of the white doll from age three to age four years and from age four to age five years[14]

(F=4.35, p≤.025). These results provide additional evidence for Allport's assumption that color preferences may actually precede sophisticated cognition of racial categories. The means for color match, color terms, and white preference show that children of both races exhibit high white preference even before they are able to match families and classify correctly into racial categories (see Figure 2).

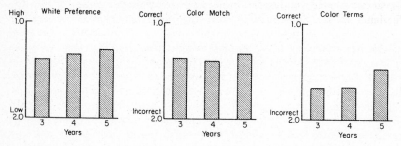

2. White preference, color match, and color terms by age, controlling for race, sex, and class.

Other data also indicate that these doll choices begin to reflect incipient racial attitudes by four and fully developed attitudes by at least five years of age. Choice of the white doll as "lazy and stupid" by white children shows random choice at age three, drops sharply at age four, and further decreases slightly at age five.[15] The choices of the white children on the "lazy and stupid" question are given below, by age group and by percent.

	3 years	4 years	5 years
White "lazy and stupid"	50	32.9	29.5
Negro "lazy and stupid"	50	67.1	70.5
	N=24	N=73	N=88

Of those white children who chose the white doll as the one to invite "home to lunch," there is an increase with age in the percentage who would not also invite the Negro (see Table 10). There is again a sharp break between ages three and four, and at age five the percentage rejecting the brown doll increases even further. The selections on this particular question reflect not slight preferences but definite opinions.[16]

As black children learn these racial evaluations, many realize what their racial role implies and begin to reject their own group. The color salience measure shows that color is already a matter of concern for

Table 10   *Responses to Negro Doll by Children Choosing*
          White Doll to "Invite Home to Lunch"

	Percent of white children		
	3 years	*4 years*	*5 years*
Would not also ask Negro	13	36	42
Would ask Negro, too	87	64	58
	N=8	N=42	N=57
	Percent of Negro children		
	3 years	*4 years*	*5 years*
Would not also ask Negro	11	12	44
Would ask Negro, too	89	88	56
	N=18	N=51	N=25

even three-year-old black children; white preference choices for this group may thus already have some vague racial implications. However, white choice and unfavorable comments about blacks increase at age four and show that incipient racial attitudes are present. By age five, white choices signify not just mild or vague preferences but in some cases outright group rejection. There is an increase with age in the percentage of black children who choose a white doll to ask "home for lunch" but who refused to invite the Negro when given the opportunity to do so (the major rise comes between ages four and five). Even if they expressed a preference for whites, the vast majority of three- and four-year-old Negroes were willing to include the black doll. Yet almost half of the five-year-olds were unwilling also to invite the Negro (see Table 10).[17]

These racial attitudes may be complex by the time the black child is five years old. Rejection of their own race is not total but may be mixed with ambivalence and hostility to whites for some of these black subjects. There is a small increase in choice of white as "lazy and stupid" from 43 percent (N=100) at age four to 52 percent (N=56) at age five. For whites at the same age level, there is a very slight decrease in white choice for this question (from 32.9 to 29.5 percent).

It is not clear whether this increase in Negro children's choice of white dolls as "lazy and stupid" indicates unwillingness to negatively stereotype a Negro, hostility to whites, or both. The comments made by the black youngsters shed some light on this problem. Some of the increase in choice of a white as "lazy and stupid" among five-year-olds is due to hostility toward whites, since the small number of Negroes making unfavorable comments about whites are all five years old. Unwillingness to openly condemn one's racial group also accounts for part of these results, since the percentage of neutral comments made about the brown dolls by Negroes rises from age four to age five and is higher than either favorable or unfavorable verbalizations. Yet the general trend revealed by these spontaneous comments shows that, although ambivalence toward own race and hostility toward whites exist, choice of a white doll does reflect favorable attitudes to whites and unfavorable opinions of Negroes for some of the five-year-old black children (see Table 11).

Table 11   *Percent of Negroes by Age Who Made Racial Comments*[a]

	Comments about white dolls		
Content	3 years	4 years	5 years
Favorable	0	3.9	19.6
Unfavorable	0	0	6.0
Neutral	4.5	13.0	13.7
	N=22	N=77	N=51

Table 11   Percent of Negroes by Age Who Made Racial Comments[a]
(continued)

	Comments about Negro dolls		
Content	3 years	4 years	5 years
Favorable	0	3.9	3.9
Unfavorable	0	6.5	10.4
Neutral	22.7	10.4	21.6
	N=22	N=77	N=51

[a] Percentages based on the number of children in each age group who actually spoke.

Table 12   Percent of Whites by Age Who Made Racial Comments[a]

	Comments about white dolls		
Content	3 years	4 years	5 years
Favorable	10.5	12.3	16.9
Unfavorable	0	0	0
Neutral	15.8	7.0	7.2
	N=19	N=57	N=83

	Comments about Negro dolls		
Content	3 years	4 years	5 years
Favorable	0	8.8	4.8
Unfavorable	10.5	22.8	16.9
Neutral	15.8	15.8	9.6
	N=19	N=57	N=83

[a] Percentages based on the number of children in each age group who actually spoke.

Analysis of comments indicates that by age five, white children also have quite complex racial attitudes. There is a slight increase in favorable own-race comments from three to five; however, unfavorable verbalizations about the opposite race increase sharply at four but dip at five (see Table 12).

Reference to actual comments suggests the reason for the puzzling dip in unfavorable verbalizations about Negroes. Many of the white five-year-old children have high term knowledge but give totally irrelevant answers to explain their choice of the white doll. Although the doll sets are completely similar in all respects but skin color and hair, some subjects gave as reasons for rejecting the Negro: "Her shoes are dirty"; "It has a scratched leg."[18] These responses and accompanying emotional discomfort suggest an extremely important result. The "American dilemma" may begin to operate at an early age for whites: the child rejects Negroes but knows it is somehow not acceptable to voice these opinions openly. Slips of the tongue when explaining white doll preference confirm this interpretation: "Because he's white—I mean a blue shirt." "Different hands—I mean hair."[19] One child who rejected brown dolls even told the investigator, "I have a reason [for doing this] but I can't tell you." Later, she confided, "I'll tell you why I really didn't choose any of the colored children. I don't like colored children." Thus, learning the need for rationalizations and equivocation seems to be part of the process of learning prejudice.

On the basis of the entire analysis of attitudes and age, Allport's theory of three stages of attitude development should not be thought of as an absolute progression. To summarize, he suggests that in the first stage of pre-generalized learning, the child may have vague preferences but is still not clearly aware of differences between racial categories. When he becomes aware of race, however, he completely verbally rejects the disvalued status. The third stage of this process is "differentiation," when the child's prejudices become less total to make them more acceptable to him. But this process is not as clear-cut as Allport makes it seem. The presence of ambivalence and hesitation accompanying white doll choice suggests that the dimensions of rejection and differentiation occur together at five years of age, when the child rejects blacks but begins to find rationalizations for his attitudes. Thus, the age levels at which the components in Allport's scheme are supposed to occur are also inaccurate.

Robert Blake and Wayne Dennis[20] say that although pre-generalized learning begins early, the stage of total rejection is present by the fourth grade and differentiation occurs by the tenth or eleventh grade. Although we have already indicated that pre-generalized learning seems to be a primary process of attitude development, the age at which differentiation and rejection begin is lower for our sample than for the Blake and Dennis group. This age discrepancy may be due to the fact that attitudes are developing earlier and are more complex now because of increased emphasis on race, but the Goodman and Clark results demonstrate that racial preference among preschool-age children has been present for a number of years. The lack of agreement seems to be due to techniques, since Blake and Dennis' variation of the adjective checklist may be too insensitive an instrument for use with a young sample and for investigation of subtle variations in attitude.

On the basis of my data, some typical patterns of response can be proposed. In the third year the child is aware of color but little social meaning is attached to these color differences. Yet even at age three, color seems to be of great importance to the black child and already has some vague social implications for him. By the age of four the child is beginning to make an affect-laden connection between color and people. The responses of four-year-olds indicate incipient racial attitudes: white and brown are beginning to be classified in terms of good and bad, and people of these colors are evaluated accordingly. The child does not have a sophisticated cognition of racial differences, however. By the fifth year, the connection between color and race becomes clear and vague preferences have developed into real social attitudes. These attitudes are not as fully differentiated as adult opinions; the correlation matrices in Appendix 2 demonstrate that the three dimensions of stereotypes, social distance, and preference are highly related. The child is, however, beginning to develop strong preferences and indicate reasons for them. This process is more complex than has formerly been supposed. Negro children manifest ambivalence toward their own race and some hostility to the opposite race, while whites begin to show internalization of the American creed as well as anti-Negro feelings.

Conclusion

Both white and black children exhibit a strong affinity for white dolls. The difference between black and white youngsters in preference for the doll of their own race seems to reflect rejection or ambivalence toward themselves on the part of many black children. The fact that for Negro children color is highly salient yet white doll choice is still high confirms this explanation. For many white youngsters, choice of a white doll also reflects a racial preference for white over black.

These findings are further clarified by considering data on age. By five years of age, children of both races have clear knowledge of racial differences and their racial attitudes are already rather sophisticated; white children may realize that blatant and overt expressions of prejudice are somehow unacceptable, and the black child may be developing complex feelings toward both his own and the opposite race. But even at age four, children have internalized the affective connotations of color and begin to generalize these meanings to people. Although the three-year-old white child does not, on the whole, invest color with social meaning, the black child of this age does perceive vaguely that color differences are important and may be personally relevant. It is thus evident that even preschool-age children are not exempt from the racial attitudes which are characteristic of a large segment of adult American society.

On the basis of these data, it can thus be concluded that *white doll selection measures racial feeling for the majority of our sample. Depending on the age of the child, these feelings range from actual attitudes to preferences attached to social categories which are dimly perceived.* And these attitudes may indicate either rejection of blacks or mild preference for whites without accompanying hostility toward Negroes, although for some of the young white children selection of white dolls is probably unrelated to racial affect.

In the next chapter new findings are presented on the effect of social class, sex, interracial contact, and shade of skin color on attitude development. *It is assumed that since there are controls for age and race, differences in white preference responses by class, sex, contact, and color actually measure differences in incipient racial attitudes.* These results also further elucidate the content of these racial feelings.

5 Social Class, Contact, and Shade of Skin Color as Correlates of Racial Attitude Formation

James Baldwin says that even before the black child fully understands racial distinctions, "he has begun to react to them, he has begun to be controlled by them."[1] Data in the preceding chapter substantiate this statement. We saw that white children also develop feelings about race before they are clearly able to differentiate between racial categories. By age four for whites and even younger for blacks, white preference begins to have vague racial connotations. But although many youngsters show white preference at an early age, these feelings manifest themselves with different degrees of intensity in different social environments. In this chapter the focus is upon how the child's social environment influences his racial attitudes. First, socioeconomic status is shown to be an important factor in the development of prejudice among black and white children. Then the relationship between attitudes and amount of interracial contact is studied for children of both races. It is demonstrated that contact and sex influence the racial preferences of white children and that contact and shade of skin color determine the image the black child has of his racial group.

Effect of Social Class on Development of Racial Attitudes

Since it has been clearly shown that social class bears a strong relationship to the adult American's racial attitudes, we must investigate its effect on children's prejudices. It has already been suggested in Chapter 2 that working- and lower-class children may be more aware of the existence of racial differences than their middle-class counterparts are. Children in lower socioeconomic brackets tend not to be as overprotected as those in the middle class, and there may be less attempt to shield the lower-class child from threatening social realities. If they live in neighborhoods which are changing in racial composition, lower-class children may be exposed not only to members of the opposite race but to discussions about race in the home.

This hypothesis of greater awareness among the lower classes is supported by trends on both the color match and the color terms index.[2] On the color terms index, the overall class effect indicates that, controlling for sex, race, and age, ADC children tend to have more term knowledge than either their middle-class or their working-class counterparts ($F=1.84$; $.11 \leqslant p \leqslant .20$). The overall trend on the color match index also shows a tendency for correctness of matching to be inversely related to class ($F=1.84$; $.11 \leqslant p \leqslant .20$). These results obtain even when we control for contact.[3]

This awareness trend, however, is not great enough to explain the race and class effect on the attitude index. Although the class differences are greater for blacks than for whites, the means for whites go in the direction predicted by our hypothesis. At most levels, ADC and working-class whites choose the white dolls *more* frequently than their middle-class counterparts do. For black children, the trend is reversed. Working-class Negroes choose white dolls on the attitude questions *less* often than middle-class Negroes do. But the ADC group exhibits less preference for the brown doll than the working class and is close to the middle class in white preference choices ($F=4.49$, $p \leqslant .025$).[4]

These class results will be discussed separately by race. Consider first the white results. In a re-analysis of a number of studies, Charles Stember found that middle-class subjects had fewer stereotypes but more social distance responses than did the working class. But Brink and Harris show that "Affluent" whites have fewer social distance attitudes as well as fewer stereotyped attitudes about blacks.[5] Although the relationship between class and social distance attitudes remains unclear, Robin Williams concludes that in general negative attitudes toward blacks are less frequent among the well educated than among relatively uneducated whites.[6] Particularly in the generation below age forty, attitudes of people of various educational levels below college do not vary greatly, but there is a strong tendency among the college educated toward clearer recognition of discrimination and stronger support of Negro civil rights.[7] Data on this age group are especially relevant for this study, since people in this category are close in age to the parents of the subjects here.

These results among white adults suggest that a class difference in attitudes may appear among young white children. And we did in fact find a difference in means between the white middle-class, working-class, and ADC samples. The data show that most working-class and ADC whites manifest slightly higher white preference than the middle class on the attitude index. The content of comments made by the children suggests that, for some of the working-class youngsters, these preferences definitely reflect unfavorable attitudes toward Negroes. Five-year-old Debbie, for instance, states in an explicit fashion: "That one [Negro] can't come home to lunch cause he's colored. Father wouldn't like it if he came!"[8]

The middle-class whites are by no means highly favorable toward Negroes, since their choices are still well on the white side of the scale, but they do select the brown dolls slightly more often than the lower class does. This means that although white preference is high, it is not so intense or so likely to be accompanied by strong anti-Negro feelings as it is in the lower classes. This explains why the middle-class child will occasionally choose a brown doll. The spontaneous comments provide evidence that at least some of the middle-class subjects do not necessarily harbor strong prejudice toward Negroes:

This one [Negro] is nice because she's black and brown. That means she's nice.
                                    Mark, white, five years old

Sometimes you can pretend he's [Negro] not a Negro with a black face and you can pretend he's [white] a Negro with a mask on. They're just the same, 'cause God made them that way, I think.
                                    Martin, white, four years old

No verbalizations of this type are made by working- and lower-class white children. Although the meaning of rejection of the brown doll may range from an expression of mild preference for whites without accompanying hostility toward blacks to strong pro-white and anti-Negro feelings, it appears that the former response may be more characteristic of the middle and the latter of the lower class. But the data do not allow us to draw any more definite conclusions.[9]

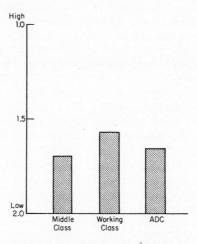

3. Own-race preference by class for
Negroes, controlling for age and sex.

We also find a significant variation by social class in the way black children react to their own group. The middle class shows the lowest and the working class the highest choice of Negro dolls. The ADC group falls in between but is somewhat closer to the middle class (see Figure 3). Additional data help interpret the meaning of these responses. Spontaneous comments indicate that, for some of the middle-class blacks, white choices were indices of black rejection and corresponding white preference:[10]

He doesn't want to be her friend because of her dark color.

Penny, four years old

The teacher says to this boy [Negro]; "Boy, get out of that school! You're colored!" She says to this little girl [white], "You're a nice girl. Have a seat."

Aaron, four years old

The spontaneous verbalizations show that for some of the working-class subjects, choice of a Negro doll reflects not only preference for the brown but also hostility to the white doll. Only a small number of subjects made anti-white comments (see Chapter 4), but those who did were almost all working-class children:

This is me! [Picks up white doll and looks at it.] No! Not that ugly one! [Throws white doll down and picks up Negro doll.]

Lynne, five years old

She's nice because she's the darkest. The other one is lazy and stupid because he's white — and he's the dirtiest because he's white. Mommy wouldn't like him to bring this one [white] home.

James, five years old

On the "lazy and stupid" question, 52.9 percent (N=87) of the working class and 40.4 percent (N=47) of the middle class selected the white for the unfavorable stereotype.[11] Although part of this choice may only reflect a reluctance on the part of the working class to negatively label the brown doll, some of the differential may be due to the actual presence of anti-white feeling among working-class subjects. Additional evidence for this interpretation is provided by studies of adults indicating that Negro hostility to whites seems to be less in the middle class than in the lower class.[12] The unstructured material cannot be used to interpret the ADC group's feelings toward whites, since very few of the ADC children spoke at all. Selection of a white doll in a forced choice situation suggests either that these ADC subjects like whites and dislike blacks or that they dislike both whites and blacks but dislike blacks slightly more. The results unfortunately do not allow us to decide between these alternatives.[13]

Interpretation of the class data for the black subjects is aided by using census categories as a measure of social class instead of the Reiss social-class scale on which the previous results are based. This scheme gives us a general idea of variations within class. The ADC group ranks below the blue-collar group and is close to the clerical/sales group in own-race preference. The blue-collar categories have more brown doll choice than does any white-collar group. But the most interesting phenomenon, demonstrated by Figure 4, is the big difference between the lower-middle-

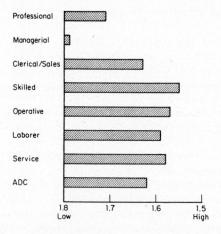

4. Black children's own-race preference
by census categories.

class clerical/sales and the upper-middle-class professional and managerial categories. The latter exhibits the least own-race preference of any black group.

These additional data suggest an interpretation of the difference in white preference choices between the three social class groups for blacks. Middle-class people are in a marginal social position and are also more likely to compare themselves socially with whites. This is particularly true in the upper middle class.[14] These factors create status deprivation which seems to result in either rejection of their own group and/or white preference. The working class, however, is not faced as much with the problem of marginal status, and the individuals in this group, although they may have contact with white employers, are more isolated from whites in terms of purely social rather than work contacts. The working class finds many positive compensations within institutions of the black community itself. For a combination of these reasons, its members may be more accepting of their race than the middle class is and may also exhibit more hostility to whites. The ADC group, on the other hand, is forced to contend with numerous problems based on a combination of race and poverty; an individual on welfare must play the subservient black role most fully. Because of personal and economic problems, this group derives fewer benefits from ghetto life than does the working class. An individual in the ADC category may respond to these pressures by disvaluing his own race more than the working class does. These factors explain why the rate of white doll choice of ADC children is similar to that of some portions of the middle class. Since findings on self-identification presented in Chapter 6 clarify the meaning of the responses presented above, they will not be discussed further at this point.

The findings in this study for both black and white children thus demonstrate that social class is a key factor affecting the development of racial attitudes. White children learn general cultural evaluations of race and all exhibit high white preference, though there is variation by class. Working-class and lower-class white children internalize slightly more negative attitudes toward Negroes than do their middle-class counterparts. Class differences for blacks are also significant, and characteristic class-related modes of reaction to racial status occur. Persons in the middle class are less accepting of their race than are those in the working class, and the ADC group also demonstrates high white preference.

Effects of Sex and Contact on Formation of White Attitudes

Social class is a key factor for consideration in any analysis of children's racial attitudes, but other sociological variables, such as amount of interracial contact, are also important. Thus far we have analyzed the effects of class, controlling for contact. Holding other variables constant, we now turn to an investigation of contact itself.[15]

Since we were not given access to the home addresses of many of the youngsters, we defined amount of interracial contact by the type of school the child attended instead of in terms of the neighborhood in which he lived. A segregated classroom is defined as one in which 90 percent or more of the children are of the same race. All other schools are considered desegregated. (The rationale for this division is presented in Chapter 3.)

There are two problems in utilizing school type to measure contact. The type of school a child attends, particularly if it is not a public school, may tell us little about the racial composition of his immediate neighborhood. Yet the classroom environment is still a good indication of interracial exposure. A large part of the child's day is spent in school; therefore, a child in a segregated classroom has less opportunity to play with children of the opposite race than does his desegregated counterpart. Another difficulty arises from the fact that enrollment in a particular type of school may be determined by parents' feelings about race. If this is true, pure contact effects would be contaminated by self-selection due to parental attitudes. Many of the children in our sample either were placed in schools on a geographical basis or were assigned by a central agency on the basis of space or financial need. Thus the self-selection factor should be minimized.

We have already suggested that the presence of children of different races in the classroom would increase the awareness of race as a social category. Although the child may see members of the opposite race in the street or on television, daily contact with other children causes him to perceive variations in skin color more clearly and to wonder about them. My data provide some support for this assumption, since at most levels children matched families more correctly in desegregated than in segregated schools (F=4.33, p≤.05; see Table 13). Since recognition of color per se is presumably uniform for our sample if age is controlled, children

Table 13   *Color Match — Analysis of Variance by Race, Class, and Contact*

1 = Correct
2 = Incorrect

WHITES

| | Middle class | | | Working class | |
	Male	Female		Male	Female
Segregated	1.38	1.38	Segregated	1.36	1.58
	N=25	N=31		N=11	N=8
Desegregated	1.24	1.34	Desegregated	1.22	1.32
	N=15	N=18		N=10	N=15

| | ADC lower class | |
	Male	Female
Segregated	1.20	1.33
	N=8	N=16
Desegregated	1.34	1.17
	N=10	N=7

NEGROES

| | Middle class | | | Working class | |
	Male	Female		Male	Female
Segregated	1.42	1.44	Segregated	1.54	1.36
	N=11	N=18		N=10	N=21
Desegregated	1.31	1.43	Desegregated	1.36	1.43
	N=9	N=8		N=27	N=21

Table 13   Color Match – Analysis of Variance by Race, Class, and Contact (continued)

	ADC lower class	
	Male	Female
Segregated	1.36	1.39
	N=11	N=16
Desegregated	1.26	1.35
	N=7	N=11

[a] Contact effect, controlling for sex, class, and race:

$$\begin{array}{l} \text{Segregated}=1.38 \\ \text{Desegregated}=1.32 \end{array} \quad F=4.33, \ p\leqslant.05$$

[a] Mean cell contact = grand mean + mean segregated (desegregated).

in desegregated settings are more sensitive to the fact that people of the same color belong together.

Some of the comments show that in desegregated schools, even children with low awareness begin to make the connection between color and social categories. One three-year-old white subject continually pointed to the brown dolls during the test, and said, "That's Jane. These are all Janes!" (Jane is a Negro girl in the class.) When she returned to the classroom, she announced loudly, "I played with Jane's doll!" This, of course, is not prejudice. The comment only indicates that the young child in a desegregated environment may perceive differences in color. in human terms.

In Chapter 1 the possibility was discussed that contact would affect not only awareness but attitudes as well. As the child becomes more cognizant of race, his attitudes also should become more clearly defined; however, attitudes are not a simple function of awareness. Interracial interactions which take place in school also give substance to this process of attitude development. The type of attitudes engendered is probably due to the nature of the contact situation the child encounters. On the basis of their re-analysis of the Coleman data, the United States Civil Rights Commission report (*Racial Isolation in the Public Schools*) draws a distinction between schools which are "integrated" and those which are merely "desegregated."[16] Desegregation involves only a specification of the racial mix of students but includes no description of the quality of the interracial contact. The Civil Rights Commission report suggests that merely desegregated schools can provide the setting for either interracial hostility or interracial acceptance; in an "integrated" school, a climate of interracial acceptance predominates.

This distinction suggests the hypothesis that in an "integrated" nursery school, positive attitudes toward their own and the opposite race may be fostered among children of both races. A nursery school which is merely "desegregated," however, may have negative effects on the formation of racial tolerance. For instance, Stephen, a white child in a desegregated classroom, stated that "I like white boys. They're my friends. Black boys are bad, because one kicked me one time." White boys have undoubtedly also hit Stephen, but he does not dislike all whites. He rejects only the individual who kicked him. Yet all blacks are categorized together. If no attempt is made to teach the children that people vary within each race, such an incident may reinforce vague preferences Stephen already has.

The type of contact situation is also important for the black child. If he is accepted by whites, he may develop positive attitudes toward children of both races. However, if he perceives hostility toward him, the black youngster may be negatively affected. In one of the schools studied, Timmy (white) says to four-year-old Chucky, "You're a black nigger and you stink like the kitchen sink." It is not difficult to imagine how Chucky feels when he hears this. Negative incidents like these can have a strong effect on the child if he is in the process of learning about racial differences and if this type of occurrence is not properly handled by the teacher. Thus, in a "desegregated" setting, children of both races can be exposed to more direct and personal confrontations with prejudice than their segregated peers are. But in what the Civil Rights Commission report describes as an "integrated" setting, teachers would not ignore these incidents but would attempt to create a climate of interracial acceptance. Even if occasional occurrences of this type escaped the teacher's attention in such a situation, they would be offset to some extent by the racially tolerant atmosphere of the classroom. In this type of environment, a large body of theory and research indicates that positive attitudes toward both ones' own and the opposite race may be developed. This and other evidence and practical measures which can be taken to create such an "integrated" atmosphere are discussed in Chapter 11.

My research was done before publication of either *Racial Isolation in the Public Schools* or the Coleman report, both of which suggest that the quality of desegregation may be an important variable to consider. Thus, I never investigated this area systematically and have no objective measure of quality of contact. But while the data were being collected, I was struck by the lack of attention to racial matters in perhaps the majority of the desegregated classrooms. Many teachers seemed to assume that it was improper to deal with race in this age group. Although the children in fact played together with little tension and racial incidents were rare (see Chapter 8), when these incidents did occur they often were by and large unnoticed or ignored by the staff. Little attempt was made by teachers to stress the importance of racial tolerance in either direct and/or subtle fashion. In a few classrooms, the middle-class teachers (black as well as white) even seemed to prefer the white middle-class children above all others.[17] Despite these factors, the atmosphere in these classrooms was not one of overt racial hostility; instead, in many classes, race was simply ignored. The attitudes of the children either were left to develop with no countervailing pressures or were reinforced in some classrooms by subtle factors introduced by teachers or curriculum that communicated that white is better than black.

There were, of course, some exceptions to the above description, but because of the time lapse since collection of the data, I feel that the introduction of impressionistic ex post facto measures of "quality of integration" for each classroom would be unsuitable. In Chapter 10 possible measures of this variable are suggested that might be utilized by future investigators. On the basis of the quality of many of the desegregated classrooms, however, I initially hypothesized that white doll choice would be greater for children of both races in desegregated than in segregated environments. But this hypothesis was not supported. Instead of an over-all contact effect I found trends far more complex than expected. When class was controlled, a race-sex-contact trend appeared. The data reveal that although white doll choice is generally high, white males in a de-segregated setting chose brown dolls *more* often than did white males in a segregated environment. White girls, however, chose the brown dolls *less* frequently in desegregated schools (F=2.14,.11≤ p≤.15; see Table 14). This result may be due in part to differing sex-role expectations for males and females. Jerome Kagan finds that children from five to ten years view the male in relation to the female as more competent, aggres-sive, and fear-arousing.[18]

Both Goodman and I have noted that black children tend to have higher rates of activity than whites do.[19] Perhaps, then, white boys who have contact with blacks admire them because the Negro boys are the ones who best embody the male sex-role expectation of competence in active and athletic pursuits. It is important to note that white males in desegregated situations still show high white doll choice. This sex-role factor only to some extent tempers the racial evaluations that the child is learning.

White girls, however, prefer white dolls more in a desegregated than in a segregated setting. This may also be due to differences in sex-role expectations. Physical prowess is not so important for girls as it is for boys. The female sex role involves a concern with physical appearance, as the data in Chapter 6 show. Blond hair and white skin are considered attractive in the dominant value system of this society. If knowledge of negative cultural evaluation of blacks is sharpened in a desegregated setting, white girls might respond by preferring the doll which most closely approximates feminine standards of beauty.

These data indicate that the effect of desegregation for whites is to sharpen knowledge of race. For my sample, this new information seems to be evaluated in terms of the norms which structure the child's sex role.

Table 14   White Attitudes — Analysis of Variance by Class, Contact, and Sex

1 = High white choice
2 = Low white choice

	Middle class				Working class	
	Male	Female			Male	Female
Segregated	1.27	1.31	Segregated		1.26	1.29
	N=25	N=31			N=11	N=8
Desegregated	1.38	1.29	Desegregated		1.30	1.16
	N=15	N=18			N=10	N=15

	ADC lower class	
	Male	Female
Segregated	1.23	1.31
	N=8	N=16
Desegregated	1.35	1.19
	N=10	N=7

Attitude effect, controlling for class for whites:

Male	Female	
Segregated = 1.25	Segregated = 1.29	$F=2.14, .11 \leqslant p \leqslant .15$
Desegregated = 1.33	Desegregated = 1.21	

Whether the preference responses that were found would have still appeared if a majority of classrooms in our sample had been truly "integrated" is an important question for further research. No comparable sex trend appears for the black sample. This may be due to the fact that race is so highly salient for blacks in any type of environment that sex differences in attitudes are unaffected by a desegregated setting.[20]

Effect of Contact and Shade of Skin Color
on Racial Attitude Formation

Although a sex-contact effect does not appear for Negroes, contact does influence the formation of racial preference for them. School type and shade of skin color interact to produce a complex pattern of response on the doll-play attitude index: controlling for class, there is a color and contact interaction effect on the attitude index. At all levels, light-skinned children exhibit *more* own-race preference in a segregated setting than dark-skinned children do. In desegregated environments the relationship is reversed: light children select brown dolls *less* often than their darker counterparts ($F=6.53$, $p \leqslant .01$, see Table 15).

Status deprivation provides one explanation of these data. In a segregated setting, the light child is the one who most closely approximates dominant cultural standards of beauty. Thus, he is admired by the darker children and/or preferred by the teacher. Although he is cognizant of the fact that he is Negro, he may be relatively favorably disposed to his group because he has high status within it. In a desegregated environment, however, the light-skinned child is no longer the object of envy but becomes a true "marginal man." His skin color may be closer to that of his white friends than to that of many of his black playmates, yet he still is classified with his darker counterparts as a member of an inferior category.[21] Although the teacher or his white classmates still prefer him to the darker child, he cannot completely escape the stigma of the Negro role. He may feel deprived of his rightful status and respond by rejecting the brown doll. The data show that in a desegregated school, light-skinned children not only exhibit more white preference than do the dark children but they also select the white doll far more frequently than do their light-skinned peers in a segregated environment. A color and contact trend on the salience index demonstrates that color is, in fact, more salient for the child in a marginal position. At most levels, the lighter children in both segregated and desegregated environments are somewhat more preoccupied with color than the darker children are ($F=1.95$; $.11 \leqslant p \leqslant .20$).[22]

Table 15   Attitudes — Analysis of Variance by
Color, Class, and Contact for Negroes

1 = High own-race preference
2 = Low own-race preference

	Light-skinned		
	Middle class	Working class	ADC
Segregated	1.65	1.53	1.61
	N=11	N=5	N=10
Desegregated	1.77	1.61	1.73
	N=11	N=18	N=5

	Dark-skinned		
	Middle class	Working class	ADC
Segregated	1.76	1.58	1.68
	N=17	N=26	N=17
Desegregated	1.50	1.52	1.55
	N=6	N=30	N=13

Color/contact effect, controlling for class:
  Segregated: Light/light medium=1.59
  Dark/dark medium=1.67
  $F=6.53$, $p \leqslant .01$
  Desegregated: Light/light medium=1.71
  Dark/dark medium=1.51

The contact differential by attitude for the dark-skinned group is puzzling. In desegregated schools, dark-skinned children select more brown dolls than both the light integrated children and their dark counterparts in segregated classrooms. It is not clear how this result should be interpreted. Because the subjects were young, it was necessary to use a simple questionnaire. Selection of a brown doll may mean several things. It may indicate positive Negro and negative white feelings, dislike of both whites and blacks but slightly greater dislike of whites, or a favorable attitude toward both races but slightly more positive feelings toward Negroes.

We have already pointed out that, where there was interracial contact, a large proportion of the classrooms were "desegregated" rather than truly integrated. Children did play interracially in a relaxed fashion, and racial incidents or comments were observed only occasionally. However, such incidents or comments may exert an effect far disproportionate to their frequency, especially if they are either unnoticed or ignored by the staff and not counteracted by a stress on the importance of racial tolerance. Since his group membership is highly evident, the dark child may bear the brunt of any unfavorable evaluations of blacks which do occur, either directly or in subtle fashion.

Thus the doll choices of the dark integrated group may represent one of the first two alternatives (positive black and negative white feeling, or dislike of both groups but slightly greater dislike of whites). Evidence that brown doll choice may show hostility toward whites is provided by analysis of the results of the "lazy and stupid" question. In a segregated situation, 42 percent (N=71) of the dark-skinned subjects chose the white doll as "lazy and stupid." However, 61 percent (N=56) of the dark children in desegregated schools selected the white for the unfavorable stereotype. Although interpretation of this question is beset by the difficulties discussed above, the results suggest that at least some of the difference between segregated and desegregated dark children may be explained by increase in negative feelings toward whites in the latter type of environment. It is important to note, however, that analysis of the entire range of means for this group shows that most dark-skinned desegregated Negro youngsters do not show an extremely low degree of white doll choice. But we would expect low white preference scores if anti-white feeling were strong.

The theory that certain types of contact lead to prejudice reduction[23] points to a contrasting explanation of the doll choice of the dark segregated youngsters. If the dark-skinned children are on the whole accepted by their white peers (and Chapter 8 suggests that this is the case in terms of actual play patterns), the factor of acceptance may override the occasional incidents of racial name-calling or subtle racial factors in the classroom setting. The children may thus feel more positive about both whites and themselves. On my test, the child is forced to choose one race over the other for each attitude question; thus, the only way that racial tolerance can be expressed is by approximately equal choice of brown and white dolls. Most of the children in the dark-skinned desegregated sample do, in fact, have means which are approximately at the midpoint of the attitude continuum. This finding shows that the third alternative of favorable feelings toward both races is also an important possibility which must be considered in interpreting these data.

Because of the limitations of the test, it is not possible to determine whether the choices of the dark-skinned desegregated youngsters indicate a favorable response to both races with a slight preference for brown or a negative feeling toward both races with slightly greater dislike of whites. The fact that most of the means for the individual children in this group show relatively equal choice of brown and white dolls eliminates the first alternative of strong preference for blacks and highly negative evaluation of whites. Because of its policy implications for school integration at this age level, this area is an extremely crucial one for research. Further studies which clarify the meaning of these results are imperative.

When this study began, I initially predicted a simple relationship between contact and shade of skin color for blacks. It appeared that if social class were held constant, contact would be a more important predictor of white preference than skin color would. Because the relationship between color and class had not been controlled by other investigators, I thought that skin color might have far less effect on choice of a white preference figure than previous studies seemed to indicate. Instead, it was found that skin color and contact are not simple effects;

rather, controlling for class, they interact to form a complex relationship. The order predicted and the order found, going from *least* to *most* choice of the brown dolls, was as follows:

Predicted	*Observed*
desegregated light	desegregated light
desegregated dark	segregated dark
segregated light	segregated light
segregated dark	desegregated dark

The dark segregated and dark desegregated are in reverse order from the hypothesis. Part of this effect may be explained by status deprivation among the light-skinned children, but the results for the dark-skinned group are difficult to interpret on the basis of my evidence.

This color and contact pattern held true within each class group. In turn, the predicted class ordering appeared: middle-class subjects chose the least and working-class subjects the most brown dolls, with the ADC group in between for most of the color and contact categories (see Figure 5 and Table 15).[24]

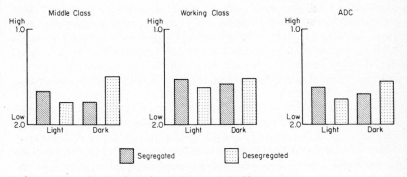

5. Own-race preference by color and contact for Negroes.

Conclusion

It is clear that class, contact, shade of skin color (for blacks), and sex have some effect, alone or in interaction, on the development of children's racial attitudes. The white child's feelings are determined in part by social class, since working- and lower-class children show more white doll preference than middle-class children do; they also tend to express tolerant attitudes less frequently. Contact must also be considered for whites. In a desegregated setting, racial awareness is sharpened and any newly learned cultural evaluations seem to be mediated by sex-role expectations: white girls show slightly greater white doll preference in desegregated than in segregated situations, but for boys this preference is reversed.

Thus, it seems that for whites the most consistent own-race doll preference exists for those groups where whiteness is an especially valued or important concomitant of a role definition and where it reinforces the major goals of the group. The working class and lower class place a high value on whiteness because this gives them an advantage in competing with blacks for status and jobs, and this attitude is transmitted to their children. Part of the female role definition involves concern with physical appearance, and whiteness as an attribute of beauty assumes particular significance for those girls whose awareness of race is sharpened in a desegregated setting. It is important to note, however, that the attitudes of white boys seem to be somewhat favorably modified by contact. Their sex-role expectations are more focused on achievement than on ascriptive criteria; racial distinctions are thus less overtly significant for them than they are for the girl.

Sociological correlates of racial attitude formation also exist for blacks. Socioeconomic status is one important factor affecting this process. Attitudes among black children seem to be subculturally patterned: working-class children exhibit more preference for brown dolls (and more overt verbal hostility toward whites) than do their middle-class peers. The ADC group falls in between in doll choice but is somewhat closer to the middle class. Socioeconomic status is not the sole explanation for doll preference, since a color and contact relationship is also important. Light-skinned children show more white preference in a desegregated than in a segregated environment, but for dark-skinned children this choice pattern is reversed. The explanation of this latter finding is unclear, however.

Thus, it is those groups of black children in marginal social situations, such as the middle-class children and the light-skinned children in desegregated schools, who exhibit particularly high rates of rejection of their own group. And white preference also tends to be high among the least advantaged groups of blacks, who are placed in a doubly difficult situation due to a combination of race and poverty. In both the above categories, race is a particularly important issue for the child to consider; his racial membership puts him in either an ambivalent or a subordinate situation which threatens major goals; he cannot attain either the status or the comforts which he desires because he is black.

The data presented in Part Two thus show that incipient racial feelings are already present for most preschool children, but a uniform pattern of response does not appear within each racial group. Variations in attitudes are not solely due to differences in individual personality. Age, class, sex, contact, and shade of skin color all prove to be important correlates of intraracial variations in attitude formation. Part Three analyzes the effects of these attitudes the child is internalizing.

Three   The Effects of Racial Attitudes
on Personality and Interaction

I begin to suffer from not being a white man to the degree
that the white man imposes discrimination on me . . . robs me of
all worth . . . tells me that I must bring myself as quickly as
possible into step with the white world. . . Then I will quite
simply try to make myself white.

       Frantz Fanon, Black Skin, White Masks

Sabrina (Negro, age five): "I don't want to be colored.
             I want to be white."
Stephen (Negro, age five): "Let's take white paint and paint
             ourselves all over."
Seth (white, age five): "If you do that, it'll all come off
             when you sit in the bathtub."
  Conversation recorded in desegregated kindergarten

Racial evaluations are assimilated by the child as part of the total pattern of ideas he acquires about the society in which he lives. The data presented in Part Two indicate that whites tend to be positively evaluated and blacks negatively evaluated by children of both races. In an appendix to the Supreme Court desegregation decision of 1954, social scientists suggested that these prejudices, as well as actual discrimination, may "potentially damage the personality of all children — the children of the majority group in a somewhat different way than the more obviously damaged children of the minority group." But "personality" is a broad concept; the effect of prejudice on different dimensions of personality is left vague in the Supreme Court statement. In this chapter, we see the effects of racial attitudes and their social concomitants on a specific dimension of personality. This dimension is the "group identity" component of self-concept, or how the individual feels about himself as a member of a racial group, whether he has high or low esteem for himself on the basis of his race. In other words, group identity refers to the child's racial self concept, or his personal reaction to his racial membership. ("Racial self-concept" and group identity are used synonomously in this chapter.) Many black children are shown to have a negative or ambivalent group identity; that is, they dislike the fact that they are black. But the racial self-concept of blacks is far from uniform. My data indicate that black girls and middle-class blacks are particularly likely to be affected negatively by their minority status.

As pointed out in Chapter 2, self-identification questions are the most frequently used measure of group identity for preschool children. The young child is asked to identify himself with the doll or picture which he most resembles, and his choice is interpreted as indicative of his desire to be a member of that race. The rationale for this operational definition of group identity is based on a set of assumptions about the relationship of attitudes and classification of the self with a racial group. As the average child learns to judge racial differences in terms of the standards of society, he is at the same time required to identify himself with one or another group. This identification necessarily involves a knowledge of the status attributes connected to the group with which he classifies himself. The child cannot learn his racial membership without being involved in a larger pattern of conflicts and emotions which are part of his growing knowledge of what society thinks about his race. Thus, racial self-classification is in many cases not an affectively neutral process. Particularly for young minority-group children, self-identification as white may often indicate a rejection of their group status or ambivalence toward it.

But it has never been clearly proved that self-classification is an adequate measure of racial self-concept for preschool youngsters.[1] Black children classify themselves less correctly than do whites, and they also have less positive attitudes toward their own racial group than white children do. In addition, there are differences in the accuracy of self-identification between subgroups of blacks. Although many investigators have interpreted variations in self-classification between groups as indicative of differences in racial self-esteem, none of these studies has fully specified whether a relationship in fact exists between self-identification and racial attitudes for the individual child. Instead, researchers have based their analysis of group differences on the untested assumption that there is actually a correlation between attitudes and identification of the self. This problem is complicated by the fact that other investigators analyze group differences in purely cognitive terms and ignore any possible attitudinal influences; that is, if the child misidentifies, he is simply considered to be unaware of his personal appearance and/or his racial membership. In some cases, white identification is interpreted as due to the fact that the black child actually looks more like the white doll.[2]

Thus, before self-identification is used as an indicator of differences between groups in racial self-concept, it is extremely important to clarify whether this measure actually indicates emotional reactions to racial status. For this reason we must begin by explaining the meaning of the self-identification index for black and white youngsters. My data demonstrate clearly for the first time that self-identification is indeed a measure of self-acceptance or rejection on racial grounds for many blacks: they either wish that they were white or at least are ambivalent toward the fact that they are Negro. The meaning of self-identification for whites is less clear, but, for many white children, self-identification does seem to demonstrate a strong attraction to their own racial group. On this basis we present new findings which show how group identity differs among subgroups of children within each race.

Meaning of Racial Differences in Self-Classification

The self-concept of every child is determined by answers to the questions: Who am I? What am I like as a person? How do I feel about myself? Racial evaluations may play a highly important part in determining the black child's response to these questions. He cannot be neutral, for the dominant culture negatively stereotypes blacks. He must learn to adapt to these pressures in some way.

One mode of adaptation is hostility toward minority-group status and an identification with the majority. Andrew Billingsley has suggested: "In one major area of life after another, strongly held values in our society assume that white is right and black is wrong . . . What is even more devastating and crippling . . . is that many Negroes have fallen victim to these same illusions. How else could it be? It is a most human characteristic to define oneself and one's behavior in terms sanctioned by the most powerful and relevant persons in one's larger social environment."[3] Of course, other reactions are also possible. The black child may respond to his racial membership by in-group pride or by ambivalence. But since most blacks are faced with the necessity of coping with negative evaluations of their racial status it seemed that self-identification should measure not just cognitive factors like awareness of race and personal appearance but also how they feel about themselves as blacks. Of course, some black children may be incorrectly classifying themselves because they are genuinely confused about the race to which they belong, and others may identify correctly on a purely cognitive basis. However, it appeared that differences between subgroups of blacks could be interpreted as racial self-concept if factors which influence awareness are controlled.

The meaning of self-identification for the white child is more ambiguous. The evidence presented to the Supreme Court suggested that prejudice had a more severe effect on the minority group child than on his majority group counterpart. And this statement applies to the group identity component of self-concept as well. Irrespective of his social position, the white child internalizes a favorable image of his racial group. Bernard Kutner and Else Frenkel-Brunswik both indicate that racial membership may not be an integral part of the self-image of the white child; his reaction depends to a large extent on his particular personality structure and the region of the country in which he lives. The fact that he is white, then, cannot be expected to have an unfavorable effect in most circumstances on the way the white child views himself; whiteness may be a favorable or neutral factor in the determination of his ego structure.[4]

Since they do not have to come to terms with a negatively evaluated status, the whole question of racial membership may be less affectively laden for whites than for blacks. Thus, I initially thought that response to self-identification questions should measure cognitive factors more than purely emotional ones: for many white children, correctness of self-classification would signify knowledge of personal appearance with little emotion or explicit racial connotations attached. Of course, I thought that some white children would identify on the basis of favorable evaluation of whites as well as cognitive factors and show a positive attraction to the favored status; in this case, correct self-classification measures racial self-concept. But it seemed that incorrect self-classification among whites should indicate not negative group identity but genuine confusion about personal appearance or identification on the basis of other factors like hair rather than skin color.

Because of these widespread negative evaluations of blacks and positive evaluations of whites, I hypothesized that many black children would reject themselves on a racial basis or be ambivalent toward their minority-group status. Thus, if self-identification did in fact measure group identity, black children should exhibit less correct self-identification than their white peers. My data support the hypothesis that, at most levels, Negro youngsters identify themselves less correctly than white children do. Controlling for sex, class, and age, there is a difference by race in correctness of self-classification which is significant at the .01 level ($F=8.89$.[5] See Table 16).

The child had three possibilities of response in the two self-identification questions: correctly identifying twice, identifying once correctly and once incorrectly, or consistently misclassifying himself. In the multivariate analysis the latter two categories were considered as "incorrect."[6] Yet a frequency analysis of the entire sample on a three-category basis confirms the self-identification findings: twice as many blacks as whites misclassify themselves consistently (Negroes: 30 percent, N=196. Whites: 15 percent, N=185). For the entire sample of this study, 52 percent (N=185) of the whites and 37 percent (N=196) of the Negroes consistently said they resembled the doll of their own race.[7]

Further analysis of the data is necessary before we determine what this difference in correctness of self-classification means. First, we consider the incorrect responses of the whites. Some whites clearly misclas-

Table 16   *Self-Identification Means — Analysis of Variance by Sex, Class, Race, and Age*

1 = Correct self-identification
2 = Incorrect self-identification

Males[a]

Middle class				Working class		
	3 yrs.	4 yrs.	5 yrs.		3 yrs.	4 yrs.	5 yrs.
White	1.67	1.43	1.57	White	2.0	1.50	1.42
	N=3	N=14	N=23		N=1	N=8	N=12
Negro	1.67	1.71	1.60	Negro	1.60	1.47	1.53
	N=3	N=7	N=10		N=5	N=17	N=15

ADC lower class

	3 yrs.	4 yrs.	5 yrs.
White	2.0	1.50	1.63
	N=3	N=4	N=11
Negro	2.0	1.50	1.40
	N=1	N=12	N=5

Females

Middle class				Working class		
	3 yrs.	4 yrs.	5 yrs.		3 yrs.	4 yrs.	5 yrs.
White	1.50	1.57	1.30	White	1.33	1.45	1.33
	N=8	N=21	N=20		N=3	N=11	N=9
Negro	2.0	1.89	1.75	Negro	1.64	1.75	1.57
	N=4	N=18	N=4		N=11	N=24	N=7

Table 16   Self-Identification Means — Analysis of Variance by Sex, Class, Race, and Age (continued)

	ADC lower class		
	3 yrs.	4 yrs.	5 yrs.
White	1.0 N=1	1.50 N=12	1.40 N=10
Negro	1.43 N=7	1.50 N=14	2.0 N=6

Total race effect, controlling for class, age, sex:

Whites = 1.49
Negroes = 1.65 $F=8.89$, $p \leqslant .01$

[a]The means for the white working class and ADC boys are misleading, because there was no control for contact. The segregated white boys in these two groups conform to the general hypothesis, while the desegregated boys do not. These two desegregated groups, however, are in a highly specific type of contact situation discussed in the section on contact.

sify themselves on the basis of factors other than race. The Negro dolls had dark and the white dolls had blond hair (see Chapter 3 for the rationale behind this decision). Some of the white double-misidentification (incorrect on both opportunities to identify the self) seems to be due to hair color, since twenty-one of the twenty-nine consistent misclassifiers had hair which was brown. The comments of several of the very young subjects even indicated that this factor was important in determining choice of the doll that looked like them. For the entire white sample, blonds identified more correctly than did brunettes. Even when we control for color salience, blonds classified themselves more correctly than brunettes did. As will be indicated shortly, other factors than hair color account for misidentification among whites, but these data on hair color suggest that incorrect self-classification may not be a measure of negative group identity for white children. It is still not clear, however, whether positive racial self-esteem is actually indicated by correct identification for the white youngsters.

The high rate of misidentification among black children does suggest that self-classification measures other factors than purely cognitive ones for the black group. The Negro subjects cannot misidentify on the basis of hair color, since all the white dolls are blond. Dislike of themselves as black and wish fulfillment (the desire to be white) may be exhibited by the 30 percent of blacks who consistently misidentified themselves. Some of the 33 percent who categorized themselves inconsistently (once correctly and once incorrectly) may actually be confused about their race. But for others, this inconsistency may express ambivalence toward their own racial status; that is, they may prefer to be white but they do not totally reject themselves as blacks. From these data we still do not know whether correct self-identification for blacks means classification on a purely perceptual basis or, in addition, a positive attraction to racial status. A review of the results on awareness and attitudes provides answers to some of these questions.

Consider the data on racial awareness. Although blacks identify less accurately than whites do, we have already seen in Chapter 4 that color salience is high among black children and that color is more salient for them than for whites. The child for whom color is extremely important is more likely to realize what his own shade of skin looks like. Thus, other factors than purely cognitive ones should be involved in misidentification; wish fulfillment must explain the self-classification responses of at least some of the black youngsters.

Additional evidence on color salience and self-identification confirms the assumption that incorrect self-identification is a measure of negative or ambivalent group identity for many black children. When we control for color salience, blacks still identify less correctly than whites at every level, but we also see that color salience and self-identification are inversely related. Those black children with higher color salience identify *less* accurately.[8] The percentages of children in different color salience categories who correctly identify themselves are shown below.[9]

	High	Medium	Low
White	52.7	46.7	54.9
	N=72	N=60	N=51
Negro	30.4	39.0	47.4
	N=162	N=41	N=38

These data demonstrate that for blacks, self-identification is not a function of degree of awareness alone. Incorrect self-identification accompanied by high color salience suggests that many Negro children dislike or are ambivalent toward themselves as black, and white identification for many Negroes is a response which seems to indicate wish fulfillment.

Data on attitudes provide additional substantiation of the fact that self-identification measures group identity. If Negro children not only misidentify themselves but also have highly favorable attitudes toward whites, self-identification may indicate concern with their racial membership. It has already been demonstrated in Chapter 4 that this is the case. Blacks have significantly lower preference for dolls of their own race than whites do, and both black and white children tend to prefer the white dolls. Since white preference is high and correct self-classification is low for black children, it seems that the black child's self-identification may be strongly affected by his feelings about race.

Thus far most of our discussion has been based on analysis of variance results for self-identification, attitudes, and awareness indices treated separately. Yet these data only point out differences between the black and white groups. To avoid the fallacy of generalizing from the group to the individual, we need additional proof that it is actually those children who have negative attitudes toward their own race who are misclassifying themselves. An analysis of variance of self-identification, controlling for attitudes, color terms, and race, was computed for the entire sample. These data clarify the meaning of self-identification not only for the black but also for the white youngsters.

An extremely important finding about the connection between attitudes and self-identification is revealed by these data. The F-ratio for the attitudes and self-identification relationship was highly significant

(F=43.66, p≤.01), indicating that those subjects who had high own-race choice on the attitude questions were identifying themselves the most correctly (see Table 17). Many more whites than blacks, however, exhibited high own-race preference. The percentages are shown below.

Own-race preference	Whites	Negroes
High	51	13
Medium	38	28
Low	11	59
	N=184	N=191

Table 17   Self-Identification Means[a] — Analysis of Variance by Race, Attitudes, and Terms

1 = Correct self-identification
2 = Incorrect self-identification

	Whites Own-race preference		
Term knowledge	Low	Medium	High
High	1.86 N=7	1.66 N=35	1.20 N=44
Low	1.92 N=13	1.53 N=36	1.41 N=49

	Negroes Own-race preference		
Term knowledge	Low	Medium	High
High	1.76 N=50	1.50 N=18	1.00 N=11
Low	1.80 N=63	1.56 N=36	1.23 N=13

Table 17   *Self-Identification Means*[a] *— Analysis of Variance by Race, Attitudes, and Terms* (continued)

Total Attitude Effect, Controlling for Terms and Race[b]

Low own-race preference — 1.84
Medium own-race preference — 1.56   F=43.66, p ≤ .01
High own-race preference — 1.22

Total Terms Effect, Controlling for Race and Attitude[c]

High terms — 1.51   F=2.98, p ≤ .10
Low terms — 1.57

Terms-Attitude Effect, Controlling for Race[d]

Term knowledge	Own-race preference		
	Low	Medium	High
High	1.82	1.59	1.12
Low	1.86	1.53	1.32
	F=2.44, p ≤ .10		

[a] It appears that at each level, Negroes actually identify better than whites. However, this race effect disappears when we control for hair color among white children. Blond-haired white children identify much better than brown-haired whites, and the brown-haired results affect the overall white mean.

[b] Cell own-race preference=grand mean + mean cell own-race preference.

[c] Cell term knowledge=grand mean + mean cell terms.

[d] Mean cell terms — preference=grand mean + mean cell terms + mean cell own-race preference + mean cell terms/preference.

But the clinching argument that self-identification measures group identity comes when we control for racial awareness. Self-identification is influenced by awareness of racial differences. If a child has high knowledge of racial terms, he will classify himself more correctly than the child with low knowledge, though the relationship between self-identification and color terms[10] is not as strong as that between attitudes and self-identification (F=2.98, p≤.10. See Table 17). It is important to note that attitudes influence self-identification even for children with low term knowledge. Although a child does not have a sophisticated understanding of racial terms he still may have an incipient racial self-concept. Even a vague feeling that white is good and brown is bad may create a desire to be white.

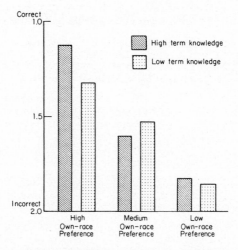

6. Self-identification by own-race preference and term knowledge.

The terms and attitude interaction effect provides further information, since it indicates that terms knowledge affects self-identification most when positive own-race attitudes are present. If a child has both highly favorable own-race attitudes *and* high term knowledge, he has the greatest likelihood of correctly identifying himself (F=2.44, p≤.10; see Table 17 and Figure 6). This effect holds for both whites and blacks, but even when we consider only children with high term knowledge, we still find that whites have a higher percentage of own-race preference than blacks do:

Own-race preference	*Whites*	*Negroes*
High	51	14
Medium	41	22
Low	8	64
	N=86	N=79

These results also demonstrate that awareness alone cannot explain the self-identification data for Negroes, since forty-seven blacks with high term knowledge still misclassify themselves. It is important to note that 81 percent of these children also have low own-race preference. *All* the black youngsters with both high own-race preference *and* high term knowledge classify themselves correctly. It is also important to note that of the entire sample, only six whites with high term knowledge had low own-race attitudes and misclassified themselves, and that over six times as many blacks did so.[11]

The self-identification index, then, does not reflect only awareness of race and/or personal appearance. For many children, and particularly for black children, self-classification seems to measure group identity, or feelings about their own racial status. And correct self-identification for whites is a better image of group identity than I had initially thought. The analysis of variance of self-identification by attitudes, terms, and race suggests that, even when we control for term knowledge, identification among children of both races becomes more accurate as white preference increases. Also, children of both races who show low term knowledge and high own-race doll choice identify even more accurately than their peers with more sophisticated knowledge but less consistent preference for their own color. Thus, a strong element of attraction to the favored status as well as purely cognitive factors seem to be involved in the *correct* self-identification of many children. *Incorrect* self-classification, however, is not as adequate a measure of negative group identity for whites as it is for blacks. White children may misclassify themselves on the basis of either lack of knowledge of race or personal appearance or on the basis of other factors like hair color. Yet the few whites with low own-race preference, high term knowledge, and incorrect self-identification suggest that, for some white children, incorrect self-classification may in fact indicate negative or ambivalent response to their racial status and/or a desire to be a member of the opposite race. (These youngsters are discussed in the section on contact).

To summarize the results, the analysis of self-identification, controlling for attitudes, terms, and race demonstrates that *for children of both races, correct self-identification measures a positive attraction to racial membership as well as knowledge of race or personal appearance alone. Incorrect self-classification also measures group identity for many black children.* All of the data confirm that the high rate of identification with the white dolls among blacks is accounted for to a large extent by wish fulfillment.

The fact that terms knowledge has a significant effect, controlling for attitudes (see Table 17), shows that for some blacks, identification (both correct and incorrect) is based only on cognitive factors. They know what they look like and identify appropriately. Positive identification for whites does not measure group identity for every child for the same reason. But if we control for age and other factors which might influence identification on a purely cognitive basis, *we assume that differences among subgroups of black children measure in most cases differences in group identity.* For whites, the meaning of variation is less clear. Though racial self-evaluation clearly plays a part in correct self-identification responses, inaccurate self-classification is less of an index of personal evaluative factors than it is for blacks. These findings give us a basis for analyzing important differences in self-identification within each racial group. We now consider the effect of class, contact, shade of skin color, and sex on the racial self-concept of black and white children.

Racial Self-Concept and Social Class

In Chapter 5 we saw that social class exerted an effect upon racial attitudes of children of both races. This section shows that there is also a class difference in racial self-concept for blacks. On the attitude index, among Negro children the middle class had the lowest and the working class the highest choice of brown dolls. The ADC group fell in between but was somewhat closer to the middle class (see Chapter 5, Figure 3). The comments made by the black children indicated that hostility toward whites and a degree of own-race acceptance might be more characteristic of the working-class youngsters than of other groups, but the comments of the middle class showed that dislike of blacks might be a more typical response for middle-class youngsters.

These data suggest that the group identity component of self-concept should be most negative among the middle class and most positive among the working class; the ADC group should be nearer to the middle than to the working class in racial self-concept. The self-identification data provide an interesting qualification of these assumptions. There is in fact a trend indicating that the working-class children identify themselves more correctly than the middle class, but results for the ADC group are different from the predictions: these youngsters are more similar to their working-class peers than they are to the middle class in correctness of self-classification ($F=2.2$, $.11 \leqslant p \leqslant .15$ for the entire trend).[12]

If we combine the attitude and self-identification data, it seems that the middle-class child shows a high rate of rejection of both other blacks and either rejection or ambivalence toward his own racial membership. The working-class child manifests a higher rate of brown preference and more correct self-classification than any other group. Yet even though the ADC subjects show almost as much white preference as the middle class, their self-identification results are more similar to those found for the working class.

Differences in racial awareness may play some part in explaining all of these class results, but analysis of spontaneous comments strongly suggests that within the middle and working class, there actually may be subculturally patterned means of adjustment to minority racial status. The ADC group rarely spoke during the test. Although we have little unstructured material for these ADC youngsters, an interesting theoretical explanation of their responses in terms of racial self-concept is possible.

One pattern of reaction seems to be especially characteristic of the middle class. According to social evaluation theory, higher economic and social status should lead to more comparison with whites. The results of such comparisons might be feelings of dissatisfaction with racial status, since whites are generally more advantaged.[13] The middle-class individual may not be burdened by the full impact of a subservient racial role, but he is still exposed to annoyances and humiliations in his contacts with whites. He has all the symbols of success and frequently has a light skin, but his ascribed position denies him the respect he is due in the wider community and he may feel this status deprivation keenly. He is thus a "marginal man" in both a sociological and a psychological sense.[14] One of the several possible modes of resolution of this dilemma is dislike of the in-group and an ambivalent or negative group-identity component of self-concept. It is important to point out that the children of the professional group, which is the most marginal of the whole middle class, not only show less brown doll choice than the lower middle class on the attitude questions but also have the least correct self-identification of any middle-class group. Of the professional group, 94.7 percent (N=19) identify inaccurately compared to 68.7 percent (N=16) of children with parents in the clerical and sales occupations. This "marginality" pattern of response may now be less characteristic of the middle class than it was at the time of this study; in Chapters 9 and 10 this possibility is discussed more fully.

The working-class individual is not faced with this problem of marginality. He may be forced to play a subservient role to a greater extent than is the middle-class black; however, the ghetto community not only provides him with compensations for his racial status but helps insulate his social life from the white world. The working-class individual is the "ambivalent": he may not completely accept his ascribed status, but he has a more favorable response to it than the middle class does; and he also retaliates more frequently with hostility toward whites. His "racial self-concept" is the most favorable of any class group.

The results for the ADC youngsters are puzzling. These children show a rate of white preference similar to the middle class but their self-identification results are more similar to those of the working class. Although we do not have unstructured material to aid us in interpretation of the ADC responses, a theoretical possibility does suggest itself. These data can be tentatively explained by Erik Erikson's concept of "negative identity," which is "an identity perversely based on all those identifications and roles which, at critical stages of development, had been presented to them as most undesirable or dangerous and yet also as most real . . . The history of such a choice reveals a set of conditions in which it is easier for the patient to derive a sense of identity out of a total identification with that which he is least supposed to be than to struggle for a feeling of reality in unacceptable roles which are unattainable with his inner means."[15] Of course, "negative identity" does not exclusively or specifically pertain to racial identity, yet Erikson suggests that "the individual belonging to an oppressed and exploited minority, which is aware of the dominant cultural ideals but prevented from emulating them, is apt to fuse the negative images held up to him by the dominant majority with the negative identity cultivated in his own group."[16]

This statement seems to be particularly applicable to the ADC group, since the full implications of being black strike them with greatest force. The recipient of welfare is more frequently forced to adopt a subservient posture and is also more likely than individuals in other social classes to have an extremely dark skin color. Although the individuals on welfare have some of the compensations of ghetto life, appreciation of these benefits is lessened by economic and personal problems. "Black" may thus become equated with "bad."[17] But the child may not be able to escape the fact that he is black, even in fantasy. He knows full well who he is. Even if he lives in a segregated neighborhood, he cannot avoid evaluations of his role, by both those within the ghetto community and those without. Thus, a higher rate of positive self-identification than initially predicted for the ADC youngsters may indicate not positive racial self-concept or greater awareness but instead the fact that the child is forced to accept a negative or disvalued identity in order to define himself at all. The middle-class child, who is more protected from the need for playing a really subordinate racial role, is at least able to pretend he is white. The ADC child, because of his social situation, does not have even this escape. This reaction, of course, would not apply to every individual on welfare, as the recent growth of the militant Welfare Rights Organization shows, but this area is an important one for further research.

Although there are black differences by class in self-identification, there are no class differences for whites.[18] These findings may indicate that self-identification is not as adequate a measure of group identity for white as for black children. The results in the following section, however, suggest that for at least some white groups, accuracy of classification is indeed indicative of racial self-esteem.

Effect of Contact on Racial Self-Concept of Whites

The effect of contact on both attitudes and self-identification demonstrates that the "group image" of whites can in fact be affected by the child's social environment. As we found in Chapter 5, racial attitudes for white children vary by contact and sex. White males in a desegregated environment prefer Negroes *more* often than white males in segregated schools do. For white girls, this relationship is reversed: the white girls in desegregated schools choose the brown dolls *less* frequently than do their segregated peers. From these data it seems that in a desegregated classroom, developing racial evaluations are influenced by sex-role expectations. For the white boys, racial attitudes are mitigated somewhat by positive feelings toward the active Negro boys, who best embody masculinity (see note 19, Chapter 5), but the girls seem to respond in terms of personal appearance. Their awareness of race is sharpened in a desegregated environment, and they thus prefer the doll which most closely approximates the dominant feminine standard of beauty.

Contact creates differences not only in attitudes but also in self-identification among some groups of white children. These differences suggest that the group image of whites is affected by the numerical racial composition of the classroom. And the effect of contact on racial self-concept is not always positive. The attitudes of all white males are slightly more favorable to blacks in a desegregated situation than in a segregated one. However, contact actually seems to have a negative effect on self-identification for two groups of boys. Desegregated working-class and ADC boys have an unusually high rate of misidentification (six out of ten working-class and eight out of ten ADC boys incorrect).[19] These two groups are far more likely to classify themselves inaccurately than are either their segregated peers or the desegregated male middle-class sample; in fact, the middle-class males identify more correctly in desegregated schools than in segregated ones. These middle-class boys, though they are more favorable to blacks than their segregated counterparts, are still aware of racial evaluations which stereotype blacks negatively (their preference scores are clearly on the white side of the continuum; see Table 14, Chapter 5). This combination of racial awareness and positive attraction to the favored status causes them to identify more accurately in desegregated classrooms.

It should be noted that the middle-class desegregated boys are in schools where whites outnumber blacks. But most of the boys in the working-class and ADC desegregated groups attend schools where Negroes constituted 50 percent or more of the student body. The white boys in predominantly black schools are the ones who are in the most constant contact with black males who, because they are active and aggressive in their play patterns, best typify sex-role expectations. Although the white boys may have positive attitudes toward their own race, they may still be more likely to use blacks as a reference group for personal comparison than would those white males who are in a classroom where their own race is a numerical majority. In addition, the white boy in a predominantly Negro school may have more opportunity for exposure to hostility against his race. (We find in Chapter 5 that working-class black children exhibit anti-white feelings, and our predominantly black schools did contain a large group of working-class blacks). These findings suggest the hypothesis that attendance at schools where Negroes are in the majority may affect the racial self-esteem of white boys in either a negative or an ambivalent fashion. The white integrated male sample in largely black schools is too small to permit investigation of this hypothesis with proper controls for social class: we do not know if middle-class boys in predominantly black schools would also exhibit this reaction.

The results for white girls substantiate the sex-role explanation of our male ADC and working-class results. White females not only tend to prefer whites but also identify slightly more correctly in a desegregated than in a segregated situation; and this is true even for the white girls who attend predominantly black schools, that is, the working-class and ADC girls.[20] Girls in desegregated situations are not only more aware of race but are also less likely to utilize blacks as a group for social comparison because their sex-role expectations stress the importance of personal appearance rather than physical activity.

Thus, the racial composition of the classroom may exert an effect on group identity for at least white males.[21] The relationship between percentage of Negroes in the school and self-identification should be further investigated for white boys with adequate class controls. It is highly important to find out whether the quality of the desegregated setting (that is, whether the atmosphere is one of racial tolerance) affects the racial self-concept of either sex.

Effect of Contact for Black Children

The self-identification of black children is also affected by contact. Controlling for skin color, there is an interaction effect between contact and social class. Negro middle- and working-class children in desegregated environments identify *more* correctly than they do in segregated classrooms. For the ADC group, the relationship is the reverse. The ADC children classify themselves *less* accurately in desegregated than in segregated environments[22] (F=3.53, p≤.05). This finding is difficult to interpret. The light- and dark-skinned children within each class group do not differ in self-identification, even though the attitudes of these two skin-color groups are affected in different fashion by contact. (Controlling for class, the light-skinned youngsters show *less* and the dark-skinned youngsters *more* brown doll choice in desegregated than in segregated schools.)

We have no basis for interpreting the greater accuracy of self-identification for the middle- and working-class children as a positive effect of desegregation on group identity. This self-identification result appears for these two groups regardless of the effect of skin color on attitudes. The unstructured questions on my test also do not provide any clarification of the meaning of the middle- and working-class findings. But since greater awareness of race does have a positive influence on accuracy of self-identification (see Table 17), the middle- and working-class results can be tentatively explained as due to greater cognizance of race in a desegregated situation.

The ADC results are particularly puzzling. In this group, the children in desegregated classrooms identify *less* accurately than they do in segregated schools. This is true even of those ADC children who show a *higher* rate of brown doll choice than their segregated peers do (i.e., the dark-skinned ADC group). I cannot explain this result, and I have no additional data to help in the analysis. I hesitate to interpret this finding as a negative effect of contact on racial self-concept, because it characterizes the entire ADC group in desegregated classrooms, no matter what their attitudes.

This is an extremely important area for research. If these results are actually indicative of more favorable group identity among some of the middle and working class, and less positive self-concept among some of the ADC group in desegregated situations, this would have major implications for integration at the preschool level. At this point, we can only say that *a desegregated setting does not seem to have a negative effect on the racial self-concepts of working- and middle-class children.* This is an important finding, because our schools were not optimally integrated; there was no attempt made to create an atmosphere of racial tolerance and understanding (see Chapter 5).

Effect of Skin Color on Racial Self-Concept

Although contact does influence self-identification for some groups of black children, shade of skin color does not have an effect. Controlling for contact and class, both dark and light-skinned children misidentify at approximately the same rate. This is true even when we look only at differences between children of each skin color who consistently misclassify themselves (two out of two choices incorrect).

Some of the Clarks' data on skin color are thus questionable. In their doll-play and line-drawing studies, the Clarks find that light-skinned children identify as white more frequently than their darker counterparts do. This result is interpreted as the fact that the light-skinned children are identifying on a purely perceptual basis alone: they actually resemble the white doll more closely and select it for this reason. There are two differences between my method and the Clarks'. I combined the color ratings into two categories ("light" and "dark"), while the Clarks use a three-category scheme which includes a "medium" group. My "light" group has both "light-medium" and "very-light" children, while the Clarks' "light" category contains only the latter group. Since their skin-color effect was so strong, my collapsing of the color ratings into two categories might reduce the effect but should not completely cancel it out.[23]

Another difference between my method and the Clarks' is that they do not control for social class, and middle-class status and light skin color are probably highly related in their sample as well as in mine. My data show that, controlling for color, the middle class has a high rate of misidentification. The fact that I hold social class constant and the Clarks do not indicates that their skin-color results were actually due partially to a class effect. Interpreting misidentification among light-skinned children in terms of purely perceptual factors is not wholly accurate; controls for class cancel out at least part of any possible effect of skin color.

Effect of Sex and Age on Racial Self-Concept

Thus far, we have seen that class and contact create differences in racial self-concept for some groups of children, though skin color does not. Sex and age are two other factors which also can theoretically be expected to influence racial self-esteem. We find that sex does exert an important effect on group identity; however, there is no effect by age on the self-identification index.

Let us begin by considering the relationship between sex and racial

self-esteem. Even if boys and girls do not always differ in racial attitudes, girls should be particularly likely to judge themselves personally
in terms of these evaluations. According to Freud, children of preschool
age are in the process of internalizing the norms defining their sex roles.
Since attractiveness is a key ingredient of the feminine role, physical
appearance becomes a highly salient factor for girls in this culture. The
little girl's complexion is a constant source of comment, and dress and
hair style are also stressed more for her than they are for the boy. Even
though the white girl may not be fully cognizant of racial differences,
she still may know not only what she looks like but also that white is
somehow better than brown. She thus will make a correct identification
on the basis of self-knowledge, reinforced, perhaps, by a vague conception
that her complexion is favorably evaluated. If she is aware of racial differences, she will in addition be strongly attracted to the favored status.

The black girl, however, may dislike her appearance and wish to look
white. She is the possessor of a complexion that the dominant culture
deems unattractive; advertisements for skin lighteners and hair straight-
eners in the Negro media only help to reinforce this conception. It is important for her to be pretty, but the image she often sees reflected back to
her is one that is disvalued.[24] William Grier and Price Cobbs state that
there is "heightened concern over all the criteria of femininity — all the
criteria of physical beauty thrust upon [black women] by a society which
held beauty to be the opposite of what they were."[25] Negro comedienne
"Moms" Mabley succinctly summarizes this problem with the following
anecdote: "there lived a little girl . . . You-all call her Cinderella . . .
She had long black hair, pretty brown eyes, pretty brown skin. Well, let's
face it — she was colored. Cindy-Ella turns to the mirror and says 'Mirror,
mirror on the wall, who's the fairest one of all?' The mirror replies,
'Snow white — and don't you forget it!' "[26]

Since these conflicts and concerns are less important for boys than they
are for girls, I expected that white girls would identify *more* correctly
than white boys and Negro girls would classify themselves *less* correctly
than their male counterparts. With controls for class, age, and race, the
results support this hypothesis. There is a strong race and sex interaction

effect; at most levels, white girls identify more accurately than white boys and the reverse is true for blacks (F=6.15, p≤.025, see Figure 7, Table

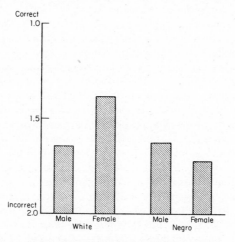

7. Self-identification by race and sex,
   controlling for age and class.

16).[27] The interpretation of these findings in terms of differences due to sex-role norms is verified by analysis of additional data. A higher percentage of white girls than of white boys made spontaneous references to appearance both verbally and in free play, as shown in the tabulation below (percentages based on number of children of each sex who spoke or engaged in free play at all):

Comments concerning:	Male	Female
blond hair	38 (N=74)	55 (N=85)
brown hair	23 (N=74)	51 (N=85)
Play patterns concerning:		
dress match	7.0 (N=60)	20.0 (N=87)

When class, age, and race are controlled, the overall sex effect on the color salience index also shows that appearance characteristics are more important for girls than for boys. At most levels, girls of both races match by dress and sex more frequently than boys do (F=6.77, p≤.01).[28] These data, however, should not be interpreted to mean that skin color is a minor factor of consideration for females, since the girls' score on this index is still at the color end of the scale. These results merely demonstrate that dress and sex are generally of greater concern to girls than to boys.

Although these data show that factors connected with personal appearance are more relevant for girls of both races than for boys, skin color seems to be more emotionally involving for the Negro than for the white girl in evaluation of personal attractiveness. The overall race-salience effect (Chapter 4, Table 7), shows that this is true, since at virtually all levels color is more important for the Negro girl than for the white girl. A frequency analysis over the entire sample on the two questions composing the color salience index gives additional evidence for all of these suppositions. For Negro girls, dress is much more important than sex, and both are generally less important than color. Any differences between Negro boys and girls on the color salience index thus seem to be due to a greater amount of dress matching among Negro girls. It should be noted that these girls are still high on color choice. For white girls, sex and color are of approximately equal importance and dress is more important than either of the other two alternatives. Dress and sex are much more important for white girls than they are for boys, confirming the fact that concern with appearance is an important sex-role expectation (see Table 18).

Spontaneous verbal comments also show that color seems to be a more relevant characteristic of appearance for the black girl than for her white counterpart. It is clear that color is also important for the white girl, since almost half of the white girls who spoke commented spontaneously about the color of the dolls. But if a white girl spoke, she was slightly more likely to comment about hair than about color. The black girls, however, were much more likely to comment about color than about

Table 18   Percent of Children of Each Race for Whom Dress and
Sex Were More Salient Than Color

Choice	White boys	White girls	Negro boys	Negro girls
	Dress v. color			
Dress rather than color	35	57	33	42
Color rather than dress	65	43	67	58
	N=81	N=100	N=78	N=97
	Sex v. color			
Sex rather than color	32	49	25	25
Color rather than sex	68	51	75	75
	N=81	N=100	N=78	N=97

hair,[29] as the following tabulation shows (percentages based on number of girls who spoke at all).

Race	Hair comments	Color comments
White	59(N=85)	49(N=85)
Negro	13(N=83)	39(N=83)

Thus, although personal appearance is more salient for girls of both races than it is for boys, skin color seems to be a more important concomitant of beauty for Negro than for white girls. The color terms index provides additional evidence that Negro girls' choices on the self-identification question reflect not lack of awareness but instead a negative or ambivalent racial self-concept. A race and sex interaction trend, controlling for age and class, reveals that black girls are more aware of racial terms than are black boys. For whites, however, the trend is reversed (F=2.34, p≤.12).[30]

I had originally thought that girls, because of their concern with physical appearance, might be more aware of race than boys are, but the awareness results for whites do not support this hypothesis. The greater awareness shown by boys, however, is probably due to the fact that the white male three-year-old sample was small and atypical. The seven boys in this group not only chose the Negro, white, and colored dolls more accurately than did their female counterparts (male=1.41; female= 1.87), but in some cases made more correct selections than either the four- or five- year-old boys did (see Chapter 4, Table 9). It is noteworthy that there is no overall sex difference within each race on the attitude index, though there was a trend for white girls in desegregated schools to prefer whites more than the boys did (see Chapter 5, Table 14). Yet, the data on self-identification show that racial evaluations tend to be particularly salient for the self-image of most girls of both races, even if their attitudes do not differ from those of the boys.

Black girls are generally more concerned about physical appearance than boys are, and they are sensitized to the part skin color plays in determining attractiveness. They realize that physical beauty is an important female asset; but cultural attitudes, transmitted by the mechanisms discussed in Chapter 1, tell them that they somehow do not measure up to acceptable standards. They are more aware of race in a cognitive sense than are males, but they identify themselves less correctly. This lack of correct self-identification indicates a higher rate of negative or ambivalent racial self-concept among black girls than among their male peers. Marion Radke's data suggest that this incorrect self-identification may indeed be an indication of wish fulfillment for the black girl. In her grammar school sample, there is greater acceptance by girls than by boys of the majority group's evaluation of the minority.[31]

Among the white children, boys seem to have a more cognitive orientation to race than girls do, but the proper interpretation of this result is unclear. Even if girls do not have a sophisticated understanding of racial differences, they may still identify correctly because of the stress on feminine personal appearance in this culture. They are more aware of what they look like and classify themselves on this basis, but many also have a vague conception of evaluations attached to color. Concern with appearance makes these positive feelings toward white skin more relevant to them personally, and positive group identity provides an incentive for correct self-classification.[32]

I not only predicted a sex difference in accuracy of self-identification but also expected to find variations by age. Because positive attitudes toward whites increased among both races from three to five years, it seemed that older whites should exhibit more and blacks less correct self-identification than their younger peers. However, we find no differences in self-identification by age on the analysis of variance index. When we look only at those children who misclassify themselves consistently (two incorrect choices), there are still no significant age differences for blacks, but the white three-year-olds consistently misclassify themselves more frequently than the white children of age five do. This difference, however, is not great (25 percent, N=20, of the three-year-olds and 13 percent, N=85, of the children of age five consistently misclassify themselves). I cannot explain why we do not find the predicted results; however, a large increase in accuracy of identification with age should appear if six- or seven-year-olds are included in the sample; by age six or seven, most children recognize what they look like and are forced by reality factors to identify themselves correctly, regardless of race.[33]

Conclusion

Self-identification is an index of group identity for preschool youngsters. Attitudes and self-identification are highly related, although the two measures are not completely congruent (see Table 17). *It is clear that many black children have low esteem for themselves on a racial basis; white children are positively attracted to the favored status.*

But racial self-classification varies among subgroups of black and white youngsters. Black girls are sensitive to evaluations which characterize their personal appearance as undesirable and show a high rate of self-rejection on a racial basis. Social class differences in group identity are also important for Negroes. Middle-class black children show higher rates of rejection of their racial status than other social classes do. The ADC group also seems to have a high proportion of children with negative feelings about their racial membership. The working class has the most positive racial self-concept of any socioeconomic group. Although the contact results for black youngsters are extremely difficult to interpret, it seems that the racial self-esteem of middle- and working-class children is not adversely affected by desegregation. This finding is of particular interest since the quality of desegregation in our classrooms was on the whole rather poor. There is only one white group that has low racial self-esteem. The white boys attending predominantly Negro schools seem to reject themselves on a racial basis. White girls, however, identify themselves accurately regardless of their environment.

When we consider the entire range of identification results presented in this chapter, a pattern appears which suggests a relationship between most of the group differences in self-classification. Within each race, differences between groups on the self-identification measure appear for those groups whose racial membership is most salient to their major goals. For instance, the group identity of those statuses in which physical appearance is of prime importance should be particularly likely to be affected by racial attitudes. These evaluations help tell the girl whether she is pretty. And the sex results for black and white girls show this is true: black girls have a more negative and white girls a more positive racial self-concept than their male peers. To take another instance of this general principle, occupants of statuses characterized by marginality or status discrepancy are particularly likely to compare themselves socially with the more successful group.[34] Minority membership may become especially important to them because it prevents or hinders them from attaining high status in all respects. This is true not only of the black middle class but of white boys in predominantly Negro schools, and both these groups do have high rates of misidentification. Thus, among blacks, those groups whose major goals are threatened are more apt to identify inaccurately. For whites, the groups whose major goals are positively reinforced by racial membership are especially likely to show high rates of correct self-classification.

Self-identification, however, indicates other factors than racial self-esteem, since it is related to awareness of racial differences as well as to attitudes (see Table 17). Thus, differences between subgroups within each race on a relatively rough index of racial self-concept are particularly likely to appear in cases where racial attitudes are highly salient for the goals of the group in question.[35] Whether factors like age or social class for whites actually affect group identity is a matter for further research with a more sensitive indicator. These variables either may not exert much effect on racial self-concept or may have an effect which our rather crude index does not uncover. It is difficult to gain an understanding of these issues from the studies reported in Chapter 2, because most of them do not have adequate controls for other relevant variables.

Group identity is only one component of self-esteem. We still do not know how it affects other dimensions of personality. In the next chapter, some exploratory findings are presented which suggest that a poor group identity may negatively influence other dimensions of self-concept for Negro children.

7 The Personal Dimension of Self-Esteem

[The secretary told me] that Mr. Upshur would see me . . .
and Mr. Upshur came in. When he said he was Mr. Upshur,
I knew he couldn't help me. He was colored. What
could he do for anybody?

Claude Brown, Manchild in the
Promised Land

This crayon is brown. I'll take pink because I
like pink. It's a lighter color, and it's better
than all the rest. Myself's not pink.
Gregory, Negro, 5 years old

The cultural evaluations of race that some black children are learning unfavorably affect their self-esteem. We have just discussed the effects of prejudice on the child's group identity or racial self-concept. Group identity refers to how the individual feels about himself *as a member of a racial group,* whether he accepts or rejects his racial membership, but other theorists have suggested that self-concept is not unidimensional. This chapter deals with one other component of self-concept which I call the "personal identity" dimension.[1] Personal identity means one's esteem for himself *as an individual,* how he feels about himself on a deep, personal level. In other words, it is one's *basic sense of personal worth and adequacy.*

Devaluation of one's racial group can create not only a negative group identity but feelings of inadequacy and insecurity on a deeper level as well.[2] My data showed that the group identity component of self-concept is indeed lower among blacks than among whites: many black children reject themselves on a racial basis and dislike or are ambivalent toward the fact that they are black. I felt that because of prejudice and its social concomitants, the *personal identity* dimension of self-esteem might also be less favorable for black youngsters.

My major interest was the relationship between racial attitudes and group identity, but I had also hoped to do a preliminary investigation of differences in personal identity between children of each race. It is difficult to measure personal identity at the preschool level because of problems with existing techniques, yet during the course of the research I accidentally discovered a picture-drawing and story method which may provide an operational definition of personal self-esteem. In this chapter we find that personal self-esteem varies by both race and class. Higher rates of negative personal identities are found among blacks than among whites. But within each race, the ADC group has the least and the middle-class group the most personal self-esteem. These findings have important implications for both theory and public policy.

Self-Portrait and Story Technique: A Measure of "Personal Identity"

The Thematic Apperception Test is one of the best known of the measures of children's personal identity and has frequently been utilized in child psychology. A common TAT variation for youngsters is the "Blacky Test," in which the child is asked to make up stories about a family of dogs.[3] There are several reasons why this measure was unsuitable for my purpose. Because of both its name and its focus on color, it has problems for use with Negro children. Also, the scoring scheme stresses Oedipal themes and does not focus on possible personality effects of social factors like race or class. Any TAT technique is dependent on the subject's ability to verbalize; thus, it is not reliable as the sole measure of personal identity for preschool, lower-class children who may have limited facility with words.

Another frequently used instrument is the adjective check-list, where the subject designates adjectives which describe him, but this of course is inappropriate with pre-literate subjects. Sentence-completion tests cannot be used with this age group for the same reason. The "evaluative" dimension of Osgood's Semantic Differential is another possible technique.[4] Here the child is asked to rate himself with respect to a number of bipolar adjectives. I tried to adapt it for use with my sample by rewording some of the choices and illustrating them with stick figures. But the Semantic Differential seems too sophisticated for this age level, because the children quickly became confused and lost interest.

Picture drawings (House-Tree-Person test, in which the individual is asked to draw each of these objects) have been used with adults and occasionally with children.[5] But the available scoring procedures for such drawings are based upon either conventional psychoanalytic schemes in which sociocultural factors do not play an important role (Machover) or upon drawing as a function of intellectual capacity (Goodenough).[6]

Dale Harris, in fact, states that "children's drawings of the human figure do not appear to be valuable as measures of . . . personality factors. The large part of the variance seems to be accounted for by cognitive, conceptual factors."[7] Other investigators, however, feel that children's figure drawings are both intellectual and emotional indicators.[8]

Besides being used as measures of intelligence or emotional adjustment, children's art work has also been utilized to measure social values. Wayne Dennis claims that if asked to draw a man, children usually draw men they admire and who are thought of favorably by their societies.[9] Robert Coles, on the basis of numerous drawings of Negro and white children, also says that social factors have an important influence on the content of children's portraits; the way children draw is "affected by their racial background, and what that 'fact' means in their particular world (society) at that particular time (period of history)."[10] Coles is one of the few investigators who has used art work as an indicator of the effect of social values and events on children's self-esteem. However, he concentrates only on the intensive study of individual cases and provides no scoring scheme for analysis of group differences.

Both because of lack of agreement on what children's art work actually measures and because of lack of an adequate scoring scheme for determining the effect of social factors on personal identity, I decided to avoid use of artistic productions as a measure of group differences in personal self-image. During the course of research, however, I accidentally discovered one type of drawing technique which I thought might be suitable.

As a check on color preference, each child was asked to choose a piece of paper and draw a picture of himself. I expected that those Negro children manifesting strong Negro preference on a variety of other measures would choose brown paper for their self-portraits. It soon became obvious that the artistic productions themselves were of much greater interest than the actual color of the paper selected. Although most children chose white or green paper, there was a wide range of difference in the details of their self-portraits. The child's experience with crayons or with viewing himself in a mirror did not seem to be a relevant explanatory factor, since most of these five-year-olds had either been in nursery school for several years and received practice in drawing or had just completed a summer program in which drawing and body image were strongly emphasized.

Intellectual differences presented a conventional interpretation of these variations. Goodenough's Draw-a-Man test has been used as a measure of children's intellectual capacity, and Martin Deutsch shows that scores on children's IQ tests are related to factors such as race and class.[11] If our pictures were only class-related tests of intelligence, they would of course be inappropriate for use as a measure of self-esteem. But Dale Harris, one of the chief proponents of drawings as a measure of intelligence, has suggested that self-portraits may be the most useful type of drawing for studying nonintellectual, psychological factors.[12] My study provides additional evidence on the value of self-portraits as emotional indicators. We asked each child to tell a story about his self-portrait. The relationship between the content of the stories and the form of the self-portraits precludes intellectual capacity as the only explanation of these observed differences, since those pictures which indicated poor self-image tended to be accompanied by stories in which themes of fear and powerlessness were stressed.

To see if it suggested hypotheses about the relationship of race and personal identity, this self-portrait technique was utilized with a group of fifty-eight five-year-old children (thirty-nine Negroes, nineteen whites). With the exception of twelve Negroes, these youngsters were in desegregated schools.[13] The children were familiar with the investigator and felt at ease with her, since she had already tested each child once before on the attitude index. Each youngster was brought into the room to "play a new game." He was given three pieces of paper (white, green, and brown) and told to choose one and to draw a picture of himself. After completing the picture, he was asked whom the figures represented. In each case, the child acknowledged that it was a self-portrait. He was then requested to tell a story about the figure, including what it liked to do or knew how to do.

A survey of existing literature revealed little that would aid in interpretation of these results. Since this was only a preliminary attempt to investigate general group differences, an uncomplicated scoring procedure was developed. The assumption was made that the most detailed, colorful, lively pictures indicated a more favorable self-image; therefore, the coding scheme consisted of a list of physical features (such as body, eyes, mouth) that could be included in the portrait.[14] (It is important to point out that correctness of racial membership was not included as one of the physical features in the scoring categories; this drawing technique was to be independent of the self-identification measure). Several other factors, such as the facial expression of the figure and its size and position on the page, were also added, since these items have frequently been used as emotional indicators in other scoring schemes.[15] Each item was specifically defined in easily measurable terms. Two coders working together determined the presence or absence of each category in the picture. Agreement was necessary for a feature to be marked present.[16] A code was also devised for the thematic content of the stories, which included such categories as "personal efficacy," "powerlessness," and "lively daily descriptions." Each verbal production was scored by a third rater who had not seen the pictures and was unfamiliar with the hypotheses (see scoring scheme for the drawings and stories in Appendix 4).

An item-by-item correlation indicates that the picture categories seem to be related to one another. These intercorrelations for the entire group of children range from about +.10 to +.65, and several item clusters seem to appear within the total set of drawing indices.[17] There is a connection between several of the themes in the stories as well. In the white stories, for instance, "personal efficacy" correlates positively with "lively daily description" and negatively with "powerlessness." For the white youngsters, there is also a correspondence between the verbal and the artistic productions. White children whose pictures indicate a generally favorable self-image also tend to tell stories containing themes of personal efficacy and of lively daily description. Powerlessness and dull daily descriptions accompany the less detailed and less colorful portraits.

Although these story themes correlate well with the overall raw score on the drawings, it is interesting to note relationships between the stories and particular picture categories for whites. The white children who place their self-portraits in the corner (instead of the middle) of the page tend to express powerlessness in the verbal descriptions of the portraits. A connection between personal efficacy in the stories and presence of limbs in the pictures also exists.[18]

No negative self-descriptions or physical harm imagery are included in the verbal productions of whites, but these themes are present in the stories of some of the black children. Although low positive correlations appear, there tends to be less connection for blacks than for whites both among the story themes and between the verbal descriptions and pictures. In the stories told by black children, personal efficacy seems to accompany positive self-description and lively daily description. There are also similarities between the stories and the portraits, since positive self-description accompanies lively facial expression. Also, personal efficacy in the stories and presence of arms in the pictures appear together.[19]

It appears that for Negroes the lower relationship between verbal and artistic productions may be due in part to bias in regard to the experimenter. Since the child is specifically asked to draw and then verbally describe himself, this technique is more anxiety provoking than the projective attitude test. This threat, plus the presence of a white interviewer, might lead to suppression of anxiety-arousing material and thus particularly affect verbal output. Yet low positive correlations still exist, so bias due to a white interviewer or other factors unrelated to self-concept cannot be a complete explanation of data gathered by this method.

These correlations indicate that the self-portraits may, in fact, be an adequate indicator of self-esteem. In a study of ten- to seventeen-year-old children's responses to the Draw-a-Person test, R. F. Bodwin and M. Bruck provide additional evidence of the validity of this assumption. Their scoring procedure, which also emphasized among other factors completeness of the portraits, was significantly related to independent psychiatric ratings of self-concept.[20]

We thus decided to use the self-portrait and story technique as a measure of personal identity. The comparison for each child of the group identity (racial self-identification) and personal identity (self-portrait) results confirms the validity of this decision as shown below (in percentages):

Personal	Group	Blacks	Whites
high	high	8	42
high	low	23	21
low	high	20	16
low	low	49	21

For 57 percent of the blacks and 63 percent of the whites, the personal and racial identity components are consistent; however, since 43 percent of the blacks and 37 percent of the whites were high on one measure and low on the other, I conclude that these components are in fact distinct.

Some important race and class differences in personal self-esteem are found by use of this self-portrait and story technique. These results must be interpreted with caution because of the small size of the sample and the nature of the test. The technique was discovered accidentally as a measure of personal identity, and a scoring scheme was not developed prior to the administration of the test. Thus, the analysis is based on categories derived from the data. The findings are meant as hypotheses rather than firm conclusions.

Race and Class Differences in Personal Self-Esteem

Because of the low evaluation of blacks in American society, it seemed that Negro youngsters should have less positive personal identities than whites on my measure. There is, in fact, a significant difference in overall picture-drawing scores by race. Whites, in general, appear to have better personal self-concepts than blacks do.[21] Sixty-three percent of the whites versus 31 percent of the blacks have high personal self-esteem (p ≤ .05; see previous tabulation). It is important that *only 8 percent of the blacks compared to 42 percent of whites are high on both personal and racial self-concept; 49 percent of the blacks and 21 percent of the whites are low on both dimensions (see previous tabulation).*

The stories they told about their self-portraits also show lower self-esteem among black youngsters. Stories told by whites tend to show significantly more "personal efficacy" than do the stories of the black children (see Table 19). Few black children gave portrait descriptions which expressed the strong sense of personal efficacy and self-confidence contained in the following story of a white child.

> He knows how to put his head up in the air without his hands. He likes to stand up with one hand and roll like an airplane. He knows how to lift a spoon with one finger and can hold a brick on top of his finger. He can even pick up a chair with one hand.
>
> White boy, middle class

Physical harm, however, is a more frequently mentioned theme among black children than it is among whites (see Table 19). Lower rates of adequate personal identities among black children have also been found by other investigators. Suzanne Keller as well as Martin Deutsch have demonstrated that black children exhibit more self-devaluation than their white counterparts do.[22] Baughman and Dahlstrom find that on MMPI ratings, southern blacks have less sense of personal worth than do southern white children,[23] and in intensive studies of individual subjects, Coles finds more or less the same result.[24] Black children also have a lower sense of control of the environment, as the Coleman data show.[25] This particular piece of evidence supports the low rate of personal efficacy in the stories told by the Negro youngsters we tested. My data thus confirm other evidence that prejudice and discrimination have a destructive effect on the black child's personal identity—his feelings about himself as an *individual* — as well as on his group identity — his acceptance or rejection of himself *as black*.[26]

Controlling for social class, we find that racial differences in personal identity still appear. In each case, whites' self-portraits have higher personal self-esteem scores than those of blacks of the same social class.[27] But a pattern is also present by class: within each race, the middle class has the highest personal self-esteem and the ADC group the lowest personal self-esteem scores on the drawings (see Table 20). Martin Deutsch, with a different technique and a sample of older children, also finds that a high percentage of lower-class children have poor self-esteem, but more blacks than whites in his lower-class group have poor self-concepts.[28]

This difference by race and class in the drawings can be illustrated by a comparison of some extreme cases. One white middle-class girl drew a

Table 19   *Differences in "Personal Efficacy" and "Physical Harm"*
   Story Theme by Race

	Personal Efficacy	
	White	*Negro*
Present	47%	16%
	N=9	N=6
Absent	53%	84%
	N=10	N=32
	χ^2=4.99 (continuity corrected)	
	p$\leqslant$.05	
	Physical Harm	
	White	*Negro*
Present	0%	21%
	N=0	N=8
Absent	100%	79%
	N=19	N=30
	χ^2=3.1 (continuity corrected)	
	p$\leqslant$.10	

Table 20   Self-Esteem by Social Class for Whites and Blacks on Self-Portraits

Personal self-esteem	Whites, class		
	Middle	Working	ADC
High	89% N=8	50% N=3	25% N=1
Low	11% N=1	50% N=3	75% N=3
	Negroes, class		
	Middle	Working	ADC
High	42% N=5	31% N=5	20% N=2
Low	58% N=7	69% N=11	80% N=8

large figure, centered in the middle of the page. The body was outlined in yellow and pink, and the figure had not only eyes, nose, and smiling mouth in appropriate colors but also curly brown hair and a colorful blue and white dress. Arms, legs, hands, and feet were present (see Figure 8). The opposite end of the spectrum is exhibited by the lower-class Negro boy who drew himself as a small, grey blob in the corner of the page, asking that it be labeled with his name (see Figure 9), or by the lower-class Negro girl who carefully drew a person and then picked up a blue crayon and obliterated the figure completely with systematic strokes. When asked what she had drawn, the child said sadly that she had produced a picture of herself.[29]

Differences in story content also appear by class within each race and provide additional evidence that personal identity and class may be related. "Powerlessness" and "dull daily description" are more frequently expressed in the verbalizations of white working-class and ADC children, and "lively daily description" is more often found in the stories of the white middle class,[30] as the percentages for each group show in the listing below:

Theme	Middle (N = 9)	Working (N = 6)	ADC (N = 4)
Powerlessness	0	33.3	50
Dull daily description	11.1	0	100
Lively daily description	88.9	66.7	0

Following is a story typical of the white middle class:

This little girl is five. She has a brother named Michael and a sister named Sally and a dog named Poppy and a mother named Mary and a father named Harry. She goes to school at— —nursery. She does what her mother says. Her name is Rachel. She picks flowers for her mother and goes to bed when mother tells her and does what teacher says and does lessons. She went to the circus one time and fed the pigeons one time and she lives on— —Street and her dog has blond hair and her father mows the lawn and my brother and me help our mother and father wash the car and plant the grass. She watches men build buildings and helps her mother put up the curtains and she had a tooth out.

White, middle class
(See Figure 8)

No middle-class white child, however, told a story like that of David, a white boy in the ADC group:

I don't know how to draw a picture of myself very well, but I'll do the best I can. This will turn out lousy like all of mine. A lot of my David pictures turn out lousy.

White, ADC
(See Figure 10)

8. Rachel, white, middle class.

GIANT

ROCKET

EUGENE

9. Eugene, Negro, ADC.

10. David, white, ADC.

ROBBIN

. Robbin, Negro, working class.

The ADC child may, of course, actually have less stimulation at home, and this group is also less able to control the environment because of their dependent welfare status. But these class differences in "daily description" and "personal efficacy" do not seem to be simply an objective reporting of reality; they affect self-concept as well. The youngster in the ADC group has little self-confidence; he feels that he, personally, is inadequate and that his efforts will all "turn cut lousy." The "dull daily descriptions" of the white ADC children indicate a lack of interpersonal stimulation in their environment. There is little of the emphasis on emotionally positive parent-child interaction that we find in the middle-class stories, and this type of relationship is of course important in the development of healthy self-esteem.

The "powerlessness" trend also appears by class in stories told by black children. The most interesting class difference for Negroes, however, appears in the physical harm dimension: 9 percent of the middle, 19 percent of the working, and 40 percent of the ADC lower class tell stories which express fear of physical assault:

A giant comes out of a rocket, the boy is afraid of him. He's going to scare the boy. The boy is crying.

> Negro, ADC
> (See Figure 9)

(Child draws picture of a snake and then a portrait of herself which is a smaller version of the snake.) I had a snake in my bed and I got in Mother's bed. I'm running from the snake. It's a bad snake.

> Negro ADC

She put some of her mother's lipstick on. Mother beat her and couldn't get it off. Then she sneaked out from her mother when mother sleeps. Mother found her and beat her. She said, "Go 'way, Go 'way daughter—

don't come back again." Mother said that because she didn't like ' ɘr said little girl.

Negro ADC

The following story seems to sum up the ADC child's approach to life:

I can't draw myself—I can't draw a body. I don't know how. I didn't do it right—I walked down the street and saw a boy and he hit me and I punched him. He took his bullets and rifles and when he tried to shoot me, I shot him. I was going to see his feet—I'm walking on a rainy day. Me and my feet walk down to the cellar and saw a pigeon bird who never finds his way home—They (the pigeon and a mouse) went home with me and I kept them. I took the mouse and put it and the poor little pigeon in my bed.

Negro, ADC

Fear of physical attack is not present in any white story. (The presence of "harm" stories among the black sample replaces the "dull daily descriptions" of the white ADC group.) One other theme appears too infrequently to be coded, but it is also present only in the ADC Negro verbal productions. Some of these children seem to concentrate on feet (see the story above). This emphasis may be due to the fact that feet carry one away from danger. One child even drew sixteen legs on his picture and specified that they were "legs to run with."

Paul Mussen finds that more Negro than white lower-class children tell stories in which the hero is hated, scolded, or reprimanded, or is the victim of physical assault, and David Palermo finds that black children show high levels of anxiety.[31] Caution must be exerted in interpretation of these results as indicative of poor personal identity. For children in certain situations, responses indicating a high degree of fear are a realistic reflection of life conditions rather than an indication of deep personal

12. Frank, white, working class.

disturbance or hostility. On the attitude test, the responses of some of the ADC children indicate that the former factor is important and must be taken into consideration (e.g., "These two dolls are going to jail." "These children are sad, because they don't have enough to eat.") However, the actual content of the stories does suggest that more than a simple reporting of reality is involved. The children seem to be emotionally affected by an environment in which deprivation and fear are present (for instance, in some of the stories the children actually state that they are frightened and unhappy). Many of these youngsters thus have identities as individuals to whom bad things will happen; they see themselves as the potential victims of attack and/or rejection.

All of these stories suggest an interpretation of the relationship between social class and personal identity. The ADC child lives in an environment of economic deprivation. He is less likely than the middle-class child to have enough to eat and an adequate place to live. He is also more likely to be a member of a large family in a home without a father. These difficulties created by poverty may also negatively affect the quality of personal relationships within the family.[32] Thus, the ADC child is less likely than his middle-class counterparts to be secure in terms of both physical and emotional needs, and a high rate of poor personal self-esteem among ADC youngsters of both races can be attributed to these factors. The black ADC child is in a doubly difficult position, however. Not only must he face all of these poverty-related problems but he is exposed to negative evaluations on the basis of race as well.

Because of the effect of racial evaluations on self-esteem, the middle- and working-class blacks also seem to have a lower rate of positive personal identity than whites do. But middle- and working-class families are better able to provide emotional and physical necessities for the child, and this positively affects his sense of personal worth, regardless of race. And it is important to note that black middle- and working-class children exhibit higher personal self-esteem than the white ADC group does. Thus my data suggest that life patterns related to the family's economic situation have an extremely important effect on personal identity, a finding with obvious policy implications.

When we combine these class findings on *personal identity* with the class results on *group identity* in Chapter 6, an interesting pattern emerges. There are no class differences in racial self-concept for whites. But for blacks, personal and group identity seem to vary separately by class. The black middle class has *more positive personal self-esteem* but *less positive racial self-esteem* than the working class does. The ADC children have low self-esteem on both dimensions.[33]

These findings can be explained in the following manner. The middle class is socially marginal and thus may be more directly frustrated by dominant cultural attitudes about blacks than the working class is, but, since the middle class is advantaged economically, there is less likelihood of family disruption and tensions and the other side-effects of financial insecurity. This whole complex of structural factors (inadequate education, economic difficulties aggravated by job discrimination, and family tensions stemming from these sources) is more pertinent to the working class and may create a higher rate of poor personal self-esteem in this group. Yet the working class is not in a marginal social position and thus may show less rejection of their racial status. The ADC group, because of its dependent welfare status, is exposed to a combination of both highly negative evaluations of blacks and problems created by a precarious economic position. The self-esteem of these children is subjected to a double-barreled attack.

I have stressed that, because of the small size of my sample and the nature of my method, the data in this chapter are meant to generate hypotheses rather than to provide conclusions. Thus, I hypothesize that because of negative evaluations of their race blacks have lower rates of positive personal self-esteem than whites do. But social class also has an extremely important influence on personal identity. Within each race, the middle class should have the most and the ADC group the least positive personal self-esteem. Although blacks differ by class on the racial as well as on the personal dimension of self-concept, these two components do not completely coincide within the black community. Group and personal identity vary separately for blacks by social class, with *group identity affected more by class differences in reaction to racial attitudes and personal identity more influenced by such class factors as economic and familial stability.* These hypotheses suggested by my data provide an important clue to the clarification of discrepancies in existing theories of the effect of prejudice on the personality of black Americans. These theories are discussed in Chapter 9.

8   Actual Playmate Choice in a Desegregated Setting

Racial attitudes may affect not only self-concept but also behavior patterns, yet the connection between preschool-age children's racial attitudes and their actual play has not been fully explored. This chapter presents results of a preliminary attempt to relate the racial feelings of five-year-old children to their actual behavior in the classroom.

Two studies of preschool play patterns found that race seems to be unimportant in selection of friends. On the basis of observation of children two and a half to three and a half years old in an Austin, Texas, nursery school, Harold and Nancy Stevenson concluded that children of this age respond to one another as individuals rather than as members of racial groups.[1] Mary Ellen Goodman discovered among her "New Dublin" (Boston) four-year-olds that white-Negro interaction was at the chance level but white-white interactions were below chance and Negro-Negro interactions above chance.[2] She attributes this differential to the more active, aggressive personalities of the Negro children.

There are several studies of the effects of prejudice on the interaction of slightly older children, but the results of these investigations differ. Paul Mussen finds that in a northern interracial camp, the elementary school-age boys who revealed a greater degree of prejudice in his test also showed more prejudice in the behavioral situation.[3] Using a sociometric technique, J. H. Criswell discovered that in the North prejudice may affect friendship choice by the fifth grade.[4] But even though racial feelings did exist among Joseph Rosner's sample of white northern twelve-year-olds, these attitudes were not expressed in the behavior of his subjects.[5]

Part of the discrepancy in these studies undoubtedly results from differences in method. Rosner draws his conclusions from observations of actual behavior, while Criswell bases her interpretations on a sociometric picture technique. A number of studies show that prejudice is more easily expressed in the latter type of situation. The disagreement between the Rosner and Mussen studies may be due to the fact that in Rosner's sample whites were in the minority and, perhaps, were afraid to express their feelings openly in behavior.

Data on the relationship between adult prejudice and actual behavior also yield conflicting results. Bernard Kutner and R. T. LaPiere found little connection in their separate studies between attitudes and inter-action in adults, but they focused on instrumental activity in a com-mercial setting rather than on behavior in less impersonal situations.[6] Other studies have suggested that attitudes may have a moderate effect on interaction. Robin Williams has demonstrated that those individuals who have the most favorable attitudes toward a minority group are also most likely to interact with members of that group.[7] It is not clear, though, whether this is a cause, an effect, or both.

In view of this conflicting evidence even for adults, I suspected that there might be little connection between friendship choice and attitudes among preschool children. This seemed particularly likely, since racial feelings are still in a formative stage at this age level. If a relationship did exist, we predicted that the children who expressed the most own-race preference on the test would also exhibit the highest percentage of own-race friendships in an actual behavioral setting.

In order to investigate these hypotheses, it was necessary to find a method of recording children's actual playmate choices in an unstruc-tured situation. In the pre-test to this study, several observers were situated at different locations in the playground, scanned the entire class at five-minute intervals, and recorded all interactions. Since in a large and constantly shifting group it is difficult to observe all children equally well, the observer's attention was focused on the highly active children. The subjects who had low rates of interaction tended to be ig-nored when this procedure was used. For this reason, this technique was unsuitable for an intensive study of the play patterns of each child.

Since my purpose was to investigate the behavior of the individual child rather than to study the overall classroom pattern of interracial play, it was decided to observe each subject at close range and record both his playmate choice and his actual comments. "Playmate choice" was defined as a conscious verbal or physical attempt to approach or make contact with another child. It should be made clear at this point that playmate choice is different from "interaction." An *interaction* involves a child's choosing and being chosen in return. Playmate choice focuses only on the child's approach to others rather than on patterns of mutual response. Since I was interested in the relationship between selection of dolls and selection of actual friends, it seemed more appropriate to concentrate on behavior in which the child himself took the initiative.

Each child was observed for half an hour while he was engaged in spontaneous, unstructured play. Everyone he selected to play with and everything he said or did, as well as any behavioral or verbal response to his actions by others, was recorded. The behavior samples were collected on two days, several weeks apart; and on each day the subject was observed for three five-minute periods approximately twenty minutes apart. We hoped that observation of each child on two widely separated days would control for the effect of absence of other children from school on playmate choice. The division of data collection on any given day by twenty-minute intervals produced a more representative picture of the subject's play, since this procedure precluded observation of a long, atypical play sequence with another child.

Reliability problems are minimized by this technique. Because she observes only one child at a time at close range, the interviewer is able to accurately record with whom the child plays and what he says. The data were collected by someone totally unacquainted with the children's performance on the structured test. Her presence did not seem to affect the children's play in any way, since she had spent several days in each classroom prior to the commencement of the data-gathering process. She was thus accepted as a familiar figure by the time she appeared on the playground. It should be noted that the teachers were always on the playground, so the presence of another adult was accepted without comment.

We decided to observe five-year-old youngsters, because children of this age level manifest the most sophisticated racial feelings of any preschool age group. Data were collected in two desegregated kindergarten classes which had different proportions of Negroes and whites. It was hoped that this would provide at least some control for effects due to percentage of children of each race in the classroom. The number of children of each race and sex in the two schools is shown below.

	School A				*School B*		
	Negro	*White*			*Negro*	*White*	
Male	9	4	13	Male	2	6	8
Female	5	2	7	Female	6	3	9
	14	6	20		8	9	17

After the data were collected, the percentage of white playmate choice was computed for each child. The final correlation between this figure and the score on the attitude index yielded somewhat surprising results. In one kindergarten (School A), there was no correlation between attitudes and actual interracial friendships for either whites or blacks. There was also no significant relationship between the indices for the blacks in School B. For whites, however, there was a strong relationship in the opposite direction from that predicted by the hypothesis. The whites in School B who *rejected* Negroes most on the attitude test were also the ones who *selected* Negroes most frequently as playmates in a real life setting.[8] This finding seems to have little to do with a disproportion in racial composition of the classroom, since there were an almost equal number of whites and Negroes in this school. An explanation of this puzzling correlation for the School B whites is suggested by other data. For all children, sex is the factor which is most highly related to play-mate selection. In each class, approximately 80 percent of the actual choices take place between children of the same sex. By use of a socio-metric technique, Evelyn Helgerson also finds that sex is more important than race in determination of friendships among preschool children.[9]

This own-sex preference is due to the fact that sex-role norms sanction different types of behavior for males and females. The boys engage in more active, aggressive play than the girls do; they are more interested in playing war than in playing house. If play style is important in ex-plaining why children generally choose friends of their own sex, it also may determine particular friendship patterns within each sex group. This factor sheds light on the puzzling correlation between the high Negro doll rejection and high Negro playmate choice among whites in School B. In this group of white children, the connection between attitudes and interaction seems to be confounded by a chance relationship between attitudes and play styles. The black children on the whole are somewhat rougher in their play than the whites are. The more active, aggressive whites of each sex play with Negroes, regardless of their racial attitudes; and in this classroom, the white children who are the most aggressive also give the most anti-Negro responses on the test.

Ralph (white),[10] for instance, has the highest white preference score possible on the attitude index. It is clear that his answers on the questionnaire are indicative of highly negative attitudes toward the brown dolls, since he specifically mentions "Negro" several times in a disparaging way. Yet 79 percent of the children he actually chooses to play with are Negroes. Ralph is the most active child in the class; during the half hour he was observed, he made contact with twenty-nine children. The only child who can keep up with him is Stanley, a Negro, who is the only boy who has a similar play style. Ralph and Stanley are together most of the time, and their play is characterized by rough, aggressive activity.

Michael (white) on the other hand, is a shy, retiring child. In the test he selects the brown doll 50 percent of the time, and he even comments in a racially tolerant manner that "she's black and that's good, because God made her that way." However, only 17 percent of the children he actually chooses to play with are Negro. He is afraid of Stanley, because he cannot defend himself against Stanley's aggression the way Ralph can:

Stanley to Michael: Watch out or I'll hit you in the mouth. You'd better watch out or I'll knock you in the mouth [hits Michael].

Michael to Stanley: Now, Stanley, let's go on the swing. [Stanley hits him again. Michael runs away.]

An analysis of the verbalizations which accompanied each choice of an actual playmate suggests that yet another factor may influence the child's behavior patterns. Friendship selections seem to be determined not only by style of play but also by personality. Patty (white) says that the white doll should "come home for lunch because he's white." Although she exhibits the highest white score possible on the attitude index, 78 percent of her actual playmate choices are Negro. Patty whines and is unkempt and unpopular with the other children. A typical play sequence is:

Patty approaches Judy (white), who walks off. She goes to Ruth (Negro): "I want to play with you, Ruth." Ruth: "Get out of here."

She makes numerous attempts to be friendly, but her initiatives are ignored. She thus plays most of the time with the only child who will accept her: a Negro girl who is also rejected by the other youngsters.

An investigation of the attitude-behavior correlation among the School B whites suggests that sex, play style within sex, and personality are three factors which may account for most of the playmate selection of kindergarten-age children. In both schools, race seemed to play little part in determining friendship patterns. We have already seen that interracial choice seems unrelated to the attitudes of the individual child. Additional evidence for the lack of racial preference in behavior lies in the fact that overall patterns of Negro-white interaction are at the chance level in both classes.

For every child, we counted only the number of actual friendship choices and did not code whether these contacts were friendly or unfriendly. It seemed possible that data on the affective tone of the behavior might prove more illuminating than a gross numerical description of number of children of the opposite race that the subject approached. Analysis of comments made during play, however, indicated that it was not necessary to use such a coding scheme. Race was very rarely mentioned, and there seemed to be no difference between each child's type of play with his own and with the opposite race. There were several cases where hostility was expressed between a Negro and a white, but these seemed to be determined much more by the children's personalities than by their racial feelings. The Stanley-to-Michael sequence was one such occurrence. Another incident took place in School A, where Grant (Negro) constantly taunted Donald (white) with the cry, "Fatso! Fatso!" Donald actually is fat, clumsy, and a natural target for aggression in any classroom. He was unmercifully bullied not only by Grant but also by the white boys in the class.

Actual racial incidents do, of course, sporadically occur in kindergarten classrooms. Even though none of these incidents took place while we were collecting the interaction data, we did observe occasional racial comments in these and other desegregated schools. And racial name-calling can have an effect on the minority group child far disproportionate to its frequency, especially if it is reinforced by teachers' attitudes or subtle factors in the curriculum. Yet with children at the age of five, these incidents are the exception rather than the rule.

Our observations thus suggest that five-year-olds have already internalized cultural evaluations of racial categories; in a highly structured situation like the attitude test, where race is the focus of attention, racial feelings are often expressed explicitly. However, these feelings are clearly secondary to other factors in affecting actual behavior. Play patterns are situationally determined. Factors like sex, personality, and play style seem to be more salient determinants of friendship than race does. This is true for even those five-year-olds with the most intense racial attitudes. We cannot predict Ralph's actions in a classroom where he would have the opportunity to choose between a Negro and a white boy with play styles similar to his. We do know that, given the alternatives he has, despite his expressed dislike of the brown dolls he actually plays with rough, aggressive Stanley, who is Negro, rather than with shier, more passive Michael, who is white.

Thus, one important prerequisite for real "integration" is already present in kindergarten classrooms: actual interaction between children does not, for the most part, seem to be marked by intense interracial hostility. But this factor is not enough to create a truly tolerant atmosphere. Just because racial incidents occur infrequently in play, teachers must not assume that racial factors are wholly irrelevant to young children, as our attitude data clearly demonstrate. The teacher's own attitudes and actions and subtle curricular factors must reinforce these relatively nondiscriminatory behavioral patterns for integration to have a real effect on attitudes.[11]

Four   Implications of the Data

The findings in this study indicate that two groups of theories concerning racial attitude formation and its effects should be modified. The existing paradigms of attitude development must be changed. In particular, attitudes at an early age are more complex than was previously thought. Also, the results give evidence for new hypotheses which clarify some contradictory results on the relationship between social class and self-concept for blacks.

Formation and Content of Racial Attitudes

Gordon Allport suggests that the first stage of attitude development is "pre-generalized learning"; the child has vague preferences rather than clearcut evaluations attached to social categories. The second stage is "rejection": the youngster becomes fully aware of racial attitudes and verbally rejects the poorly evaluated status. "Differentiation" is the final stage: the child begins to rationalize his prejudices.[1]

My data show that the phase of pre-generalized learning is indeed highly important. Even before they have a sophisticated knowledge of racial categories, children of both races have a positive evaluation of "white" and a negative feeling about "brown." Color associations and their cultural connotations are important influences on these preferences. Many children spontaneously associate "brown" with dirty and "white" with clean, and in this culture the positive value of cleanliness is stressed. These feelings about color are reinforced by racial factors. The youngster may not quite understand what a Negro is, yet he begins to sense that "nigger" is a derogatory term. He also may have a vague idea that his family and others think that brown people are less acceptable than whites or inferior to them.

The preference for white during this stage is an "incipient attitude." The child thinks that white is better than brown, and, even though he has no clear knowledge of racial categories, this preference may generalize to individuals he knows. But his feelings still indicate more of a heirarchy of preference rather than clearcut acceptance or rejection.[2] He does not as yet have a fully developed set of attitudes which have a definite social referent. My results show that this stage of pre-generalized learning occurs at about the age of four, although Negro children of three already begin to perceive these factors.

"Rejection" and "differentiation" are not entirely separate stages but occur together at about age five. When the white child becomes fully aware of the existence of racial categories and the evaluations attached to them, he rejects the unfavored status and almost simultaneously begins to provide rationalizations for his feelings. White children learn at an early age the peculiar double-talk appropriate to prejudice in a democracy. For black children, awareness of the way the dominant culture evaluates them is accompanied not by just outright rejection of blacks but by more differentiated reactions, for instance, ambivalence and/or positive feelings toward their own race. Subculturally learned hostility toward whites is also present at this age.

In this second stage of attitude formation, the several components of attitudes (social distance, evaluative, and stereotypic) are not fully differentiated from one another. Yet the feelings are more intense and begin to signify racial acceptance and rejection rather than the earlier vague heirarchy of color preference. It should be noted that although attitudes have developed in sophistication by kindergarten age, they do not seem to affect the child's actual behavior. His play patterns are situationally determined. We call this second stage of development "generalized racial attitudes," to distinguish it from the "pre-generalized learning" of the first stage and the "fully developed" prejudice of adults.

Many children pass through the first two stages of attitude formation during the preschool years, but sociological factors create differences in the extent to which these attitudes are held. The child's socioeconomic position is an important influence on his attitudes. Among whites, working-class children are more anti-black than middle-class children are. And among blacks, the working class seems to exhibit less rejection of their racial group and more hostility to whites than do their middle-class counterparts.

In a desegregated setting, racial evaluations seem to be mediated through sex-role expectations for whites. Both sexes become more aware of racial differences and the evaluations attached to them, but if the black boys in the class have a high rate of activity, the negative attitudes of white boys seem to be modified somewhat. The effect of contact on the attitudes of black children is also important, but it depends on skin color rather than on sex. In a desegregated classroom, light-skinned Negro children, who are in a more marginal position, show particularly strong white preference. The dark-skinned children prefer their own race more in a desegregated setting, but it is not clear whether this preference indicates increased racial acceptance or hostility toward whites.

The process of attitude formation in children is more complex than had previously been supposed. The content of racial biases and the extent to which they are held differ among subgroups of youngsters. These attitudes are still not as sophisticated as fully developed adult prejudice. However, during the preschool years racial evaluations start as pre-generalized learning or incipient attitudes and develop into "generalized attitudes." By the time the child enters first grade, his opinions about race are fairly well formed.

Effects of Prejudice on Personality

Pettigrew has suggested that "the socially stigmatized role of 'Negro' is the critical factor of having a dark skin in the U.S."[3] Existing theories have focused in large part either on a generalized response pattern to the "subordinate" Negro role or on specific variations in response due to social class.

Theorists have been primarily concerned with black people's disparate modes of response to a negatively evaluated role. Alexis de Tocqueville suggests that the Negro "having been told from infancy that his race is naturally inferior to that of whites, assents to this proposition and is ashamed of his own nature."[4] Much modern theoretical work has suffered from the same overly simplistic bias, which might be called "the mark of oppression" approach. The implicit paradigm of this orientation seems to be: white cupidity leads to black suffering. The most notable attempt to elaborate upon this theme is Abram Kardiner and Lionel Ovesey's psychoanalytically oriented study of personality, in which they conclude, "the Negro has no possible basis for a healthy self-esteem and every incentive for self-hatred."[5] They propose the following scheme as one set of elaborations of this paradigm: low self-esteem → white ideal → unattainable effort to be white → introjected white ideal → self-hatred → projection of self-hatred onto group → hatred of blacks.[6] They also stress the presence of rage among blacks, which is kept under control by a variety of mechanisms like submission, guilt, and depression. Although admitting that this process varies somewhat with social class, they consider that the formula of low self-esteem and repressed anger is generally applicable to all groups. This paradigm does not allow for much functional autonomy of motives; many of the responses made by their subjects, no matter how unrelated to race they appear on the surface, are traced back to a racial basis. It should also be noted that Kardiner and Ovesey's sample is uniquely qualified to substantiate their thesis of personality damage, since half of the twenty-five subjects were patients in psychotherapy.

Franklin Frazier expresses much the same orientation in *Black Bourgeoisie,* where he states that the Negro middle class lives in a world of fantasy in order to compensate for their feelings of inferiority; however, "despite their attempt to escape from real identity with the masses of Negroes, they can not escape the mark of oppression any more than their less favored kinsmen."[7] Frazier's a priori assumption of the deleterious effects of minority group status among the middle-class seems to affect strongly the validity of his explanations. In his determination to prove that a mark of oppression exists, he overstates his case by interpreting almost every action of the black middle class as a manifestation of self-rejection. For instance, as evidence of middle-class Negro self-hate, he suggests that the middle-class Negro church is extrinsically oriented and divorced from the "real religion" of the masses, that there is an unrealistic desire for success in business ventures which signifies an attempt "to identify with the white propertied classes . . . and escape identification with the masses,"[8] and that the Negro middle-class press echoes the opinions of the white community and encourages conspicuous consumption. However, these criticisms apply just as well to white middle-class society. Although these phenomena may, indeed, be indicative of escapism and self-rejection, they may only indicate the fact that the black American has internalized much of the content of middle-class culture. Thus Frazier's assertions can be read as his condemnation of American middle-class culture in general rather than as a criticism of the fantasy life of the middle-class black. Since he offers no feasible alternatives to these values, he does not seem to have considered this possible interpretation of his findings.

In their recent work, William Grier and Price Cobbs seem to come close to this orientation. They state: "No man who breathes this air can avoid [white supremacy] and black men are no exception. They are taught to hate themselves . . . [so they] identify with the oppressor psychologically . . . From his new psychologically "white" position, [the black man] turns on black people with aggression and hostility and hates blacks and, among the blacks, himself."[9] There are some important qualifications, however, that Grier and Cobbs add to the "mark of oppression" orientation. They stress the fact that many traits like suspicion and repressed aggression are adaptive devices. These traits are not pathological but instead are a cultural "Black norm," that is, realistic and survival-oriented responses in an oppressive environment. They also stress that not all adaptations to the Negro role are negative, since "in their adaptations [blacks] have developed a vigorous style of life . . . Their genius is that they have survived."[10] In addition, since they have been able to incorporate recent events into their theory, Grier and Cobbs give more importance than Kardiner and Ovesey to the alternative that repressed rage will build up and explode. Despite these modifications, their approach is similar to Kardiner and Ovesey's in its stress on problems stemming from the Negro role. Most "character traits" are seen as defenses against it.

Within the last few years, however, some investigators have suggested that this mark of oppression paradigm is not universally applicable. Positive, nondefensive orientations to racial status are beginning to be emphasized. Erik Erikson asks: "is 'the Negro' not all too often summarily and all too exclusively discussed in such a way that his . . . identity is defined only in terms of his defensive adjustments to the dominant white majority?"[11] Ralph Ellison has stated the same idea in *Shadow and Act:* "But can a people . . . live and develop for over 300 years simply by reacting? Are American Negroes simply the creation of the white man? . . . American Negro life is, for the Negro who must live it, not only a burden (and not always that) but also a discipline. There is a fullness, even a richness here . . . To deny that such possibilities of human richness exist . . . is . . . to deny us our humanity."[12]

Although Robert Coles does not deny the mark of oppression, he also feels that the emphasis on personality damage is one-sided. Many of the black children he studied showed resilience and emotional strength, and he concludes that "sometimes when I read descriptions of 'what it's like to be Negro,' I have to turn away in disbelief . . . [I must be] skeptical of some of the rhetoric that sees only . . . irreparably damaged, brutalized" blacks.[13]

The recent movement toward black pride has substantiated the position that American blacks may have a healthy self-esteem despite the presence of oppression. Many of the important ideologists of the black revolution, however, seem to have combined parts of the "mark of oppression" and the "positive, nondefensive" approaches and developed their own theory of the effects of racism on personality. A simple dichotomy differentiating between the self-hating "Uncle Tom" and the proud and self-confident militant is implicit in much of this writing:

The social effects of colonialism are to degrade and to dehumanize the subjected black man. White America's School of Slavery and Segregation . . . has taught the subject to hate himself and to deny his own humanity . . . Black people must redefine themselves, and only *they* can do that . . . When we begin to define our own image, the stereotypes — that is, lies — that our oppressor has developed will begin in the white community and end there. The black community will have a positive image of itself that *it* has created.[14]

The implication of many of the militant black writers and activists is that presently the black community is in a transition period in terms of self-esteem; blacks are beginning to cast off the mark of oppression characteristic of the past and develop a new race pride emphasizing that "perfect, radical love of Black on which our fathers thrived"[15] which will be characteristic of the future. There is still disagreement, however, on whether blacks should work with whites in the implementation of this black political and spiritual revolution.

Although it is clear that some sort of typology of personality effects of racial status is necessary, this implicit division between the self-hating "Negro" and the militant "black" misses some of the complexities of adjustment to the present situation. Gordon Allport has suggested that the minority group member may make a wide variety of responses to both his own and the majority group and that his typical mode of reaction depends partly on his personality structure. Several typologies have been constructed by social scientists to classify a wider range of alternative responses to the Negro role. But these analyses of reaction to oppression are characterized by several problems.

One set of typologies has focused on black reactions to their own racial role but has neglected to investigate the relationship between this factor and response to whites. Martin Grossack's typology exemplifies this trend. He classifies "group belongingness" into categories of nondefensive group pride, ethnocentric group pride, ambivalence, defensive reactions, and hostile reactions to one's own group.[16] But it is obvious that the orientation toward whites should be included in any scheme of blacks' responses to their racial membership; the relationship of attitudes toward the in-group and reciprocal prejudice toward the majority group must be investigated in order to understand the effect of oppression on self-concept more fully. Pettigrew's scheme of categorization has avoided this problem by outlining three broad classes of responses Negroes may make toward whites: "moving towards" (seeking full acceptance as a human being), "moving away from" (avoidance reactions), and "moving against" (aggressive reactions). However, his typology does not include a similar classification of reactions of Negroes to themselves.[17]

Robert Johnson has made an attempt simultaneously to classify Negro reactions to both whites and other Negroes. He isolates several major continua of reaction to minority group status and to whites. In terms of these continua, he distinguishes between the "Old Negro" creed of self-hatred and hostility toward whites and a "New Negro creed" of militance and friendliness toward whites.[18] Donald Noel is another investigator who classifies reactions to the out-group and in-group into several categories. His dimensions basically include acceptance, ambivalence, and rejection. He also finds that blacks who identify with their race and have militant group pride exhibit low prejudice toward whites. Gary Marx' study again demonstrates this relationship between militancy, favorable self-image, and low degree of anti-white feeling.[19]

All of these data, however, show that an *inverse* relationship between anti-white feeling and in-group identity also may exist: a substantial number of blacks with positive group identity are also anti-white, but these alternative cases of black pride accompanied by anti-white feeling are not analyzed in detail. Another problem with these typologies is that their indices of group identity are rather crude and measure general racial attitudes rather than more subtle degrees of personal acceptance or rejection on racial grounds. The Noel and Johnson works need further development, because these studies were completed before the onset of the current movement toward black power and black pride. The "militancy" they describe is the integrationist militancy of the 1950's and 1960's, and their categories of reactions to blacks and whites must be modified to take more recent political and social developments into account.

McCord has recently suggested a typology of various responses to oppression which avoids some of the problems of the other literature. He argues that choices in life orientation can be made along three dimensions of acceptance versus rebellion, collective versus individual mode of adaptation, and outer- versus inner-directed aggression. Presumably on the basis of these dimensions, he and his co-workers offer a categorization of life styles ranging the gamut from positive to negative reactions to the

Negro role and including response to whites.[20] This classification, however, is based more directly on behavior and styles of living than on type
of personal and group identity. Consequently, one life style may encom-
pass several different types of self-esteem.

Most of the typologies discussed thus far stress the group identity or
racial component of self-concept but do not deal as fully with what we
have called the personal-identity dimension of self-esteem. Allison Davis
and John Dollard's discussion of personality development among blacks
highlights differences in the realm of personal identity. But this scheme
is illustrative of an orientation diametrically opposed to the mark of
oppression. It can be referred to somewhat loosely as the "color blind"
theory, since personality development is discussed in terms of orientations to such variables as class, and group identity or racial self-concept
is considered to be a factor of secondary importance in determination of
ego structure. Davis and Dollard take at face value the assertion of some
of their subjects that they are not concerned with race. In a study of Negro
patients in psychotherapy, Viola Bernard has discovered that many patients maintain strongly that their problems have little to do with being
black; however, upon deeper investigation this denial proves in many
cases to be an expression of distaste for the Negro role and a desire to
leave the field of conflict.[21] The color blind approach avoids the tendency of
some of the theorists already discussed to reduce the explanation of most
behavior of blacks to racial causes. Yet at the same time, it seems to
underestimate the relationship between racial self-concept and personal
identity.

My data provide some clarification of these various positions on generalized reactions to oppression. By ages three and four, black children
are aware of racial differences, and their group identity is affected by
these newly learned evaluations. On this basis, we reject the color blind
orientation. But the mark of oppression approach is also overstated;
although many of the black youngsters we studied did reject themselves
on a racial basis, others seemed to exhibit positive identification with the
in-group, and attitudes toward whites also varied from acceptance to re-

jection. Existing literature on reactions to racial status has concentrated on the positive relationship among blacks between group pride and pro-white feeling. My data imply that an inverse relationship also exists.

Although the Negro role will have some effect on self-concept, responses to it can differ widely. It is thus clear that any attempt to characterize "reactions to oppression" must take account of the whole range of reactions from self-hate to positive and nondefensive response to racial status. Also these variations in reaction must be related to feelings about the majority group on one hand and to personal self-esteem on the other.

The interest in developing typologies of reaction to oppression lies not in the description of these reactions per se but in the sociological and psychological factors that actually create these differences. The effect of social class on variations in personal and racial self-concept among blacks has been a major sociological focus of interest, since social status is of prime importance in affecting the type of exposure one has to racial evaluations. Only a limited and largely negative range of responses to the role of Negro is admitted in much of the literature. Yet there is disagreement on which social class is the most adversely affected by racial status. *My data show that the problem lies in the fact that theoreticians are addressing themselves to two separate dimensions of self-concept.* Taking this into consideration, we can clarify some of the contradictory results in previous theoretical work and suggest a general scheme relating personal and group identity among blacks to socioeconomic status.

In the social class and personality literature on blacks, there is a contradiction between two sets of theories. One set of studies hypothesizes that the self-image of the middle-class Negro is the most detrimentally affected by racial prejudice. Frazier's *Black Bourgeoisie* is the classic work in this tradition, but John Dollard in *Caste and Class in a Southern Town* and Allison Davis and John Dollard in *Children of Bondage* also suggest that it is the Negro middle class which feels most bitterly the pressure of the caste barrier with its damaging effect on self-esteem. This conclusion is not due to the fact that the sample in the latter two studies is primarily southern, since Margaret Brenman's northern data and Robert Kleiner's evidence from Philadelphia both support the hypothesis that middle-class Negroes show more racial insecurity than the lower classes do.[22] This position is also supported by many of the current black militants, who have particular scorn for the middle-class "black bourgeoisie" and describe them as white-identified Uncle Toms.

Another body of literature, however, seems to contradict this viewpoint directly. Kardiner and Ovesey, Elliot LieBow, David Schultz, and Daniel Moynihan, among others, have suggested that a highly negative self-image is often found in the lower socioeconomic brackets.[23] The psychological picture that Kardiner and Ovesey paint of the lower-class black for instance, shows a person who is insecure and severely damaged psychologically, who "lacks every implement for self-defense."[24]

My data suggest a way of unifying these contradictory positions. The first group of writers seems to be dealing mostly with the *direct* effects of the Negro role and the individual's overt response to the prejudice this role entails. Frazier, Brenman, and Kleiner concentrate on what we have called group identity, or the individual's racial self-concept, that is, how he feels about himself *as a black man.* But the second group of studies discusses mostly the effect that poverty, with its accompanying physical and emotional deprivations, can have on self-image. They deal with what we have called the personal identity component of self-concept, or one's basic sense of esteem for himself *as an individual.* Because of present and past discrimination and prejudice, a disproportionate number of blacks are poor. Those who argue that the lower class are the most psychically damaged concentrate heavily on the *indirect* effect of discrimination, mediated through poverty, on personal self-esteem.

My data suggest that these two dimensions may be interrelated; if one's group identity is negative, it may have some general influence on a sense of personal self-esteem. Many theorists have argued that adequate self-perception, security, and feelings of personal continuity are major psychological functions of group-belonging for an individual.[25] And it also seems that, if an individual has low personal self-esteem, he may project this onto his racial group. However, despite this general relationship, my results indicate in addition that these components vary independently within the black community. The middle class, for instance, seems to have higher rates of positive "personal identity" and lower rates of positive "group identity" than the working class does. These findings suggest a way in which previous theories can be integrated into a conceptual scheme that relates the two dimensions of self-concept to social class. Individuals differ widely in response within each category; the purpose of this scheme is only to delineate characteristic differences between groups.

Considering first the middle class, my data suggest that the middle-class black has a more negative "group identity" component of self-concept than the working class does. Stonequist's concept of marginality provides theoretical substantiation for this hypothesis. He describes a marginal man as one who is poised between two cultures, wishing to be accepted by one of them but excluded by barriers of birth or ancestry.[26] Although the classical treatment of marginality is vague and confusing, the notion can be recast in terms of Lewinian psychology. Lewin states that if the sum of forces away from the group is greater than the sum of forces toward it, the individual will desire to leave the group; however, if barriers prevent him from doing so, he may respond with ambivalence and dislike of his ascribed status. Lewin further suggests that a near goal creates a very strong force in its direction. The middle-class Negro, with highly developed skills, enough money to live comfortably, and often with light skin, is more likely to compare himself with whites and suffers frustrations because the social system keeps him half in and half out.[27] The caste barrier may be especially intolerable to him because it is arbitrary and cannot be surmounted by any degree of excellence in social traits or skills. Although he is not forced to assume the subservient "racial role" to as great an extent as is the lower class, his status inconsistency of high-achieved and low-ascribed status leads to stressful cross-pressures and social incertitude. The presentation to others of these inconsistent status cues may cause them to behave toward him in an unpredictable manner; he may frequently suffer various types of strain and dissipation of energy over petty annoyances and deprivations.[28] One possible response to these pressures is dislike of his minority group membership or ambivalence toward it.[29]

The middle-class black may feel the most victimized by status deprivation connected with the Negro role; however, he still suffers less from
the physical and emotional deprivations which are related to lower-
class status. He does not suffer from hunger or constant ill health. His
family life is more likely to be stable, since it is less frequently disrupted
or threatened by tensions created by poverty or job insecurity. Nurtured
in a stable family and a secure environment, the "ego strong Negro may
. . . [have more of an opportunity] to dissociate . . . his basic personality
from his socially defined role of 'Negro' [and] maintain his self-respect
as a unique and worthwhile human being."[30] Although the group-identity
component of self-image may be more negative for him than it is for the
lower class, his personal-identity dimension may be more favorable.

My data on the middle class suggest this theoretical possibility. But
there is another pattern of response which may be occurring with increasing frequency. Status inconsistency may lead either to social with-
drawal on one hand or to desire for social and political change on the
other.[31] A number of studies have indicated that the middle class is more
militant or at least more willing to participate in organized protest activity then the lower class is;[32] and the protests led by college students over
the past decade have provided a clear illustration of this principle. Thus,
a "new" middle-class type of response may be the prototype of the future:
positive personal *and* group identity. It is interesting that the self-concept of the black middle-class youngsters we tested was still highly negative, even though other studies done at that time showed that the adult
middle class was the most militant or activist group.[33] Activism in the
middle 1960's, however, was defined in terms of integration. Although I
have no data on the parental attitudes of the middle-class children in my
study, my data in conjunction with these other studies of adults do at
least suggest the interesting possibility that militancy in terms of "integration" alone, without a concomitant stress on the more recent cultural
pride and cultural identity component of the black revolution, is not
sufficient to create a change in the racial self-concepts of the middle class.

Although the status inconsistency of the middle class may lead to
conflicting responses, the working-class individual is not in a status-

inconsistent situation;[34] his ethnic and economic statuses are more crystallized or similar to each other. His social boundaries are more clearly defined, and he does not suffer from the frustrations of marginal status. In his contact with whites, the working-class black may be forced to assume a subservient role to a greater extent than his middle-class counterpart is. However, both because his leisure time activity takes place within the confines of the ghetto and because he has developed a set of avoidance reactions, he may be less exposed to the direct unfavorable effects of the Negro role in informal situations.

The ghetto is not only a spatial but also a sociopsychological community, with a range of institutions which reinforce positive identification. These institutions include those of the social network — the extended kinship system, the street system of buddies, the institution of entertainment by which ghetto dwellers instruct, explain, and accept themselves. "The arguments in the barbershop, the gossip in the beauty parlors . . . are all theirs, and the white men . . . are aliens, . . . intruders on the black man's turf."[35]

Although these factors indicate a more positive sense of group identity for the working-class black, his sense of personal esteem may be affected by factors connected to his economic position. Discrimination in the skilled crafts and inadequate education combine to keep many working-class blacks from rising to more lucrative positions. The difficulties of managing on an inadequate budget may create family tensions which affect the socialization of the children, and they also may lead to feelings of inadequacy arising from inability to successfully affect one's environment. These factors may cause a less adequate personal identity among the working class as compared with the middle class.

The lower class, however, is hit most heavily of any group by this combination of race and class factors. The individual in this group must cope not only with the direct effects of prejudice but with its indirect effects, mediated through poverty. Poverty itself, with its accompanying ill health and deprivation of food and other basic necessities, may decrease feelings of security and self-confidence.[36]

In *Tally's Corner,* Elliot LieBow vividly describes the connection between economic and attitudinal factors and family relationships. The man, armed with models who have failed, poorly educated and unskilled himself, and convinced that he cannot control the environment, enters the job market with the smell of failure all around him. His inability to support his family, coupled with his wife's expectation based on her adult role models that he will fail to be an adequate husband and father, may lead to family tensions and often to the breakup of the marriage.[37] This process is aided by the fact that employment opportunities are often more available for the woman than for the man, and she may in fact be the major wage earner. The welfare system, with its stress in many states on father absence as a condition for support, also helps to encourage family disruption.

These economic factors perpetuate the historical influences of slavery, which set a precedent for matri-focal families. And as a result of these forces, more black than white families have female heads, particularly at the lowest income levels.[38] A wide range of studies has dealt with the effect of father absence or lack of a competent male role model on person-ality development. Burton and Whiting hypothesize that boys whose fathers are not present initially identify with their mothers and must later develop a conflicting secondary identification.[39] Roy D'Andrade[40] has substantiated this hypothesis for lower-class black males in Boston. Pettigrew, matching twenty-one adult Negro males whose fathers were present during childhood with those whose fathers were absent, found that the latter group was more likely to manifest disturbed sexual iden-tity and feel more victimized and distrustful of others.[41] And the Moyni-han report also pointed out the connection between father absence and such factors as school failure and delinquency.[42]

Research since the Moynihan report, however, has stressed that the functioning of the family rather than the structure per se is the important factor to consider in analysis of the consequences of lower-class status on self-esteem. The quality of emotional relationships within the household is more important than whether the husband is present or absent. A boy-friend who offers financial support and acts as a quasi-father can often cause less tension in a household and be more affectionate to the children than an actual father who lives with his family but cannot provide for them.[43] However, in this economic environment, stable and permanent relationships of any type are difficult to attain, and this has effects on the socialization of the child: "While most mothers and older children express great warmth and affection toward the younger members of the family, there is . . . a basis for an extreme amount of hostility . . . This hostility may stem from . . . having a child while still in one's middle teens and not being able to escape caring for that child; or it may derive from the anxiety incipient in the unpredictable marital situations, where one is likely to be left with the children at any time. Thus, . . . a strong covert current of hostility is very much part of the orientation toward children . . . Youngsters must cope with this as well as with the burdens of ill health and the social and racial handicaps of poverty and discrimination."[44]

These family problems may be reinforced by the fact that families in the lower class are more likely to be large: an inadequate budget must be stretched to feed many mouths, and the mother also has less time to spend with each child. Mistrust is thus built into the socialization process early in the child's life,[45] and growing up may involve an ever-increasing appreciation of one's shortcomings and one's inability to succeed: "It is in the family first and most devastatingly that one learns these lessons . . . [since] human nature is conceived as essentially bad, destructive, immoral . . . Since [the child] does not experience his world as particularly gratifying, it is very easy for him to conclude that his lack of gratification is due to the fact that something is wrong with him. This, in turn, can be readily assimilated to the definitions of being a bad person [which may be] offered him by those with whom he lives."[46]

It should be noted that this pattern of covert hostility, family tensions, and mistrust is characteristic of only one segment of the lower class. A number of investigators have demonstrated that there is a great difference among families within the lower-class group, and that many families, even under highly stressful economic conditions, can be "absorbing, adaptive, and amazingly resilient mechanisms for the socialization of their children,"[47] regardless of their particular structure. However, economic pressures have helped to perpetuate family disintegration on both a structural and an emotional level for a large segment of the lower-class black community, and these tensions are coupled with the lack of security and physical deprivations which are characteristic of poverty. Thus, we might expect a lower rate of adequate personal identities among the lower-class group. My data show that the ADC youngsters, who are particularly exposed to the set of poverty-related problems just described, do have less adequate personal self-esteem.

My findings also suggest that the lower-class child may develop a relatively negative group image as well. The full implications of the Negro role strike the lower-class black with greatest force. If the mother is a recipient of welfare, for instance, she is often forced to adopt a subservient posture. She must surrender both her status as an adult and her control over her own home, since the caseworker, who is often white, can make implications about how she is spending her money, implying that she is not mature and responsible enough to spend it properly.[48] The lower-class group, which is also more likely to contain a high percentage of dark-skinned individuals, is frequently on the receiving end of poor treatment due to a combination of race and class. The individual cannot escape early awareness that he is a member of a negatively evaluated minority. He may even be instructed by his parents in a subservient role and told to be careful of his behavior around whites. Being black may come to mean not just a subservient posture, however, but also membership in a community of persons who "think poorly of each other, who attack and manipulate each other . . . 'Black' comes to stand for a sense of identity no better than these destructive others."[49]

Although the members of the lower class may experience some of the compensations of ghetto life, racial membership for them lacks some of the positive implications it has for the working class. Any gains may be offset to some extent by personal difficulties compounded by severe economic deprivation and feelings of powerlessness. My data suggest that for at least part of the lower class, however, the individual may feel that he would rather be somebody bad than not quite somebody at all. In Erikson's terms, blackness may be internalized as a negative identity: an unattractive self is embraced so that the individual may continue to function.[50]

The lower-class group, and particularly the portion of this group who are welfare recipients, are thus affected both by direct racial prejudice and discrimination and also by poverty, which is the indirect effect of these racial attitudes. A combination of these race and class factors, as other investigators have suggested,[51] can lead to lower rates of adequate racial and personal self-esteem than are found in the working class. It is important to note that in terms of these combined effects of racial status and poverty on self-esteem, the black lower class are at even more of a disadvantage than were earlier poor ethnic groups. These immigrant groups had their own cultural tradition which could cushion the effects of ethnic prejudice directed against them, and some also had traditions of family stability which helped preserve family structure and functioning despite poverty. The black lower class, however, does not have even these buffers and thus is particularly vulnerable to both the effects of poverty on family functioning and to negative evaluations of them made by the majority group.

This framework connecting reactions to race with social class pertains to characteristic differences between groups rather than to individual cases. Individuals certainly differ widely among themselves within each socioeconomic bracket: a member of the Welfare Rights Organization is vastly different from the resigned welfare recipient; middle-class black nationalists are different from the "black bourgeoisie" that Frazier describes. Coles has suggested that "there are no easy correlations between parental ideology, class or race and 'successful' child development. Many children the world over have revealed a kind of toughness and plasticity under far from favorable conditions."[52] I present here only a general framework suggested by my data which needs further refinement. Some of the existing typologies and theories discussed in this chapter are shown in Figure 13.

This scheme is meant to suggest different degrees of intensity rather than clearcut distinctions; mixed and ambivalent feelings are highly important subjects for investigation. For instance, on some components

Figure 13: *Personal Identity, Group Identity, and Social Class*

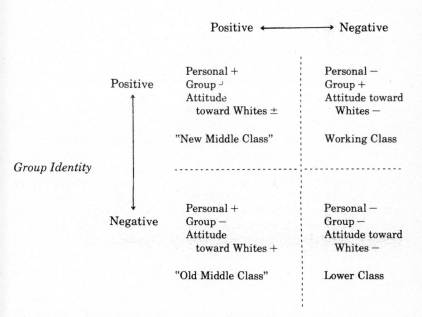

Personal Identity

Positive ←——————→ Negative

Positive

Personal +
Group ⌐
Attitude
  toward Whites ±

"New Middle Class"

Personal −
Group +
Attitude toward
  Whites −

Working Class

Group Identity

Negative

Personal +
Group −
Attitude
  toward Whites +

"Old Middle Class"

Personal −
Group −
Attitude toward
  Whites −

Lower Class

of attitudes, the working class may have more negative attitudes toward whites than the middle class does. Yet many of these same working-class individuals may still be favorable toward integration of schools and neighborhoods. Also, the working-class individuals, although they have more positive group identity than the middle class does, may still be somewhat ambivalent toward their racial membership. The "new" middle class may be less likely than other groups to see all whites as hostile but may at the same time express a great deal of anger and bitterness at exclusion of blacks from full participation in American society.

My findings, however, indicate that there are at least two separate components of identity. Neither are personal and group identity uniform for most blacks nor do they necessarily vary together within the black community. These variables, as well as attitudes toward whites, are related to social class. But the effects of interclass mobility must be investigated, and a more refined categorization of social status must be made, taking variables like income and education as well as occupation into account.

We have stressed the relationship of personal and group identity to social class, because class is one of the few major sociological variables to which a large body of work on the personality effects of racism has been addressed. Yet my own data clearly show that patterns of adjustment vary within as well as between classes. Factors like family stability, socialization patterns, and educational experience are important variables whose relationship to self-concept must be clarified. My findings do indicate that neither group nor personal identity seems to be negatively affected by desegregated (as opposed to truly "integrated") educational settings. However, the sample was very young; even though the classroom atmosphere was not optimal, it was not overtly suffused with interracial hostility. With older children or adults, it is possible that a tense or hostile contact situation might lead to more diverse effects on self-esteem, and these possibilities should be investigated.[53] The effect of militancy on self-concept is also a highly important question, but since this study was done before the onset of the black power and black pride movement, I am unable on the basis of my data to provide further theoretical clarification of the relationship between self-esteem and the more recent brands of militancy. (Some hypotheses on this issue are suggested, however, in Chapter 10).

I have stressed sociological variables in my theoretical scheme; yet psychological factors affecting response to racism are highly important and must also be included in any future theoretical framework. My findings only clarify some of the disparities in existing theories concerning the effects of prejudice and discrimination on the personality of blacks. The general pattern of all of my findings on group identity suggests that blacks whose major goals are especially threatened by their racial membership have particularly high rates of *racial* self-rejection. Those groups characterized by a host of economic and familial problems have especially high rates of poor *personal* self-esteem. These general hypotheses suggest a starting point for badly needed further theoretical development in this area.

Some people say we got a lot of malice
Some say it's a lot of nerve
But I say we won't quit moving
Until we get what we deserve.
Say it loud, I'm Black and I'm proud.
Say it loud, I'm Black and I'm proud.
Say it loud, I'm Black and I'm proud.

                                    James Brown, popular recording star[1]

What do we need to know about children's racial attitudes? It is now clear that even young children make racial evaluations and may be affected by them, but we do not know how cultural and social changes within the black community have affected black youngsters. We also must find out much more about the relationship between racial self-esteem and factors like school desegregation. In this chapter major research needs are discussed and the methodological pitfalls which future investigations must avoid are summarized.

Changes in Black Attitudes and Group Identity

The changes that have recently occurred in racial attitudes and self-esteem among blacks must be assessed; yet it is difficult to determine the effect of increased militancy by comparing recent studies with prior research. Asher and Allen have contrasted their results, collected in Newark during the riot-torn summer of 1967, with the Clarks' 1939 northern data. They do not find any increase in black preference; in fact, they find some slight but statistically insignificant increase in white preference among Negro youngsters. They interpret their findings in terms of a social comparison model: enhanced status of blacks has contributed, through more frequent comparison with whites, to increased feelings of inferiority.[2] This conclusion may not be valid, however, because of lack of controls for relevant variables. The Clarks do not hold social class constant in their study, and their northern sample was integrated while the Asher and Allen sample was largely segregated. My data show that both social class and contact affect attitudes among black children. Thus, no firm conclusions can be drawn about the changes occasioned by the events of the past decade unless careful controls for class and contact are applied.

I had initially hoped that my investigation would provide a partial answer to this question, and I had planned to compare my results with Goodman's study, which was done about fifteen years previously, also in Boston.[3] It proved impossible, however, to make any systematic comparisons because reporting of Goodman's data is incomplete (she gives figures on racial preference and affinity but it is not clear how she explicitly made these concepts operational). Despite these factors, there is general agreement between Goodman's data and my sample on the extent of white preference among black children.[4]

I did find one possible difference from the Goodman results. There seems to be more overt anti-white feeling among the black children in my study. My data on racial comments and remarks about cleanliness (see Chapter 4) show that approximately 5 percent of the Negro children who spoke expressed negative opinions about whites. On the structured questionnaire, 46.9 percent (N=196) of the Negro youngsters chose the white doll as "lazy and stupid." Part of this choice may reflect a response-set for the white doll, and, since it was a forced choice situation, part may only indicate reluctance to stereotype the Negro doll. However, hostility or ambivalence toward whites clearly exists for at least some of these children, since several youngsters actually responded that "it's lazy and stupid because it's white."

Goodman says that approximately 9 percent of her black sample expressed "out-group antagonism." Her discussion, however, seems to suggest that only one boy had a strong verbal anti-white inclination. It is not clear how Goodman judged the percentage of her sample that was anti-white, but the implications are that it was on other than a purely verbal basis. She concludes that "antagonism toward whites may be present, but it is not often expressed."[5] But our findings suggest that one effect of the black revolution by the middle 1960's may have been to make anti-white feelings more explicit: 5 percent of the black children in our sample who made comments during the test *overtly expressed verbal antagonism* toward the opposite race.[6]

It should be noted that studies of adults have shown that hostility toward whites does not seem to be increasing in the black community and the majority of blacks still support integration.[7] Thus, I tentatively suggest that one interpretation of my findings may be what Pettigrew calls an "out from under the rocks" phenomenon: hostility toward whites has always been present among blacks, but black children are exposed to it with greater frequency now because of its freer expression. Although this conclusion must remain highly tentative, the effect of the black revolution on childrens' attitudes toward whites is an extremely important area for further research.

In terms of attitudes toward the black child's own race, we can only conclude from available evidence that by the late 1960's, despite the integrationist phase of the civil rights movement and the riots, there had been no major change in the pattern of white identification and preference found by numerous early investigations. However, the effect of the growing emphasis on black identity and black pride is a highly important area for future research. The Campbell and Schuman study, "Racial Attitudes in Fifteen American Cities," finds: "Ninety-six percent of the sample affirm that 'Negroes should take more pride in Negro history,' . . . nearly as many agree 'there should be more Negro businesses, banks, and stores.' But it is striking indeed that 42 percent of this sample believe 'Negro school children should study an African language.' . . . The support for this single proposition, which a few years ago was scarcely discussed by most Negroes . . . is so impressive that it suggests a considerable potential for the growth of black cultural identity in America."[8]

The recent popularity of "Afro" hairdos and African clothing attests to this statement. This change is incorporated into the entertainment world as well. When James Brown, one of the most popular black recording stars, sings "Say it loud, I'm Black and I'm proud," the message is clear. It is thus probable that some change has now occurred in the pattern of white preference among preschool children. We suggest that this is particularly true of children whose parents are directly involved in protest activities or who have teachers that stress black pride in their classrooms. It is also likely that these changed patterns of group preference and identity are occurring especially among the middle class. (This factor is discussed in the following section.) These possibilities should be investigated immediately.

The stress on black pride has probably already changed results for some subgroups, but I hypothesize that the difference between black and white children in racial preference and self-esteem has not as yet been greatly reduced. First, cultural nationalism may not be sufficient in itself to cause large-scale changes for blacks. Studies clearly indicate that even young children are sensitive to the implication of social roles.[9] As long as race and poverty are related, "black" will still mean "stay back," particularly for lower-class black children, but many middle-class black youngsters may be aware of this connection between race and socioeconomic status as well; "black" may still mean membership in a less desirable social group.

There is also another reason why I expect that major alteration in my findings has not as yet occurred. The black revolution has the tacit support of many older people who do not protest or riot; however, the young people are "where the action is,"[10] and "it appears to be black youth in colleges and black youth on ghetto streets who are least satisfied with America."[11] Thus, a significant change in our findings on group identity among black youngsters may not occur until the present highschool and college-age group have children who are old enough to be tested. A large-scale replication of my study is thus imperative in several years.[12] If the difference in racial self-esteem between black and white children is to disappear in the future, however, elimination of the connection between race and low socioeconomic status must accompany this growing black pride. The relationship between change in the economic and social position of blacks, the growth of black cultural pride, and racial attitudes and identity among preschool-age black youngsters are the major questions for future research.

New Research on Social Class and Racial Attitudes

Important areas for further study exist on the connection between social class and racial attitudes and self-esteem among blacks. Some of my findings and nonsignificant trends must be rechecked and expanded. Changes in class patterns of response must also be investigated.

It is among the middle class that I expect at present to find the greatest change from my results. Billingsley suggests: "Not all middle-class Negro families are yet able or willing to see the connections they share with all other Negroes. Many still hold to the view that they are more middle-class than Negro, and are still seeking to convince the white middle-class of that fact . . . [But] . . . now, in every major community in the country, upper and middle-class Negroes are turning in dozens of ways toward an explicit recognition of the common destiny shared by the Negro people . . . And the country was surprised to find such substantial support among middle-class Negroes for the ghetto uprisings."[13]

We have seen that persons in the middle class are less likely to be forced to play a really subservient racial role than those in the lower class are, and the new movement toward race pride is not as frequently undercut by serious deprivations connected to racial membership as they are in the lower class. Cultural nationalism helps make the racial and economic statuses of the middle-class individual congruent in his own eyes: his ascribed status also becomes a source of pride. Because of his education, he is probably likely to be aware of the effect that racial attitudes can have on the self-esteem of his children, and he may consciously try to instill racial pride in them. Thus, it seems probable that the pattern of self- and group rejection is beginning to be replaced by racial pride and self-acceptance. This possibility must be carefully investigated, in terms of more refined class subdivisions within the middle-class group.

The working class showed the most acceptance of their own race in this study. I suggest that this pattern has not changed, since it has only been reinforced by recent events like the growth of black pride. The ADC group has probably also exhibited little change in pattern of response, but for a different reason. They have reaped fewer of the benefits of cultural and economic changes than other groups, and they are still affected most directly by the subordinate Negro role.

The lower class, including the children whose families are on welfare, must be carefully studied in future investigations.[14] These children are not highly verbal, particularly at the three- and four year-old level, and their responses are thus difficult to interpret. If the trend of correct identification and high white preference that I found still persists, its meaning should be carefully investigated. My interpretation of these findings as negative identity, or identification with an unfavorable image, is tentative. It is also not clear how lower-class children feel about whites.

Factors which create variations in response between individuals in the lower-class group are another crucial area for research. It would be most interesting, for instance, to see if involvement in a militant group like the Welfare Rights Organization or in protest surrounding community control of the schools produces changes in racial self-esteem in the lower class.

We have thus far explored the possibility of changes in black attitudes and self-esteem by class, but the attitudes of white preschool youngsters may also be changing. The Campbell and Schuman study finds that "there is no universal pattern of racial conduct among white people in this country; there is on the contrary a fundamental and perhaps growing schism between those whose basic orientation toward Negroes is positive and those whose attitudes and behavior are negative."[15] It is particularly among young whites who have attended college that there is greater acceptance of integration and stronger support of Negro civil rights. Thus, I predict a continuing difference in white attitudes by social class, with the possibility of more overt expression of anti-Negro prejudice among the working-class white youngsters. Changes in the response pattern of the white middle class are uncertain and depend in part on what course the black revolution takes.

Thus far new areas have been suggested for research on the relation between social class and group identity. One final area for investigation concerns the relationship of personal identity to social class. The theoretical framework proposed in Chapter 9 should be carefully tested on a large sample to see if in fact "group" and "personal" identity vary by class within the black community. The relationship between these two components for whites must also be investigated by social class.

New Research on Effects of Contact

Data on contact have more immediate policy implications than almost any of my other findings on racial attitudes at the preschool level. Therefore, all of my trend data on contact must be carefully rechecked, and several new problems suggested by my research must be investigated. I find a trend that racial attitudes are affected by sex-role expectations for white youngsters in desegregated classrooms. This trend must be carefully restudied with a large sample to see if in fact white boys have more positive and white girls more negative attitudes toward blacks in a desegregated setting. Play patterns should also be investigated at this age level to see if the black males are more aggressive than their white peers and thus best typify male sex-role norms.

It is difficult to interpret some of my contact data for blacks. It was found, for instance, that dark-skinned youngsters show significantly more preference for brown dolls in a desegregated than in a segregated situation. Since my technique forced a choice between brown and white dolls, this finding can mean either less rejection of the child's own race or increased hostility toward whites. It is not possible to draw any definite conclusions as to which alternative is most plausible, and the ambiguity of this result must be clarified. One way to do so is by addition of more open-ended questions which measure acceptance or rejection of the opposite race.

An even more important question which must be restudied is the meaning of increased correctness of self-identification by the black working and middle class in a desegregated situation. Does this indicate only increased awareness of race, as I have suggested, or does it actually show that contact creates improved self-esteem among these groups of black children? The ADC results are highly confusing: ADC children in desegregated environments classified themselves less accurately regardless of their attitudes. I cannot interpret the meaning of this result, and it should be carefully checked.

What effect do varying proportions of black and white children in the classroom have on attitudes and self-esteem? These findings have extremely important policy implications, since they would indicate the optimum racial composition of the classroom at the preschool level. My data suggest that white boys in predominantly Negro schools may have poor self-images. This possibility should be verified with class controls. For black children, the effect of the racial proportion of the classroom must also be investigated. Many "integrated" nursery schools are integrated in name only; there are only one or two black children in the class. The effect of such a situation on the racial self-esteem of the black child is a particularly important area for research.

We must also determine the way that racial composition of the classroom affects actual interaction patterns. Data are needed from a large number of classrooms, so that such factors as sex, personality, and play style could be controlled. Careful thought must be given to the experimental design of a project of this type. My data were based on playmate choice rather than on true interaction. A reliable method of collecting interaction data must be devised and a coding scheme and descriptive categories developed.

The effect of *quality* of integration on attitudes and racial self-esteem is another major research area. I have already suggested that the majority of our schools did not seem to be adequately integrated: race was ignored as an issue of any importance, both directly and on a more subtle level. It is important to see whether my sex and contact results for whites and my skin-color and contact results for blacks hold true in a "quality" integrated situation. A technique for differentiating desegregated classrooms in terms of quality is thus necessary. Such a measure might be based on the following set of criteria:

1. What are the teacher's racial attitudes? Does she, herself, fully support integration? Is she even aware that children at this age level have racial attitudes? The answers to these questions can be discovered

by interviews, conventional attitude scales, or scales based on observations of the teacher's behavior in the classroom.

2. Is the teaching staff fully integrated?

3. Does the play material in the classroom subtly reinforce racial tolerance? For instance, do the pictures on the wall show children of both races? Are there any blatantly stereotypic books? (This refers not only to the *Little Black Sambo* type of story but also to more subtle references to color. In many children's books which teach color differences, dark colors are given a negative connotation. For an example of this type of literature, see Chapter 1.) Is the classroom bookshelf well stocked with books featuring integrated stories or stories about black as well as white children? Are both black and white dolls available?

4. Are the proportions of black and white children in the class approximately equal? Also, the relationship between race and social class should be checked. If one race is predominantly lower class and the other is predominantly middle class, problems created by class differences in play style may acquire a racial tinge.

5. Are parents of both races given the opportunity to interact with each other in the nursery school program? Are they asked to participate in the program or are they consulted about it?

6. If any racial incidents occur, are they handled directly instead of being ignored?

7. Does the curriculum directly emphasize race? For instance, are black leaders and historical events explained to the children?

These criteria can form a scale to determine quality of integration. (This list is discussed more fully in Chapter 11.) The answers to some of these questions can be determined by simply observing the nursery school in operation. The administration of any attitude test requires some prior observation in the classroom so that the children can become acquainted with the researcher. Part of the above inventory can be made at this time. Besides the new areas for research on the effect of contact on group identity, it is also highly important to see in what ways personal identity is affected for children by the nature of the interracial situation.

Research on Age and Racial Attitudes

This study dealt only with children from ages three to five. We need to know more about the process of attitude formation over the entire grammar school age range. Longitudinal studies of individuals are an important supplement to investigations comparing differences between age groups at one time period. A modified form of the TV-story game we used is one possible instrument for investigations of this type. Harding found that a doll-play and story-telling method was appropriate for measuring the racial attitudes of grammar school children.[16] If my stories were rewritten on a more sophisticated level, it would be possible to study the entire age range from preschool through grammar school with the same technique. It would also be important to incorporate questions attempting to measure children's understanding of current racial events into such a method. New indices of racial self-esteem must be added to an indicator of this type, since other investigators find that self-identification is no longer appropriate as a measure of group identity after age six or seven[17] (see IB of the summary of methodological issues in the last section of this chapter). Data on age and attitudes have important implications. Our understanding of the process of attitude development would be expanded by studies on the relation of age and attitude, and these results might also suggest the optimum ages for various types of intervention aimed at attitude change.

New Areas for Research

Group differences in attitudes were analyzed in this study, but the research did not focus on the mechanisms by which these attitudes are transmitted. Possible sources of transmission are summarized in Chapter 1, but this area needs study; for instance, how much do parental racial attitudes actually affect the process of attitude formation in children? The influence of teachers' racial attitudes must be demonstrated as well. Do stereotypic reading materials or television affect the child's ideas about race? We must also investigate whether youngsters of this age have any conception of the meaning of political events. Part of the reason for white preference is the fact that blacks are seen disproportionately often in subordinate social roles. Thus, another important area of study is the way in which perception of the occupational role structure of society affects the development of attitudes. We also need to know how the perception of de facto segregation in neighborhoods and schools influences attitudes about race.

Individual variation in attitudes within each social group must also be considered. What is the effect of personality factors on racial attitudes? Does parental militancy affect the black child's racial self-esteem? How are family structure and functioning and socialization patterns related to both "group" and "personal" identity? The factors creating racially tolerant attitudes or high racial self-esteem in youngsters whose social attributes would lead us to predict the opposite reaction is one area which deserves intensive study.

Finally, it is of critical importance to investigate the processes of attitude change. Do programs of attitude change aimed at creating either interracial tolerance or black self-esteem have any effect at the preschool level?[18] If so, what types of programs are most suitable? These studies must be conducted in both integrated and segregated classes. Investigation of programs aimed at attitude change in segregated settings, compared with similar programs in integrated settings, can provide useful evidence on the importance of interracial contact as a factor in the development of racial attitudes and self-esteem at this age level. Research on all of these problems, as well as the problems that have been proposed in previous sections, is necessary in both the North and the South; the theoretical and social implications of these data are highly important.

Summary of Major Methodological Issues

Research on the racial attitudes and self-esteem of preschool-age children is beset by a number of problems of experimental design. These technical issues are summarized on the following pages.

I. General Problems of Validity

A. Data on racial awareness should be considered before interpreting preference responses. The awareness results indicate whether preference choices are actual racial attitudes or are based on nonracial factors.

B. Since incorrect self-identification on the part of the black child may reflect wish fulfillment, correctness of self-identification should never be used as a measure of racial awareness alone. Self-identification questions are, however, affected by racial knowledge to some extent; some black children identify merely on the basis of what they look like. For this reason, additional questions on racial self-esteem should be included in any further research; for instance, "which [of these two dolls] would[the identification figure] most like to be?" Another possibility for older children (ages five or six and above) is to present dolls of several different shades of brown and see whether the youngster identifies with a doll that is darker than, the same as, or lighter than his own shade of skin color. This method may be a more subtle index of self-perception for older children than a question with only two alternatives (see IIC2.)

C. The color of the investigator may serve as a contaminating factor. I suggest that, ideally, black experimenters be used with Negro youngsters, particularly in segregated schools. If a white must do some of the actual testing of black children, I suggest that he work only in desegregated schools. And to minimize threat, the black children should also have the opportunity to become well acquainted with the white investigator before the testing situation actually starts.

D. Class, contact, and skin color (for blacks) must be carefully controlled in any study. My results show that all of these factors affect attitudes, and these three variables may be highly interrelated. (This point is particularly important in any study of the changes created by black cultural nationalism in the self-esteem of black youngsters.) It is thus necessary to have a large sample in order for appropriate controls to be utilized.

II. Problems of Technique in the Measurement of Racial Attitudes and "Group Identity." A variety of methods have been tried in testing racial

attitudes and self-esteem of pre-literate children. These methods can
be classified into three major categories.

A. Pictures and line drawings and/or actual photos (used by Springer,
Helgerson, Trager, Clark, Horowitz, Mussen, and Morland)

1. Picture tests rely solely on children's linguistic responses and are
too dependent on passive, non-acting-out behavior. Because results may
be related to the child's understanding of language, TAT-type tests are
inadvisable, since some children may lack the vocabulary to spin extended fantasies. A picture test does permit use of a highly structured
questionnaire; however, it does not allow for observation of unstructured
play.

2. Pictures present a concrete situation. If one is interested in investigating general attitudes, he may find that responses are influenced
by specific details of the pictures he presents.

B. Puzzles: puzzles with interchangeable Negro and white parts, doll-
assemblage, picture insets (used by Goodman, Stevenson and Stewart,
Trager, and Landreth)

1. Puzzle techniques are more suitable for measuring racial awareness than they are for measuring racial attitudes or self-concept.

2. Ability to solve puzzles may reflect differences in intelligence
rather than differences in racial awareness per se.

3. Ability to assemble complicated toys or puzzles may measure
familiarity with this type of play equipment rather than racial awareness. This is particularly true if lower- and middle-class children are
being compared.

4. Special variations of puzzle technique: Coloring test, used by the
Clarks. This test cannot be used with very little children who do not have
coloring skills. Many black children also became disturbed with this type
of procedure, according to the Clarks, since it involved not just a simple
pointing response but use of crayons over an extended period of time to
color a picture "the same color you are." But they do suggest that the
technique is more sensitive than the doll test (at least with older children)
because it allows for the possibility of irrelevant responses in an attempt
to avoid the issue.

C. Doll Play: Research with preschool children presents special problems. Instructions must be simple enough for young children to understand. The children must have the physical abilities to perform whatever acts are demanded by the method. Perhaps most important, the tasks must entice and maintain interest over a brief span of attention. Doll play seems to meet these criteria better than puzzles or pictures. Goodman, Clark, Ammons, Greenwald and Oppenheim, and Asher and Allen have used doll play in measuring racial awareness and attitudes; however, their work and my own study suggest several possible problems with this technique.

1. The dolls should be realistic and well made (Ammons seemed to have problems with poorly constructed pipe cleaner figures).

2. Negro dolls should be a medium shade of brown to facilitate self-identification of both light and dark Negro children. The Greenwald and Oppenheim study shows that it would be interesting to use dolls of several different shades of skin color on self-identification questions. However, I suggest that this procedure is more appropriate for grammar school children than for preschool youngsters; I advise against using it in a sample younger than the kindergarten age group. Older children are probably more able to make subtle color discriminations and also are less confused by a variety of choices.

3. Choice of a doll in preference questions may be measuring a response-set for a type and color of doll the child actually owns. To minimize the familiarity factor, realistic dolls dressed like nursery school children should be used instead of the more popularly available baby dolls.

4. Equipment like doll furniture or houses should be used with the dolls. This additional equipment encourages free play, which is an important indicator of racial attitudes. It also helps interest the child in the test, and occasional changes of setting and furniture help to hold the attention of even the three-year-old child. A longer and more thorough investigation of attitudes is thus possible.

5. A projective or semiprojective technique of the type I used may give a more realistic evaluation of racial attitudes among children than a direct method does, particularly since my data show that children try

to rationalize their prejudices at an early age. This indirect procedure is also less upsetting to the child than a list of direct questions like "which one is pretty?," "which one looks like you?," with no attempt to disguise the purpose of the test.

      a. Structured questions as well as unstructured material must be utilized in any test of this type.

      (1) Negative attributes as well as positive attributes should be included in a measure of racial attitudes (i.e., "which one is bad [lazy, stupid]" as well as "which one is nice [good, pretty]"). Inclusion of these negative items controls for response-set for one color and also helps to indicate hostility toward the opposite race. There were not enough of these items in my test.

      (2) Open-ended questions where there is no forced choice between two racial alternatives should also be included in any attitude test (i.e., "would you like to bring this one [rejected doll] home for lunch, too?") This type of response differentiates mild preference from actual hostility. More alternatives of this type should be added in future use of my method.

      (3) Several indices of each major dependent variable (attitudes, awareness, self-identification) must be included to make interpretation of the results more valid. Different types of indicators of racial self-esteem must thus be added to my measure (see IB). I suggest that brown-haired dolls be used on the self-identification questions when white brunettes are tested. It is also necessary to include measures of the several different dimensions of racial awareness (color terms knowledge, color match, and color salience). In the index of racial term knowledge, "which dolls look like black children?" should be added.

      (4) It is absolutely crucial to include opportunities for unstructured expression in any test. This type of material is invaluable in interpreting the data on the structured questionnaire. Probing for reasons for doll choice and opportunity for free play are thus essential.

III. Measures of "personal identity": My picture and story technique should be developed further as a measure of "personal self-esteem."

This method, however, cannot be used with children under the age of five. The scoring scheme for the figure drawings must be revised and subscales developed. An attempt to devise a more subtle coding procedure would also be useful. One method is to have raters Q-sort from high to low self-concept on an implicit basis and then compute inter-rater reliability.[19] The story categories also might be refined. The effect of intelligence should be investigated; however, even if this technique does relate to intelligence, it *also* may be a self-esteem measure with which intelligence must be controlled. Because this test is relatively threatening, bias against the interviewer is another factor which must be studied.

The investigation of racial attitude formation in children is far from complete. New research with careful experimental design must be oriented to areas which have been inadequately studied, because the questions raised in this chapter have extremely important implications for both theory and public policy.

Right now I want to forget ever thing thats happened . . .
Right now I want to change the way the world is
acting . . .

Children of Cardozo Tell It Like It Is

Racial prejudices reflect the type of experiences that children have. Such prejudices can be curtailed only by altering the social environment from which they are learned. Thus the data obtained in this study have important implications for public policy.

Legal Implications of the Findings

In Chapter 2, it was pointed out that certain methodological problems of the Clark studies make interpretation of some of their data ambiguous. The Supreme Court took these studies into consideration in the momentous desegregation decisions of 1954; thus, it is necessary to clarify the possible legal implications of my criticisms.

In 1950 Kenneth Clark prepared a manuscript on "The Effect of Prejudice and Discrimination on Personality Development" for the Mid-Century White House Conference on Children and Youth.[1] This manuscript was written months before Clark became involved in the legal school desegregation cases; however, it was cited in footnote 11 of the Supreme Court desegregation opinions of 1954 and was also quoted in the Social Science Appendix to the Appellant's Brief in these cases.

Kenneth Clark's White House Conference report did not rely solely on his own data. It was a compilation of all available social science knowledge related to the problem of how racial and religious prejudices and their social concomitants influenced the development of personality. His and his wife's studies of black children were, of course, cited in this manuscript, yet his description of their research focused largely on the general finding that many black children exhibit white preference and reject themselves racially at an early age, a conclusion which is not open to methodological criticism and which my own data strongly substantiate. He did not contend that racial segregation itself accounted for his findings. Rather, he argued that black children were affected by the entire social and cultural context surrounding race in American society, of which segregation was only a part.

The Clarks' regional data are more difficult to interpret because of the lack of strict controls for such relevant variables as social class and contact. However, although in the papers based on doll play and coloring techniques the southern schools were all segregated and the northern schools were integrated, Clark is careful not to use school segregation alone as the major explanation of differences between the North and South. Instead, he attributes his findings of greater personality damage for southern black children to the total context of segregation and prejudice that was characteristic of the South at that time.[2]

Thus, my criticism of some of the methodology of the Clark studies must be separated from the general statement on the basis of his own and much other evidence which he presented to the Mid-Century White House Conference. It is the document connected with that conference which was cited in the 1954 Supreme Court proceedings; my technical criticism of parts of his own studies does not undermine the basic conclusions he draws in this report that "segregation, prejudice and discrimination, and their social concomitants" have a damaging effect on childrens' personalities.[3]

Implications for Integration at the Preschool Level

There are some investigators who feel that integration may actually have a negative effect on black children. Clairette Armstrong and A. Gregor have argued that a young black child's ego may be especially damaged if he is exposed to white rejection by attendance at a desegregated school.[4] They assume that the black child in a segregated school is more protected from negative evaluations of his race, but they do not give enough credence to the fact that even the segregated ghetto community is not isolated from the general cultural system of attitudes, values, and beliefs. A black child in a segregated school may be well aware of the implications of his racial membership, as our data show;

hence, integration may not be the intensely disturbing new experience that their framework would lead one to expect.

On the basis of social comparison theory, Asher and Allen predict that desegregation will lead to greater white preference among young black children; more frequent comparisons with whites should lead to increased feelings of inferiority. Their implication is that self- and group identity may be improved by rejection of social comparison with whites and formation of new (presumably black) political and social comparison groups.[5]

Neither Armstrong and Gregor nor Asher and Allen give specific data to prove their contention that the self-image of black children will be negatively affected by desegregation. *My data disprove this position.* I have demonstrated that the effect of desegregation on the attitudes of children of both races is highly complex; sometimes the effect may be positive and sometimes negative, depending on such factors as sex for whites and shade of skin color for blacks. I have tried to exert caution in interpreting the self-identification findings, partially because my own value position is one of commitment to integration. Yet my data show that identification as white does not increase among most Negro youngsters in desegregated classrooms. In fact, I find the opposite result: the middle- and working-class children in desegregated settings classify themselves more frequently as brown. Although I do not feel that this result necessarily indicates more positive self-image, it does clearly show that at least *desegregation does not have a negative effect on the racial self-esteem of most groups of black children.[6] This finding is particularly important because the quality of integration in a majority of the schools in the study was poor. The ADC group may be an important exception to this general conclusion, but additional evidence is needed on this issue.*

The United States Civil Rights Commission Report, *Racial Isolation in the Public Schools,* points out that desegregation is a necessary but not sufficient condition for integration. Real or "quality" integration involves in addition to racial mixture an active effort to create a climate of interracial acceptance. It is important to note that the atmosphere in the nursery schools I studied was not one of overt racial tension, as it was in some of the older groups investigated by the Civil Rights Commission.

Rather, race was simply ignored by the school as an issue of any importance. Any negative attitudes children held were of course reinforced by
occasional racial incidents; however, the entire atmosphere of the classroom, ranging from school equipment to in some cases teacher attitudes,
subtly communicated a set of evaluations that white was better than
brown. Especially at this age level, conclusions about the quality of
integration must be determined on the basis of these subtle factors rather
than on the basis of an atmosphere of interracial tension.

The Civil Rights Commission Report not only suggests a distinction
between desegregation and integration but also finds that quality integration may have positive effects on the academic attitudes and achievement of older Negro children. In schools with integration of high quality
and without racial tensions, black children had more definite educational
plans and more of a sense of control of the environment than they did in
merely desegregated settings.[7] There are indications that quality integration may have a positive effect on racial attitudes as well. It is generally agreed that prejudice can be reduced by noncompetitive, equal-
status contact. Such contact must also be sanctioned by authority.[8] The
atmosphere of the class in a quality integrated school, ranging from
books containing pictures of black and white children to an integrated
teaching staff, shows the children that authority firmly backs the concept of interracial acceptance.

Mark Chesler, Simon Wittes, and Norma Radin's study of grammar
school children in a merely desegregated school nicely summarizes my
major argument. They find that though there are occasional glimpses of
the beginning of acceptance, "the children by themselves do not appear to
be forming . . . positive attitudes towards interracial association. The
lack of specific curriculum emphasis on racial matters contributed to the
slow pace of progress . . . School desegregation can enable Negro and
white students to learn and live together, but . . . the specific outcome
depends upon the tactics each school system utilizes to marshall the best
of student, teacher, and community resources in the open admission and
treatment of things that separate us now but may yet bring us together."[9]
It is important to remember that my sample was younger than the chil-

dren in their study; thus we have already pointed out that there was little of the overt interracial hostility which may characterize older age groups in desegregated environments.

Jackson, Teele, and Mayo's study of a bussing program shows that according to parental reports, younger black children fare better than older children in terms of amount of discrimination encountered and making friends with white peers.[10] The special potency of desegregation in the beginning of the school years is demonstrated by other data. For instance, the Coleman report shows that white children who attended public school with Negroes were least likely to prefer all-white classmates and close friends; this effect is strongest among those who began their interracial schooling in the early grades.[11]

My findings show that mere desegregation has a complex effect on attitudes but at least does not have a negative effect on the self-esteem of most groups of black children. Other work suggests that quality integration may actually have positive effects on attitudes and achievement, particularly if it is instituted in the early grades. On the basis of all of this evidence I make the policy recommendation that *preschool programs should be integrated wherever possible. Federal and locally sponsored preschool programs must lead the way with firm commitment in both words and action to integration. I stress that I mean quality integration, with an active attempt to create an atmosphere of interracial tolerance, rather than simply desegregation or racial mixture alone.* Even if quality integration is instituted, my data lead me to expect complex effects on the racial attitudes of different subgroups of children. I thus add to my recommendation the qualification that these effects must be studied immediately; only then will we have a better understanding of how to create a situation which optimally affects the attitudes and self-esteem of all youngsters.[12]

Recommendations for Quality Integration

Quality integration of preschools is not based on a laissez-faire policy.[13] In order to counteract attitudes which are already in the process of development, preschool programs must stress interracial tolerance in both direct and subtle ways. My observations while collecting the data suggest ways in which a quality integrated situation may be created at the preschool level. Many of these recommendations can be followed in segregated as well as in integrated schools; however, to have the maximum effect on attitudes, there probably should be children of both races in the classroom. In a quality interracial setting, white children have an opportunity to have their stereotypes corrected by actual association with blacks, and if the black child is accepted by whites in an atmosphere which stresses the importance of all races, he learns that others respect him. This may give him a greater basis for respecting himself.

There are several important prerequisites for a quality integrated setting. The teacher's own racial attitudes are highly important for successful integration. If she does not genuinely like and accept all groups of children, these attitudes are communicated to the youngster. But good will alone is not enough. Competence in handling race relations within the classroom must also be considered. Martin Deutsch suggests: "Teachers, both white and Negro, must be helped to deal with questions of race and intergroup relations on an objective, frank, professional basis, or their embarrassment and circumventing of the issue will somehow always be communicated to the child, and to the Negro child the connotation attached will be a negative one."[14]

Thus teachers must be carefully interviewed on these issues before they are hired. For instance, it should be determined whether a perspective teacher is even aware that children of this age have racial attitudes. She might also be asked how she would handle racial incidents. Another prerequisite of a climate of interracial acceptance is presence of an interracial teaching staff in each classroom. This point cannot be considered in isolation from the general problem considered above, however. Our impressions were that some of the black teachers either did not particularly like the lower-class black children or put special pressure on them to conform to middle-class norms of behavior. Thus, the race and class attitudes of black as well as white teachers must be determined previous to hiring.[15]

It is obvious that equipment in the classroom is also important. The dolls,[16] pictures on the walls, and the reading material must reflect the interracial nature of the student body. Books about color differences should be free of negative connotations about brown or black, and positive associations with these colors should be pointed out when the occasion to do so arises. The teacher can discuss the roles of different types of community workers and use pictures as aids to her explanation; these pictures should show blacks as well as whites in all types of occupational roles. The importance of all types of occupations to the functioning of society should also be pointed out.

Successful integration also depends on the actual racial composition of the classroom. Our data on the group identity of white boys in classrooms where the majority of children were black suggest that being in a numerical minority may have negative effects on some groups. Thus, a racial composition as close as possible to 50/50 is probably most desirable. Any racial composition of less than 75/25 presents certain problems. If the classroom has a vast majority of one racial group and only one or two children of the other, personality and racial factors may be confounded. For instance, if the lone black or white child is extremely aggressive or extremely passive and withdrawn, personality patterns may either reinforce stereotypes or be generalized by classmates to all whites or all blacks. In a 75/25 racial composition there are at least enough children of each race so that play styles will vary and no child will be in a distinct minority. The effect on the self-esteem of the lone integrator has not been systematically studied at the preschool level, but any possible negative effects of such a situation would be avoided by a more equal racial division.

Another factor concerning classroom composition must be considered. Race and social class should not mutually reinforce each other. If one race is middle class and the other is lower class, then class differences in play styles as well as other factors may be attributed to racial causes by some children. Social class heterogeneity within each race or class homogeneity across both races seems more advisable in terms of positive effects on racial attitudes.[17]

It should be stressed that it is not necessary for the school to have a middle-class student body for it to be "quality integrated." The fact that the teachers, play material, and curriculum stress racial acceptance and that race and class differences do not wholly reinforce one another may be more important in affecting racial attitudes than whether the student body is of a particular socioeconomic status. Another important part of quality integration is an attempt to involve the parents. If the parents are given the opportunity to interact in the pursuit of common goals, like the planning of innovative school programs, their own racial attitudes may be modified.

All of the factors mentioned thus far do not involve direct teaching about race but rather attempt to shape attitudes indirectly. There are several times, however, where direct comments may be effective. If historical and political events are explained, important events in both black and white history should be presented. For instance, if George Washington is discussed, Martin Luther King or other black leaders should have a place in the curriculum. The same is true for music and art. In addition, differences in religious or national customs might be made a focus of interest. If the child learns to appreciate many types of differences, there may be more chance that he will regard racial variations positively.

Another evidence of a quality integrated classroom is the teacher's handling of racial incidents. These occurrences must be dealt with immediately. If a child makes negative racial remarks, he should be told firmly by the teacher that this is unacceptable behavior. It is sometimes not possible to explain further, because by doing so the teacher might attract the attention of everyone else in the class to the incident. For this reason, and because these incidents may escape the attention of a teacher, it is highly important for tolerance to be expressed in the classroom in the ways already described.

There are other factors contributing to quality integration which are necessary in any preschool program regardless of its racial composition. The development of cognitive and linguistic skills is highly important during the preschool years. Particularly for lower-class black children, training in achievement and ability skills at this age level helps to prevent low personal self-esteem which can reinforce a negative racial self-image.[18] The individuality of each child should also be stressed, and the teacher should emphasize what each youngster does well. This not only bolsters personal self-esteem but also points out individual variations within each race.

A quality integrated situation basically means a sound educational program combined with an active stress on interracial tolerance. By quality integration we do not mean that all mention of race should be allocated to a weekly "tolerance hour." The subtle atmosphere of the classroom, created by teacher's attitudes, play equipment, racial composition, and parental involvement may be more important in the creation of interracial acceptance than is direct teaching about race.

Educational programs for prospective nursery school and kindergarten teachers must thus incorporate teaching about children's racial attitudes into their curriculum. The training of preschool teachers must stress the fact that children of this age level are beginning to develop racial attitudes. Such training should provide information on available interracial play and reading materials. Opportunities to discuss the handling of racial incidents and suggestions about teaching the children to appreciate variations along racial and ethnic lines are also important.

Some teachers wish to create a quality integrated situation but lack the knowledge to translate their intentions into positive classroom situations; others do not share even this willingness to be helpful. For this latter group, opportunities for examination of their own prejudice are an instrumental part of their preparation for teaching.

Pluralism or Separatism?

Growth of black pride, positive identification with a black heritage (both African and Afro-American), and a desire to contribute to the development of the black community are gaining widespread popular support among blacks.[19] This stress on positive cultural identity is of extreme importance for changing the pattern of poor racial self-esteem among black youngsters. Numerous investigators have stated that strong group identity gives the individual a sense of security and feelings of personal continuity; it also makes it easier for him to handle the prejudice directed against his group. My data abundantly testify to the need for a movement toward black pride.

Statements concerning the desirability of black pride and the desirability of quality integration are not contradictory; these two factors may effectively supplement one another. If the black child learns at home that his heritage is a source of pride, if he has a strong black identity, then his positive image of blacks may be communicated to the white children with whom he is in contact and their attitudes may be shaped or modified. In turn, the black child's attitudes toward himself and his group may be reinforced by the atmosphere of interracial acceptance he finds in the classroom. His attitudes toward whites may also be positively affected.

Some blacks feel that "when we begin to define our own image, the stereotypes . . . that our oppressor has developed will begin in the white community and end there."[20] But blacks cannot define themselves apart from the larger society. Black communities are not entirely insulated ghettos; the living conditions and other external attributes of white Americans are perceived as the proper standards to which blacks are entitled.[21] Thus, affirmation of black identity must be distinguished from institutional separatism. Children are sensitive to the implications of social roles. Even if separate black institutions are developed, children of both races will still be aware that blacks are excluded from full participation in American society in economic and social terms. Cultural pluralism within an interracial social structure seems in fact to be the solution that most blacks desire.[22] Yet surveys show that bitterness and estrangement is growing and that there is an absence of understanding and compassion among a large segment of the white population.

Thus, it becomes a matter of immediate importance for laws guaranteeing equal opportunity in employment and education to be strongly enforced and for educational, occupational, and other institutions to become fully responsive to the needs of blacks. It is also important for every family to be guaranteed a decent level of living so that the connection between race and poverty will be diminished and the personal self-esteem of children, regardless of race, will not be damaged by poverty-related factors.

The racial attitudes of children are a reflection of the racial attitudes and actions of American society. Only if energy is redirected toward the improvement of the economic position of blacks and the full integration of American society will the pattern of prejudice among whites and self-rejection among black youngsters that I have reported largely disappear.

Appendices Notes Bibliography Index

Appendix 1 Coding Scheme for Comments and Free Play

Comments[1]

Comments about Race or Color[2]

1. Favorable: "This [brown or white] is a nice, good, pretty color. I like, want to play with, people who are this color. She is pretty because she's white [brown] or has light [dark] skin."
2. Unfavorable: "This [brown or white] is an ugly, bad color." "I don't like, won't play with, people who are this color." "He is lazy and stupid because he's white [brown]." If a child answers "no" to "would your Mommy like you to bring this one home for lunch?" it is not scored as unfavorable unless the child designates that "Mommy would not like him because he is white [brown]."
3. Neutral: "This is [brown or white]," with no favorable or unfavorable adjective or connotation attached. "These dolls match in color." "This looks just like [person of same race as doll]."

Comments about Hair

Comment pertaining to the color or style of the hair of the doll.

Comments about Dirt

1. "This one [Negro] is dirty." If the child specifically states "he's dirty because he's colored" he is scored both in this category and in the "Negro Unfavorable" category. If he points to Negro doll and just says, "he's dirty," he is scored only in this category.
2. "This one [white] is clean." If child says "he's clean because he's white," he is scored in both "Favorable White" and this category.
3. "White dirty" and "Negro clean" scored the same way as 1 and 2 above.

Free Play[3]

Discrimination by Race

1. Only white (Negro) dolls used throughout free play period.
2. Whites (Negroes) used predominantly
   a. Plays with all of the dolls of one race first and then with a few dolls of the opposite race
   b. Picks doll of one race, rejects it, and chooses same sex doll of opposite race.

Spontaneous Family Matching

Spontaneously and correctly sorting and matching families, specifically stating that this is a family.

---

[1] This and the following code sheets are abbreviated versions of the longer and more detailed code sheet used in the actual scoring.

[2] Sometimes a child picks up a doll and says, "This is the best" or "This is the prettiest." This is not scored as a comment pertaining to race unless the doll's color is specifically mentioned.

[3] No score given on free play unless child has played with at least five dolls.

Correlations between Attitude Items

	Play with	Nice	Lazy	Home-lunch	Clean
Nice	.17				
Lazy	.10	−.05			
Home-lunch	.19	.34	.00		
Clean	.23	.24	.02	.28	
Lollipop	.20	.21	.02	.24	.31

Correlations between Color Match Items

	Negro mother correct	Negro family correct	White mother correct
Negro family correct	.43		
White mother correct	.44	.30	
White family correct	.29	.52	.44

Correlation between Color Terms Items

	Negro	Colored
Colored	.21	
White	.29	.58

Correlation between Color Salience Items

Dress/color salience and sex/color salience: +.39

Appendix 3 F-Ratios for Analyses of Variance

F-Ratios for Analysis of Variance
by Terms, Attitudes, Race

	Degrees of Freedom	Self-Identification
Terms	1	2.98
Attitudes	2	43.66
Race	1	4.11
Terms/attitudes	2	2.44
Terms/race	1	.70
Attitudes/race	2	.56
3-way	2	.38
Anova error	363	

F-Ratios for Analysis of Variance by Race, Age, Class, and Sex

	Degrees of Freedom	Self-identification	Attitudes	Color match	Color terms	Color salience
Race	1	8.89	7.26	1.30	.003	6.05
Age	2	.51	4.43	.98	18.93	.17
Class	2	.26	.66	1.50	1.83	.90
Sex	1	.06	.16	.29	.45	6.77
Race/age	2	.15	.28	1.18	.60	.11
Race/class	2	1.01	4.49	.02	.97	.27
Race/sex	1	6.15	.17	.01	2.34	.98
Age/class	4	.43	.33	1.15	.65	.51
Age/sex	2	1.74	.87	.26	.71	.36
Class/sex	2	.37	1.08	.03	.05	.38
Race/age/class	4	.21	.39	.45	.80	1.07
Race/age/sex	2	.93	.52	.16	1.63	.00
Race/class/sex	2	.00	.20	.93	.01	.24
Age/class/sex	4	1.15	.32	.16	.71	.97
4-way	4	.69	1.37	.20	,83	.52
Anova error	308					

F-Ratios for Analysis of Variance by Race, Sex, Class, Contact

	Degrees of Freedom	Self-identification	Attitudes	Color match	Color terms	Color salience
Race	1	9.17	10.47	3.13	1.71	6.21
Sex	1	.24	.20	1.15	.28	8.60
Class	2	.23	.68	1.56	1.81	.32
Contact	1	.88	.45	4.07	1.12	.00
Race/sex	1	5.74	.33	.25	2.31	1.19
Race/class	2	1.96	3.41	.03	1.13	.26
Race/contact	1	.00	.32	.43	1.54	1.97
Sex/class	2	.62	1.22	.04	.44	.54
Sex/contact	1	1.92	2.13	.57	.04	.05
Class/contact	2	2.76	.31	.16	1.60	.93
Race/sex/class	2	.01	.27	1.20	.12	.34
Race/sex/contact	1	1.01	1.74	1.36	.23	.45
Race/class/contact	2	1.04	.05	.85	.89	.15
Sex/class/contact	2	1.34	.00	1.09	3.78	1.81
4-way	2	.17	.33	.88	1.76	.67
Anova error	320					

F-Ratios for Analysis of Variance by Color, Class, Contact for Negroes

	Degrees of Freedom	Self-identification	Attitudes	Color match	Color terms	Color salience
Class	2	2.78	4.33	.52	1.98	.05
Contact	1	.62	.71	1.06	.00	.49
Color	1	.52	.74	.44	.00	1.95
Contact/class	2	3.53	.02	.11	.27	1.11
Color/class	2	.52	.07	.29	.29	.36
Color/contact	1	.20	6.53	.00	.00	1.29
3-way	2	.29	.58	.40	.26	.14
Anova error	157					

Appendix 4 Self-Portrait and Story Code Sheets

Scoring Scheme for Figure Drawings

Characteristic	*Score*	
	+ 1	*+ 0*
1. Size of figure drawing	More than half the page	Less than half the page
2. Placement of self-figure on paper	More than half of drawing in middle third of paper	On side or near edge
3. Amount of color	More than three colors	Less than three colors
4. Amount of detail in face		
Eyes	Present	Absent
Ears	Present	Absent
Nose	Present	Absent
Mouth	Present	Absent
Hair	Present	Absent
Eyebrows	Present	Absent
5. Expression of face	Lively or smiling	Sad or neutral
6. Presence of body	Present	Absent
7. Presence of clothes on body	Present and clearly outlined: distinct from body[a]	Absent
8. Presence of Arms	Present	Absent
9. Presence of Fingers (regardless of correct number)	Present	Absent
10. Presence of Legs	Present	Absent

Scoring Scheme for Figure Drawings (continued)

Characteristic	Score	
	+1	*+0*
11. Presence of Feet	Present	Absent
12. Realism of Drawing	Clearly resembles person[b]	Does not resemble person or poor resemblance

[a] Regardless of number of items. One item of clothing sufficient to be scored +1.
[b] Whether the child accurately draws himself racially is not included in this evaluation.

Scoring Scheme for Stories

1. Daily description: Lively-cheerful, lively daily description. Child elaborates upon type of play or interpersonal relations and/or expresses enjoyment in what he does.

2. Daily description: Dull-lack of imagination, no elaboration of details or interpersonal relationships. Simple enumeration of features of pictures or just a list of things the child does. Typical story: "Plays and Sleeps."

3. Self-description: Positive-subject implies that he likes his appearance or his attributes and/or reiterates proudly that it is a picture of himself.

4. Self-description: Negative-negative and self-deprecating.

5. Personal efficacy: Subject discusses things he is able to do. Brags about his ability to master the environment.

6. Powerlessness: Subject deprecates his ability to do things; says he cannot do or accomplish tasks.

7. Physical harm: Fear imagery, frightening imagery. Subject is frightened of things, real or imaginary, which will injure him; says others wish to injure him or he wishes to injure himself.

Notes

Introduction

1. The term "black" is used predominantly in this book. I do, however, utilize "Negro" either for stylistic purposes or in discussions of color per se, where the designation "black" might lead to confusion.

2. Franklin Giddings, *Principles of Sociology* (New York, 1896), p. 18. W. I. Thomas, "The Psychology of Race Prejudice," *American Journal of Sociology,* 9 (1904), 593–611.

3. Arnold Gesell and Frances Ilg, *The Child from Five to Ten* (New York, 1946), pp. 338, 356–357.

4. "Text of Nixon's Address to the Nation Outlining His Proposals for Welfare Reform," *New York Times,* August 9, 1969, p. 10.

5. Ibid., p. 10.

6. Steven Asher and Vernon Allen, "Racial Preference and Social Comparison Processes," *Journal of Social Issues,* 25 (1969), 157–166.

7. Angus Campbell and Howard Schuman, "Racial Attitudes in Fifteen American Cities," *Supplemental Studies for the National Advisory Commission on Civil Disorders* (Washington, D.C., 1968), p. 17.

1 Mechanisms of Racial Attitude Transmission

1. David Krech, Richard Crutchfield, and Egerton Ballachey, *Individual in Society* (New York, 1962), pp. 139–146.

2. Gordon Allport, *The Nature of Prejudice* (New York, 1958), p. 10. I use the term "prejudice" rather than the currently more popular term "racism" because the former concept is both more clearly defined and more frequently utilized in existing social science literature.

3. *Toward a General Theory of Action,* ed. Talcott Parsons and Edward Shils (Cambridge, Mass., 1959), pp. 3–29.

4. *Report of the National Advisory Commission on Civil Disorders* (New York, 1968).

5. William Brink and Louis Harris, *Black and White* (New York, 1967), pp. 131–132; Angus Campbell and Howard Schuman, "Racial Attitudes in Fifteen American Cities," *Supplemental Studies for the National Advisory Commission on Civil Disorders* (Washington, D.C., 1968), p. 31.

6. Mildred Schwartz, *Trends in White Attitudes toward Negroes* (Chicago, 1967), p. 9.

7. Brink and Harris, *Black and White,* p. 136; Campbell and Schuman, *Racial Attitudes,* p. 31.

8. Kenneth and Mamie Clark, "Racial Identification and Preference in Negro Children," *Readings in Social Psychology,* ed. Maccoby, Newcomb, and Hartley (New York, 1958), pp. 602–611; Kenneth Morland, "Racial Self-Identification: A Study of Nursery School Children," *American Catholic Sociological Review,* 24 (fall 1963), 231–242.

9. Among many other sources, Brink and Harris, *Black and White,* p. 136; Campbell and Schuman, *Racial Attitudes,* p. 35.

10. For instance, Robin Williams, *Strangers Next Door* (Englewood Cliffs, N.J., 1964), pp. 259–263.

11. Allport, *The Nature of Prejudice* (New York, 1958), pp. 250–270.

12. T. W. Adorno, E. Frenkel-Brunswik, D. J. Levinson, and R. N. Sanford, *The Authoritarian Personality* (New York, 1950).

13. Allport, *The Nature of Prejudice,* p. 301.

14. *Ibid.,* p. 283.

15. Bernard Kutner, "Patterns of Mental Functioning Associated with Prejudice in Children," *Psychological Monographs,* 72 (1958), no. 460.

16. Virginia Axline, "Play Therapy and Race Conflict in Young Children," *Journal of Abnormal and Social Psychology,* 43 (1948), 300–310.

17. Richard Trent, "The Relation between Expressed Self-Acceptance and Expressed Attitudes toward Negroes and Whites among Negro Children," *Journal of Genetic Psychology,* 91 (1957), 25–31.

18. Eugene Brody, "Color and Identity Conflict in Young Boys: Observations of Negro Mothers and Sons in Urban Baltimore," *Psychiatry,* 2 (May 1963), 188–202.

19. Thomas Pettigrew, *A Profile of the Negro American* (Princeton, N.J., 1964), pp. 3–4.

20. Campbell and Schuman, *Racial Attitudes,* p. 25.

21. William McCord, John Howard, Bernard Friedberg, and Edwin Harwood, *Life Styles in the Black Ghetto* (New York, 1969), p. 99.

22. Brink and Harris, *Black and White,* p. 276.

23. Since I am interested in group rather than individual differences, I do not deal with psychological factors creating individual variation in type of attitudes and response to them. The section on personality causes of prejudice has been included as a reminder that this is one important area I do not cover.

24. Mary Ellen Goodman, *Race Awareness in Young Children* (New York, 1964), pp. 200–215.

25. Eugene and Ruth Horowitz, "Development of Social Attitudes in Children," *Sociometry,* 1 (1938), 301–338.

26. Robert Coles, *Children of Crisis* (Boston, 1967), pp. 333–350.

27. Erik Erikson, "Memorandum on Identity and Negro Youth," *Journal of Social Issues,* 20 (October 1964), 30.

28. Lillian Smith, *Killers of the Dream* (Garden City, New York, 1963), pp. 17, 75.

29. Eugene Brody, "Color and Identity Conflict," pp. 198–199.

30. Helen Trager and Marion Yarrow, *They Learn What They Live* (New York, 1952), pp. 185–231. Charles Bird, Elio Monachesi, and Harvey Burdick, "Studies of Group Tensions: III. The Effect of Parental Discouragement of Play Activities upon the Attitudes of White Children toward Negroes," *Child Development,* 23 (December 1952), 295–306.

31. Allport indicates that equal status contact which is noncompetitive, in pursuit of common goals, and sanctioned by authority can cause positive attitude change. This suggests, for instance, that in a setting where racial differences coincide with social class differences, the situation for positive attitude formation is probably not optimal.

32. Elliot LieBow, *Tally's Corner* (Boston, 1967), p. 88.

33. Coles, *Children of Crisis,* p. 357.

34. Trager and Yarrow, *They Learn What They Live.*

35. Janet Martin, *Red and Blue* (New York, 1965).

36. For instance, Ezra Jack Keats' famous book, *The Snowy Day* (New York, 1966), as well as other Keats books in this series (*Whistle for Willie, Goggles*). Also Don Freeman, *Courderoy* (New York, 1968), and Ann McGovern, *Black is Beautiful* (New York, 1969), are important new additions to this literature. Even if a child does not own books, most nursery schools are well stocked with juvenile literature. Thus even children from low-income families may be exposed to the influences discussed here.

37. Suzanne Keller, "The Social World of the Urban Slum Child," *American Journal of Orthopsychiatry,* 33 (1963), 823–831.

38. Slightly older children may, however, regard political events as important. A collection of drawings and comments concerning the death of Martin Luther King indicates that children in the primary grades may be well aware of the

significance of race-related events. See *Children of Cardozo Tell It Like It Is,* (Cambridge, Mass., 1968).

39. Coles, *Children of Crisis,* p. 338.

40. Helen Trager and Marion Radke, "Children's Perception of the Social Roles of Negroes and Whites," *Journal of Psychology,* 29 (January 1950), 3-33.

41. Gordon Allport, *The Nature of Prejudice,* pp. 282-295.

42. Although racial attitudes are stressed here, these general processes are also operative in the acquisition of many other types of attitudes (for instance, political socialization, acquisition of sex-role norms).

2   Review of Other Studies

1. Bruno Lasker, *Race Attitudes in Children* (New York, 1929), p. 67.

2. Ruth Horowitz, "Racial Aspects of Self-Identification in Nursery School age Children," *Journal of Psychology,* 7 (1939) 91-99.

3. Kenneth and Mamie Clark, "The Development of Consciousness of Self and the Emergence of Racial Identity in Negro Preschool Children," *Journal of Social Psychology,* 10 (1939), 591-599; "Racial Identification and Preference in Negro Children," in *Readings in Social Psychology,* ed. Maccoby, Newcomb, and Hartley (New York, 1958), pp. 602-611. The former study utilizes line drawings of Negro and white children and the latter uses dolls of both races.

4. Mary Ellen Goodman, *Race Awareness in Young Children* (New York, 1964), pp. 50-73.

5. Harold and Nancy Stevenson, "Social Interaction in an Interracial Nursery School," *Genetic Psychology Monographs,* 61 (1960), 37-75.

6. Kenneth Morland, "Racial Recognition by Nursery School Children in Lynchburg, Virginia," *Social Forces,* 37 (1958), 132-37.

7. Kenneth Morland, "Comparison of Racial Awareness in Northern and Southern Children," *American Journal of Orthopsychiatry,* 36 (1966), 22-32.

8. Graham Vaughan, "Concept Formation and the Development of Ethnic Awareness," *Journal of Genetic Psychology,* 103 (1963), 93-103.

9. Morland, "Racial Recognition," pp. 132-137.

10. Horowitz, "Racial Aspects of Self-Identification," pp. 91-99.

11. Goodman, *Race Awareness,* pp. 1-69.

12. Morland, "Comparison of Racial Awareness," pp. 22-32.

13. *Ibid.,* pp. 22-32.

14. Irwin Katz, James Robinson, Edgar Epps, and Patricia Waly, "The Influ-

ence of Race of the Experimenter and Instructions upon the Expression of Hostility by Negro Boys," *Journal of Social Issues,* 20 (April 1964), 54–59. Morland claims that in his pre-tests there were no differences in results between white and Negro interviewers; thus he used white interviewers in the final sample. Given existing research on subject bias due to the race of the experimenter, the nature of his questions, and the fact that he was working in a segregated southern setting, this finding is surprising.

15. C. Landreth and B. C. Johnson, "Young Children's Responses to a Picture and Inset Test Designed to Reveal Reactions to Persons of Different Skin Color," *Child Development,* 24 (1953), 65–79.

16. Morland, "Racial Recognition," pp. 132–137.

17. Clark and Clark, "Racial Identification and Preference," p. 605.

18. Skin color is a correlate of social class among Negro-Americans. See Thomas Pettigrew, Michael Ross, David Armor, and Howard Freeman, "Color Gradation and Attitudes among Middle-Income Negroes," *American Sociological Review,* 31 (1966), 365–374.

19. George Simpson and J. Milton Yinger, *Racial and Cultural Minorities* (New York, 1958), pp. 522–523.

20. Clark and Clark, "Racial Identification and Preference" and Morland, "Comparison of Racial Awareness," present data on segregated and integrated school experience, but their segregated schools tend to be in the South and integrated schools or play groups in the North in both these studies. It is thus impossible to differentiate any effect of contact from a regional effect.

21. Clark and Clark, "Racial Identification and Preference," pp. 602–611.

22. Steven Asher and Vernon Allen, "Racial Preference and Social Comparison Processes," *Journal of Social Issues,* 25 (1969), 157–166. R. B. Ammons, "Reactions in a Projective Doll Play Interview of White Males Two to Six Years Old to Differences in Skin Color and Facial Features," *Journal of Genetic Psychology,* 76 (1950), 323–341.

23. Doris Springer, "Awareness of Racial Differences by Pre-school Children in Hawaii," *Genetic Psychology Monographs,* 41 (1950), 215–270.

24. Robert Blake and Wayne Dennis, "The Development of Stereotypes Concerning the Negro," *Journal of Abnormal and Social Psychology,* 38 (1943), 525–531.

25. Kenneth Morland, "Racial Acceptance and Preference of Nursery School Children in a Southern City," *Merrill-Palmer Quarterly,* 8 (1962), 271–280.

26. Clark and Clark, "Racial Identification and Preference," pp. 602–611. The

Morland data ("Racial Acceptance," p. 279) seem to suggest that for many Negroes, white preference does not necessarily mean black rejection. For Negroes, no own-race acceptace results by age are provided, however.

27. Marion Radke and Helen Trager, "Children's Perceptions of the Social Roles of Negroes and Whites," *Journal of Psychology,* 29 (1950), 3–33.

28. Morland, "Comparison of Racial Awareness," pp. 22–32. All of his southern subjects are segregated, however, so it is not clear whether region or contact explains this effect.

29. Charles Bird, Elio Monachesi, and Harvey Burdick, "Studies of Group Tensions: III. The Effect of Parental Discouragement of Play Activities upon the Attitudes of White Children toward Negroes," *Child Development,* 23 (1952), 295–306. Asher and Allen, "Racial Preference," pp. 157–166.

30. Kenneth Morland, "Racial Acceptance," pp. 271–280.

31. *Ibid.*

32. Evelyn Helgerson, "The Relative Significance of Race, Sex, and Facial Expression in Choice of Playmates by the Pre-School Child," *Journal of Negro Education,* 12 (1943), 617–622. The only other study which deals with effects of contact for white children is Morland, "Comparison of Racial Awareness." He finds segregated white children reject Negroes more often than do children in integrated schools or play groups. Since his segregated subjects are in the South, however, it is not clear whether region or contact is the explanatory variable.

33. Helgerson, "Relative Significance," pp. 617–622.

34. Kenneth and Mamie Clark, "Emotional Factors in Racial Identification and Preference in Negro Children" in *Mental Health and Segregation,* ed. Martin Grossack (New York, 1963), pp. 53–63. Three separate methods are used by the Clarks in their series of studies: line drawings, doll play, and the coloring test. In the doll-play technique, they find that integrated northern subjects tend to be somewhat more favorable to the white doll and are significantly more likely to reject the brown doll than are segregated southern children. In contrast, on forced choice questions, Morland ("Comparison of Racial Awareness,") finds that his northern black subjects, most of whom seemed to be in integrated settings, exhibited less white preference than did the segregated southern ones.

35. Clark and Clark, "Racial Identification and Preference," p. 611.

36. Asher and Allen, "Racial Preference," p. 161.

37. Clark and Clark, "Development of Consciousness of Self," pp. 591–599.

38. Clark and Clark, "Emotional Factors," p. 58.

39. Thomas Pettigrew, "Social Evaluation Theory: Convergences and Applications," *Nebraska Symposium on Motivation,* 15 (1967), 241–311.

40. Clark and Clark, "Racial Identification and Preference," pp. 602–611. The Clarks' data suggest that children exhibit more correct self-identification when asked to color themselves the appropriate color than they do when asked to identify with the appropriate doll or picture. But in the coloring test, in contrast to the doll-play and line-drawing technique, it was considered a reality response for the light child to classify himself as white, and the sample was older than in the doll-play research (three- and four-year-olds were not used). Also, in the coloring test, the child was shown a picture, told that it was a picture of himself (using his name), and asked to color it the same color he was. This seems to force more of a reality response than the doll-play technique, where the subject was only asked, "Which doll looks like you?" The latter technique does not specifically tell the subject that the doll is a representation of himself by labeling the image with his own name. Therefore, it may allow more room for fantasy than the directions given on the coloring test.

41. H. J. Greenwald and D. B. Oppenheim, "Reported Magnitude of Self-Misidentification among Negro Children – Artifact?" *Journal of Personality and Social Psychology,* 8 (1968), 49–52. There are several major methodological problems with this study as well. They use subjects from ages three to five years, but they group the subjects together by age in presenting results. They also do not control for class and contact, and the interviewers were white. Since the questions were direct and the nature of the test was undisguised, a threat situation may have existed and may have enhanced bias in regard to the experimenter.

42. Goodman, *Race Awareness,* pp. 81–82. Horowitz, "Racial Aspects of Self-Identification," pp. 91–99.

43. Kenneth Morland, "Racial Self-Identification: A Study of Nursery School Children," *American Catholic Sociological Review,* 24 (1963), 231–242.

44. Kenneth and Mamie Clark, "Skin Color as a Factor in Racial Identification of Negro Pre-school Children," *Journal of Social Psychology,* 11 (1940), 159–169.

45. Clark and Clark, "Development of Consciousness of Self," pp. 591–599.

46. Kenneth Clark, *Prejudice and Your Child* (Boston, 1963), p. 46.

47. Morland, "Comparison of Racial Awareness," pp. 22–32.

48. Morland, "Racial Self-Identification," pp. 231–242.

49. Clark and Clark, "Racial Identification and Preference," pp. 602–611.

50. Clark and Clark, "Development of Consciousness," pp. 591–599.

51. Clark and Clark, "Racial Identification and Preference," pp. 602–611. This seems to be true with both the doll-play and the line-drawing techniques. With the coloring test, however, more light than dark-skinned subjects gave "reality responses" (Clark and Clark, "Emotional Factors," p. 57). The Clarks, however, consider coloring the self "white" a reality response for a light-skinned Negro child. But the subjects in this test are from five to seven years of age, and approximately 90 percent of even light-skinned children show awareness of racial differences ("Racial Identification and Preference," p. 606). This procedure is thus open to question, especially since different shades of brown crayon seemed to be available. The results of the coloring test cannot be utilized in much of the following discussion, since some of the other results are presented without controls for skin color.

52. It is interesting that even when darker children correctly classify themselves, they still may wish to be a shade lighter than they actually are (Clark and Clark, "Emotional Factors," p. 55). The data of Greenwald and Oppenheim also seem to indicate this.

53. Clark and Clark, "Skin Color as a Factor," pp. 159–169. Clark and Clark, "Racial Identification and Preference," p. 606. Even in their early studies, the Clarks do admit that wish fulfillment may be operative in the case of the dark child who misclassifies himself.

54. Clark and Clark, "Racial Identification and Preference," pp. 602–611.

55. In one of their early studies, they investigate only a segregated sample in Washington, D.C., and they find when region and contact do not vary, skin color does have an effect. However, class is still not controlled in this study (Clark and Clark, "Skin Color as a Factor," pp. 159–169).

56. Morland finds the opposite result on one of his questions ("which one would you rather be?") but this may in part be due to his use of a white interviewer.

57. Kenneth and Mamie Clark, "Segregation as a Factor in the Racial Identification of Negro Pre-school Children," *Journal of Experimental Education,* 8 (1939), 161–163. Light children show an opposite trend, however; for the light children in segregated schools, there are more choices of a white than a black identification figure, and in integrated schools choices approximate chance. In this particular paper, the Clarks' integrated schools (in terms of both students and staff) and semisegregated schools (all black students and integrated staff) were in New York City. Their totally segregated schools (both staff and pupils black) were in Washington, D.C. Therefore, some regional effect may still be operative. However, the differences between the semisegregated and the inte-

grated schools in New York suggest that contact, when color and region do not vary, does have an effect on self-identification. Social class is not controlled, however.

3 Methods of Inquiry

1. Judith R. Porter, "Racial Concept Formation in Pre-school Age Children," unpub. master's thesis, Cornell University, 1963.

2. Since young children are far more familiar with television than they are with motion pictures, the format was changed from a "Movie-Story" game on the pre-test to a "TV-Story" game in the final version used here. One stereotype question which provided ambiguous results was also replaced. The question "Which one of these two dolls [Negro and white] hit the boy and pushed him down?" was replaced by "Which one is lazy and stupid?" It was unclear whether the former question measured racial attitudes or the realities of the behavior setting, since the black children in the integrated school in the pre-test actually tended to be highly aggressive.

3. One interviewer (the author) is a sociologist, one is a psychologist, and one a speech therapist.

4. For girls, the name Judy was used. If someone in class was named Johnny or Judy, another name was substituted.

5. A pair of Negro and white dolls identically dressed are presented to the subject for each question. After a choice, the rejected doll is removed from view. The position of the Negro dolls is alternated in each successive pair to control for possible response-set for right or left.

6. Although this birthday party situation is more appropriate for middleclass than for lower-class youngsters, the fact that our subjects are in nursery schools obviates some of this class bias. In many nursery schools the children's birthdays are commemorated, so even lower-class children may be familiar with the concept of birthday party.

7. Different kinds of furniture to move around helps maintain the child's interest during the unstructured part of the test.

8. Robert Blake and Wayne Dennis, "Development of Stereotypes Concerning the Negro," *Journal of Abnormal and Social Psychology,* 38 (1943), 525–531. These figures would probably be lower at the present time.

9. William Brink and Louis Harris, *The Negro Revolution in America,* (New York, 1964), pp. 140–141.

10. *Ibid.,* p. 148. A later Brink and Harris poll shows that this figure has remained stable. *Black and White* (New York, 1967), p. 136.

11. Porter, "Racial Concept Formation."

12. Thomas Pettigrew, *Profile of the Negro American* (Princeton, N. J., 1964), p. 50.

13. John Rohrer and Munro Edmundson, *The Eighth Generation Grows Up* (New York, 1964).

14. Irwin Katz, James Robinson, Edgar Epps, and Patricia Waly, "The Influence of Race of the Experimenter and Instructions upon the Expression of Hostility by Negro Boys," *Journal of Social Issues,* 20 (April, 1964), 54. Irwin Katz, "Review of Evidence Relating to the Effects of Desegregation on the Performance of Negroes," *American Psychologist,* 19 (1964), 381–399.

15. My test seems on the whole less threatening than one which asks directed questions about race with no extraneous material between questions. The latter type of technique should be more prone to bias because of the experimenter's race, particularly in a segregated school.

16. Irwin Katz, Thomas Henchey, and Harvey Allen, "Effects of Race of Tester, Approval-Disapproval, and Need on Negro Children's Learning," *Journal of Personality and Social Psychology,* 8 (1968), 38–42.

17. One person first scored all the verbal responses and then categorized all the free play. Since verbal responses and free play were recorded on separate sheets, the coder had no way of identifying any verbal and behavorial protocol as belonging to the same child. A second individual re-scored every fifth set of unstructured responses in the same manner. The coding scheme is reproduced in Appendix 1.

18. These points are raised to show the problems of subjectivity inherent in skin-color ratings. Since two-thirds of the sample was rated by only a white interviewer, that interviewer's ratings were used on the remaining one-third of the sample to maintain consistency. Only the two-category rating scheme, on which a high degree of agreement was manifested between a black and a white rater, was used in analysis of the data; the major skin-color result discussed in Chapter 5 is so highly significant that it would not be canceled out by small variations in color coding. It should be noted that the problems I have raised are inherent in the use of skin color as a variable per se. Even in a more "objective" means of rating skin color, such as matching the skin shade to a chart, the skin shade may not match exactly and subjective judgment of the rater is still involved.

19. Albert Reiss, Otis Duncan, Paul Hatt, and Cecil North, *Occupations and Social Status* (New York, 1961). Working with information from the census tracts, Reiss constructed a rank-order scale of occupational prestige based on average income and education. On his scale 38.5 is used as a cutting point for working–middle-class differentiations. The white-collar and the most highly skilled craft positions fall above this figure. The minor white-collar and semi-skilled and unskilled positions fall below. Since a more refined indicator is needed for measurement of Negro social class, we have lowered the cutting point on Reiss' scale to 25.5 for Negroes. This figure seems to differentiate between all skilled crafts and white-collar work on one hand and semiskilled or unskilled occupations on the other. A Negro brickmason would thus be considered middle class, although an unskilled factory operative would not. This procedure seemed valid, since Drake and Cayton suggest that the skilled trades are invested with high prestige value in the Negro community. *Black Metropolis* (New York, 1962), p. 510.

20. Andrew Billingsley suggests that black middle-class families have three distinct groupings: upper middle class, solid middle class, and precarious middle class. *Black Families in White America* (Englewood Cliffs, N. J., 1968). Although my class index is not refined enough to differentiate my subjects in this manner, I seem to have few black families in the first category. Most of the middle-class black children are in one of the last two classifications.

21. Except in the case of "lazy and stupid," which was expected to have a minus or zero correlation with the other attitude items.

4   Meaning of Doll Choice: An Analysis by Race and Age

1. Part Two is entitled "Sociological Correlates of Attitude Formation." I define a sociological variable as a variable connected with group interaction or social definition of roles. Social class and amount of interracial contact are clearly sociological variables. Sex and shade of skin color are also sociological variables by this definition; although they are biologically ascribed, their meaning for the child is socially defined. Age is the only variable which strictly speaking does not fully qualify as sociological in the sense defined above. Since the subjects in this study are so young, the development of cognitive processes is a more important effect of age for my purposes than are specific role definitions attached to various phases of the life cycle. The generalizations made about the effects of each socio-

logical variable on racial attitudes do not characterize every child in each group. Variations due to individual personality are certainly important; however, they do not concern us here because we are interested only in group differences.

2. Unless otherwise indicated, this result and those following are computed on the basis of a four way analysis of variance by sex, class, age, and race. Because of unequal n's, the computer program puts undue weight on the first effect variable of an analysis of variance. In order to see if the effect is stable, it is necessary to run the analysis backward with the variable order reversed. Each analysis of variance reported was run twice in this manner, and the F-ratio reported is the lower F of these two runs.

3. This relationship is not a spurious effect of differences in racial awareness because covariance for the color match and color terms index does not affect the results.

4. For instance, Goodman; Trager; Clark; Ammons; Morland; Horowitz; Asher and Allen; and Porter (1963).

5. In the four tables on behavior and comments, the trends are more pronounced for whites than for blacks. Black children not only prefer the white dolls but also, as will be seen, are more concerned with color than are their white counterparts. It appears thus that black children tended on the whole to avoid racial or color comments as a protective mechanism. These results were unaffected by race of the interviewer. Other investigators have also found that black children are reticent to verbalize about color. See Mary Ellen Goodman, "Evidence Concerning the Genesis of Interracial Attitudes," *American Anthropologist,* 48 (1946), 624–630.

6. This was the only instance in the study in which knowledge of a local news event may have been reflected. The subject was also one of the oldest children in the sample.

7. Jane Thompson, "The Ability of Children of Different Grade Levels to Generalize on Sorting Tests," *Journal of Psychology,* 11 (1941), 119–126.

8. Negroes tended to make fewer spontaneous comments about appearance than whites did, and this result is unaffected by the race of the interviewer. It has already been suggested that avoidance of this type of comment may be a defense mechanism on the part of some of our black sample.

9. Barry Wellman, "Social Identities in Black and White," paper presented to the Society for the Study of Social Problems, August 1969. Marion Radke, Helen Trager, and Hadassah Davis, "Social Perceptions and Attitudes of Children,"

Genetic Psychology Monographs, 40 (1949), 327–447, also show that race is highly salient for blacks.

10. See Tables 8 and 9.

11. Kenneth Clark, *Prejudice and Your Child* (Boston, 1963), p. 43.

12. Ability to pair whole families correctly is lower than mother-child matching. This seems to be due in part to the fact that some children selected brothers and sisters on the basis of similarity in clothing rather than similarity in color.

13. The color match effects are closer to the "correct" side of the scale than the color terms means are. This suggests that at each age level there is some pairing on the basis of color alone without a sophisticated knowledge of the color-race relationship. The color match index, however, does seem to be a rough measure of racial awareness, since scores on color match and color terms increase together at age five.

14. The means for the total age effect, controlling for race, class, and sex are:

        3 years = 1.38   1 = high white choice
        4 years = 1.33   2 = low white choice
        5 years = 1.28

For each age level, the effect is computed by: group mean for that age + grand mean. The complete means for all groups are shown in Table 5. Since the means in these tables are presented in terms of own-race preference, it is necessary to subtract each Negro mean from 3.00 to find the white-choice score.

15. These and the following percentages are based on a frequency analysis of the entire sample by race.

16. Morland ("Racial Acceptance and Preference of Nursery School Children in a Southern City," *Merrill-Palmer Quarterly,* 8 [1962], 271–280) finds that on preference questions where choice between races is not forced, acceptance by whites of a black child as a playmate also dips at age five. Where the white child is forced to choose between a black and white playmate, white choice increases between ages three and four. Asher and Allen ("Racial Preference and Social Comparison Processes," *Journal of Social Issues,* 25 [1969], 157–166) also find that choice of white as a "nice color" increases with age for white children.

17. Clark and Clark ("Racial Identification and Preference in Negro Children," *Readings in Social Psychology,* ed. Maccoby, Newcomb, and Hartley, [New York, 1958], 602–611) show that white preference increases for black children from age three to age five. Asher and Allen ("Racial Preference") also indicate that preference for a white playmate increases with age for their Negro sample.

Morland ("Racial Acceptance") finds no significant age differences, but this may be due to either bias in regard to the experimenter or the fact that the sample was southern.

18. This type of comment seems to occur about equally in segregated and desegregated schools.

19. Morland finds a high degree of willingness by children of both races to accept a black playmate when no choice is required. He thus feels that children of this age do not exhibit real racial prejudices. My data suggest that this type of choice may instead measure an "American dilemma" type of response for some whites and an ambivalent response for blacks.

20. Robert Blake and Wayne Dennis, "Development of Stereotypes Concerning the Negro," *Journal of Abnormal and Social Psychology*, 38 (1943), 525–531.

5 Social Class, Contact, and Shade of Skin Color as Correlates of Racial Attitude Formation

1. James Baldwin, "Letter from a Region in My Mind," *New Yorker*, Nov. 17, 1962, p. 65.

2. Since this area has not previously been fully investigated, it is important to report trends. A trend for my analysis of variance results is defined in the following manner: (*a*) $.11 \leq p \leq .20$; (*b*) F-ratio is stable, i.e., similar on forward and backward runs (see Chapter 4, note 2); (*c*) there is theoretical reason to suppose that a relationship exists; (*d*) the overall effect is significant at $.11 \leq p \leq .20$. I refer here to the F-ratio over all the dependent variables instead of on a variable-by-variable basis: i.e., the class F-ratio computed over the self-identification, attitude, match, terms, and salience indices rather than on an index-by-index basis as reported in the text. This check on the overall F insures that the trend is not random.

3. Color match: class effect, controlling for sex, age, and race:

Middle = 1.42	1 = Correct
Working = 1.35	2 = Incorrect
ADC = 1.32	

Color terms: class effect, controlling for sex, age, and race:

Middle = 1.60	1 = Correct
Working = 1.60	2 = Incorrect
ADC = 1.57	

For complete means, see Tables 8 and 9, Chapter 4.

4. Race and class effect, controlling for age and sex:

White Middle	= 1.33	Negro Middle	= 1.31
White Working	= 1.29	Negro Working	= 1.43
White ADC	= 1.28	Negro ADC	= 1.34
1 = High White Choice;		2 = Low White Choice	

The complete means are presented in Chapter 4, Table 5, in terms of own-race preference. Conversion of own-race preference scores to white preference scores (and vice versa) is accomplished by subtracting each Negro mean from 3.00. Thus, overall Negro own-race preference scores would be: Middle = 1.69; Working = 1.57; ADC = 1.66, where 1 = high and 2 = low own-race preference.

5. Robin Williams, *Strangers Next Door* (Englewood Cliffs, N.J., 1964), p. 55. Brink and Harris, *Black and White* (New York, 1967), p. 136.

6. Williams, *Strangers Next Door,* p. 55.

7. Angus Campbell and Howard Schuman, "Racial Attitudes in Fifteen American Cities," *Supplemental Studies for the National Advisory Commission on Civil Disorders* (Washington, D.C., 1968), p. 35.

8. Although I had planned to do a comparative frequency analysis by class of this type of comment, few working-class and lower-class children made any type of comment at all, so such an analysis was not feasible.

9. Asher and Allen ("Racial Preference and Social Comparison Processes," *Journal of Social Issues,* 25 [1969], 157–166) find no significant social class differences in response for whites, but they do not seem to control carefully for contact. Morland's results on attitudes and social class conflict. On open-ended questions lower-class whites are more willing to accept blacks than their middle-class counterparts are, but these findings are reversed on forced-choice questions. The response on the open-ended question should be interpreted carefully, however, for reasons discussed in Chapter 4. See Morland, "Racial Acceptance and Preference of Nursery School Children in a Southern City," *Merrill-Palmer Quarterly,* 8 (1962), 271–280.

10. Asher and Allen ("Racial Preference") also find that middle-class black subjects responded with a slightly higher percentage of white choice and tended to prefer whites more consistently than their lower-class black subjects did.

11. Part of the choice in both these socioeconomic groups may also reflect response-set for a white doll by some of the younger subjects.

12. Campbell and Schuman, "Racial Attitudes," p. 19. Gary Marx, *Protest and Prejudice* (New York, 1967), pp. 188–189.

13. On the basis of both theory and data to be presented in Chapters 6 and 7,

it does not appear that the white preference response of ADC subjects means that they like both whites and blacks but have a slight preference for whites.

14. See Thomas Pettigrew, "Social Evaluation Theory: Convergences and Applications," *Nebraska Symposium on Motivation,* 15 (1967), 241–311.

15. Since the analysis of variance program I used will not work with empty cells, it was not possible to run a five-way analysis of variance because of our sample size. Instead, two four-way analyses were run: race/class/sex/age, and contact/race/class/sex. The relationship between age and contact was also checked by running a race/age/contact analysis. For Negroes, a contact/class/color analysis of variance was computed. (The relationship between sex and contact/class/color was also checked for Negroes. There appeared to be no sex/color or sex/contact effects.) Each of these was computed twice (with the variable order reversed) and the lower F reported. Thus, each variable was run, controlling for every other. Complete effects tables for all of these runs appear in Appendix 3.

16. *Racial Isolation in the Public Schools,* vol. I. U.S. Commission on Civil Rights (Washington, D.C., 1967), pp. 157–158. See also Pettigrew, "Social Evaluation Theory," pp. 284–285.

17. This was gathered from impressionistic observations of how warm the teachers were to the children (as indicated, for instance, by affectionate physical contact with the children). Although no teacher mentioned race directly, in a few of the classrooms the teachers made far more negative personal comments to us about their black pupils than about their white ones.

18. Jerome Kagan and Howard Moss, *Birth to Maturity* (New York, 1962), p. 269.

19. Mary Ellen Goodman, *Race Awareness in Young Children* (New York, 1964), pp. 311–313. Judith Porter, "Racial Concept Formation in Pre-school Age Children," unpub. diss., Cornell University, 1963. Rainwater's article, "Crucible of Identity: the Negro Lower Class Family" (*Daedalus,* winter 1966, pp. 172–216) seems to suggest that child-rearing practices and subculturally approved behavior patterns may be somewhat different in white and Negro lower-class groups. Differences in these factors may be related to differences in activity levels, even controlling for class.

20. Asher and Allen ("Racial Preference") find sex effects on the attitude measure for their sample. Boys of each race favored the white doll more often than did their female counterparts. These investigators do not seem to apply the same kind of contact, age, and skin color controls that I do, however, which may account for the difference in our findings.

21. Many of the young subjects of both races were extremely conscious of hair. Hair texture and perhaps facial features may provide the additional cues that cause even a light Negro child to be classified as black by his peers. The very light child may not be correctly categorized by his classmates, but the skin color measure combined light and light/medium ratings into one group. Many of the subjects in this category had a skin color that was different enough from white to be recognizable by other children.

22. Color and contact effect, controlling for class:

Light/light medium = 1.27	1 = *color*	
Dark/dark medium = 1.37	2 = *dress*	

On this question, the child was given the opportunity to match dolls by either color or dress. See Chapter 3.

23. Contact that is equal status, noncompetitive, in pursuit of common goals, and sanctioned by authority. See Gordon Allport, *Nature of Prejudice* (Garden City, N.Y., 1958), pp. 250–268.

24. In their doll-play studies, Kenneth and Mamie Clark find a simple skin-color effect: dark children tended to choose more brown dolls than the light children did. The coloring test, however, suggested that the dark-skinned subjects had the lowest amount of own-race preference; this result seems to be explained mainly by the high white choice of their dark-skinned integrated subjects. The Clarks do not control for social class nor use statistical techniques which uncover interaction effects, and this may explain some of the discrepancy between the simple skin-color effects on their doll-play test and my more complex findings. But I do not understand why their data on the coloring test are opposed to mine. I had a two-category as opposed to their three-category color-rating scheme, but this should reduce rather than reverse the difference in white doll preference between groups. My two-category coding scheme also did have fairly high reliability between black and white skin-color raters. Thus, I think that factors connected to color ratings per se are not the major factor in explaining the differences between the Clarks' results and my study.

6 Racial Self-Concept

1. By the age of six or seven, self-identification is definitely not a useful measure of racial self-concept for black children. Fantasy and reality become more fully separated, and most children identify correctly.

2. The Clarks' interpretation of the high rate of misidentification by light-

skinned subjects, for instance. See also the Greenwald and Oppenheim study discussed in Chapter 2.

3. Andrew Billingsley, *Black Families in White America* (Englewood Cliffs, N.J., 1968), p. 164.

4. Prejudice may have negative effects on the personality of white children, too, of course. The white child may learn to gain personal status in an unrealistic and nonadaptive way or learn to scapegoat minority groups instead of dealing realistically with his frustrations; see Kenneth Clark, *Prejudice and Your Child* (Boston, 1963), p. 170. Here, however, we are talking only about the group identity dimension of self-concept, defined as whether the child accepts or rejects himself on a racial basis.

5. It should be noted that although self-identification is a dichotomous variable, the error introduced by using statistical procedures more suitable for continuous variables is not major. See B. J. Winer, *Statistical Principles in Experimental Design* (New York, 1962), pp. 138–139.

6. Two self-identifications were consideed "correct" for the purpose of minimizing any purely random factors in self-classification. If a child identifies himself accurately twice, then it is more likely that he is aware of what he is doing. For each significant result presented, I analyzed frequencies for the "double misidentifiers" to see if type of misidentification helped to interpret the findings.

7. My results for Negroes are lower than the Clarks'. They found that approximately six out of ten black children correctly identified themselves on the dolls test. However, I used a more stringent measure of self-identification than they did, since they only had one question on self-identification while I had two. My technique also allowed more room for a fantasy or wish-fulfillment response.

8. Morland also finds that among blacks, identification with their own race tended to decrease as ability to recognize race increased. See Kenneth Morland, "Racial Self-Identification: A Study of Nursery School Children," *American Catholic Sociological Review*, 24 (fall 1963), 231–242.

9. Although in each category white correct self-identification is higher than it is among blacks, it is still relatively low. Part of this result, as already suggested, is due to hair color. The salience questions measured sex v. color and dress v. color salience, but no question was included which indicated the relative importance of hair v. skin color. Because the white dolls had blond and the Negroes dark hair, white blonds identified more correctly than white brunettes, even in the high-salience category. Although hair color of the white children affects the self-identification results, it does not affect the attitude data to any appreciable extent.

10. Color terms are used here because they constitute the most directly inter-
pretable of all the awareness indices and indicate the most sophisticated knowledge on the part of the child. These results are not affected by covariance for age.

11. Among whites with high own-race preference, thirty-five children identified correctly and nine incorrectly. Of whites with low own-race preference, one
identified correctly and six incorrectly. Of those Negroes with high own-race
preference, all eleven identified correctly. For Negroes with low own-race preference, however, twelve identified correctly and thirty-eight misclassified themselves. See note to Table 6 and to tabulations on comments about cleanliness and
type of free play in Chapter 4 for confirmation of this finding.

12. Race and class effect, controlling for age and sex:

Negro middle	= 1.75	1 = correct
Negro working	= 1.59	2 = incorrect
Negro ADC	= 1.64	

For complete means, see Table 16. This result also holds when we control for
skin color; census category data also show the ADC closer to working-class than
to white-collar groups.

13. See Thomas Pettigrew, "Social Evaluation Theory: Covergences and Applications," *Nebraska Symposium on Motivation*, 15 (1967), 241–311.

14. Everett Stonequist, *The Marginal Man* (New York, 1937). Aaron Antonov-
sky, "Towards a Refinement of the 'Marginal Man' Concept," *Social Forces*, 35
(October 1956), 57–62. H. F. Dickie-Clark, "The Marginal Situation: A Contribu-
tion to Marginality Theory," *Social Forces*, 44 (March 1966), 363–370.

15. Erik Erikson, *Identity: Youth and Crisis* (New York, 1968), pp. 174–76.

16. *Ibid.*, p. 303.

17. Lee Rainwater, "Crucible of Identity: The Negro Lower Class Family,"
Daedalus, Winter 1966, pp. 172–216.

18. Morland also finds no differences in self-identification by social class for
whites. See Morland, "Racial Self-Identification," pp. 231–242.

19. Means for white males on self-identification index:

School	Middle	Working	ADC	
Segregated	1.56	1.36	1.50	1 = correct
Desegregated	1.47	1.60	1.80	2 = incorrect

20. Because ADC and working-class white children differ by sex on self-
identification in schools where blacks are in the majority, the higher rate of white
male misidentification in these settings cannot be explained by possible subtle
class differences between the youngsters in the segregated and the desegregated
sample.

21. I analyzed the self-identification results for blacks to see if racial composition of the classroom had any effects. The results showed no consistent patterns. This area merits further investigation.

22. Means for segregated and desegregated blacks on self-identification index:

Class	Segregated	Desegregated	
Middle	1.82	1.66	1 = correct
Working	1.74	1.56	2 = incorrect
ADC	1.45	1.66	

The "negative identity" explanation suggested for ADC children in the section on social class does not seem to be operative in a desegregated environment.

23. On the self-identification index, however, if the skin color data are analyzed in terms of four categories, there were no differences in correctness of identification between "light-medium" and the very light Negro children.

24. This was particularly true at the time of this study, before "Afro" hair styles became fashionable.

25. William Grier and Price Cobbs, *Black Rage* (New York, 1968), p. 47.

26. Joseph Boskin, "Good-by, Mr. Bones," *New York Times Magazine,* May 1, 1966, p. 31. Although in the complete version of this anecdote the story is given a southern setting, it is obviously applicable to the North as well.

27. Total race and sex means, controlling for age and class:

> White male = 1.64
> White female = 1.38   1 = correct self-identification
> Negro male = 1.62   2 = incorrect self-identification
> Negro female = 1.72

Note that the black males still identify highly inaccurately, which indicates that many Negro boys also have negative group identity.

28. Total sex effect, controlling for age, race, and class:

> Male = 1.31   1 = color
> Female = 1.45   2 = dress and sex

29. Black girls make fewer comments about color than white girls do, but avoidance of color comments may be a defensive reaction for blacks. See note 5, Chapter 4.

30. Total race and sex effect, controlling for age and class:

> White males = 1.50   Negro males = 1.64   1 = correct terms
> White females = 1.66   Negro females = 1.56   2 = incorrect terms

Again, it is important to report trends in this area; see note 2, Chapter 5.

31. Marion Radke, Jean Sutherland, and Pearl Rosenberg, "Racial Attitudes of Children," *Sociometry,* 13 (1950), 164.

32. The fact that white boys misidentify more frequently than do white girls does not necessarily mean that there is a high rate of self-rejection on a racial basis. We have already suggested that misidentification does not seem to measure negative group identity for most white youngsters. (Some of the white boys do, however, seem to have negative racial self-concepts. See section on contact.)

33. Graham Vaughan finds that by age four, the majority of white children classify themselves correctly. The fact that I do not find this result may be due to the importance of hair color in self-identification of young white children. The white dolls in this study all had blond hair. See Vaughan, "Concept Formation and Developing Ethnic Awareness," *Journal of Genetic Psychology,* 103 (1963), 93–103.

34. See Pettigrew, "Social Evaluation Theory." By this theory, light-skinned Negro children in desegregated schools should also exhibit less correct self-identification. The fact that the middle- and working-class black children in this group do not do so qualifies my general hypothesis.

35. I cannot judge whether differences between middle- and working-class blacks in desegregated and segregated schools fit with my general hypothesis. These two groups identify more accurately in segregated classrooms; however, I have no additional data which show whether this higher rate of self-classification actually indicates more positive racial self-concepts.

7   The Personal Dimension of Self-Esteem

1. Erikson, for instance, has suggested the distinction between "individual" identity and "communal" identities; see *Identity: Youth and Crisis* (New York, 1968), p. 301. A comparison of theories concerning the effect of prejudice on the personality of blacks also suggests that this distinction is valid (see Chapter 9). It is important to note that by personal identity, I do not mean identity in the true psychoanalytic sense of adult ego identity; I refer rather to self-conception in terms of feelings of adequacy and personal worth.

2. For instance, see Martin Grossack, "Group Belongingness among Negroes," in *Mental Health and Segregation,* ed. Martin Grossack (New York, 1963), pp. 18–29. See also, Donald Noel, "Group Identification among Negroes: An Empirical Analysis," *Journal of Social Issues,* 20 (1964), 71–84; Kurt Lewin, "Psychosocial Problems of a Minority Group," *Character and Personality,* 3 (1935), 175–187; Erik Erikson, *Childhood and Society* (New York, 1963).

3. Charles Blum, "The Blacky Pictures with Children," in *Projective Tech-*

niques with Children, ed. Albert Rabin and Mary Haworth (New York, 1960), pp. 95–104.

4. C. E. Osgood, G. Suci, and P. Tannenbaum, *The Measurement of Meaning,* (Urbana, Ill., 1957).

5. Emmanuel Hammer, "H-T-P Drawings as a Projective Technique with Children," *Projective Techniques with Children,* pp. 258–273.

6. Karen Machover, *Personality Projection in the Drawing of the Human Figure* (Springfield, Ill., 1949). F. L. Goodenough, *Measurement of Intelligence by Drawings* (Yonkers, N.Y., 1926).

7. Dale Harris, *Children's Drawings as Measures of Intellectual Maturity* (New York, 1963), p. 225

8. See Elizabeth Koppitz, *Psychological Evaluation of Children's Human Figure Drawings* (New York, 1968).

9. Wayne Dennis, *Group Values through Children's Drawings* (New York, 1966).

10. Robert Coles, *Children of Crisis* (Boston, 1967), p. 45.

11. Martin Deutsch and Bert Brown, "Social Influences in Negro-White Intelligence Differences," *Journal of Social Issues,* 20 (1964), 26.

12. Harris, *Children's Drawings,* p. 226.

13. All Negroes were tested by a white interviewer. There was no statistically significant difference in picture-drawing scores between the twelve Negroes in the segregated and the twenty-six in the integrated schools, so they have been included together. Since this test is more threatening than the attitude test, the effect of bias in regard to the interviewer is unknown. But on the basis of an analysis of many drawings made by the same children, Coles says that "what I found significant and revealing in the drawings of black children has a consistency and persistence quite its own," regardless of the fact that he is white (see *Children of Crisis,* p. 63).

14. Koppitz uses the presence of body parts as a developmental index; however, according to her norms, all the body parts I used in my scoring scheme are "expected," "common," or "not unusual" at this age level. She does suggest that the absence of a few of the major facial features or body parts is clinically significant at age five (i.e., head, body, legs, mouth, nose, eyes). On most of these features, there are either class trends for my sample or a difference between the middle and working class on one hand and the ADC group on the other. See Koppitz, *Psychological Evaluation,* pp. 12–17, 35–37.

15. Koppitz (*ibid.,* p. 59) suggests that a tiny figure is an emotional indicator

and shows feelings of inadequacy. Dennis, in his study of twelve- and thirteen-year-olds, finds Negro boys have lower frequencies of smiles in drawings than white boys do (Dennis, *Group Values,* p. 110).

16. Although this coding method is certainly not an ideal means of checking reliability, the purpose here was only to see whether the scheme suggested hypotheses. Any systematic attempt to investigate the true reliability of this test must use several coders working separately. The scoring scheme is so simple, however, that the reliability probably would be high. See Appendix 4.

17. For instance, there is a high intercorrelation between the three items eyes, nose, and mouth. The only two items which correlated poorly with the rest of the scale were size of drawing and presence of ears. In Koppitz' scheme, however, only 25 to 29 percent of five-year-olds included ears in their human portraits, so the lack of a correlation between ears and the body parts more commonly drawn at this age level is not surprising. See Koppitz, *Psychological Evaluation,* pp. 12 and 16.

18. *For Whites:* Correlations between particular story themes and overall raw score on pictures: Daily description dull= −.46; personal efficacy= +.64; powerlessness= −.61; daily description lively= +.77. Correlation between story themes: personal efficacy and daily description lively=+.51; personal efficacy and powerlessness= −.78. Correlation between story themes and individual self-portrait items: powerlessness and placement of figure on page= −.86; personal efficacy and presence of feet= +.59, arms= +.46.

19. *For Negroes:* Correlation within stories: personal efficacy and positive self-description= +.40; personal efficacy and lively daily description= +.35; personal efficacy and powerlessness= −.58. Correlation between stories and pictures: Positive self-description and facial expression=+.36; personal efficacy and arms= +.46.

20. R. F. Bodwin and M. Bruck, "The Adaptation and Validation of the Draw-a-Person Test as a Measure of Self-Concept," *Journal of Clinical Psychology,* 16 (1960), 427–429.

21. For every child, the number of items present in the portrait was added and each picture was assigned a rating on personal self-esteem. The frequency analysis showed that the pictures fell into high and low categories. In an item-by-item analysis, whites were also consistently higher than Negroes on most of the elements in the personal self-esteem index. It should be noted that incorrect racial self-identification for whites is not a clear measure of poor group identity, since many white children misidentified on the basis of hair color (see Chapter 6).

22. Suzanne Keller, "The Social World of the Urban Slum Child," *American Journal of Orthopsychiatry,* 33 (1963), 827. Martin Deutsch, "Minority Group and Class Status as Related to Social and Personality Factors in Scholastic Achievement," in *Mental Health and Segregation,* ed. Martin Grossack, pp. 64–75.

23. In interviews these same black children showed a healthy sense of self-esteem. The authors explain this discrepancy in terms of the situational context in which behavior occurs. They feel that many of the psychological problems showing up on the MMPI will not be externalized in these children's behavior as long as they stay in a relatively untaxing segregated social situation. But if they moved to more complex and taxing environments, like a northern urban locale, overt signs of inner personality problems might be more common. See Earl Baughman and Grant Dahlstrom, *Negro and White Children: A Psychological Study in the Rural South* (New York, 1968).

24. The Negro self-portraits contain either no hint of the child's race (brown paper in infrequently chosen, and figure outlines are only occasionally drawn in brown crayon) or they manifest an exaggeration of racial characteristics. This phenomenon also appears among some of the children Coles studied.

25. James Coleman et al., *Equality of Educational Opportunity* (Washington, D.C., 1966), p. 289.

26. It should be noted that the correctness of self-identification by race for this subpopulation is about the same as that for the entire population (30 percent of the Negroes and 55 percent of the whites identify correctly on a racial basis).

27. These racial differences are not due to IQ differences. Once class is con-, trolled the IQ's of Negro and white first graders do not differ significantly. See Martin Deutsch, *The Disadvantaged Child* (New York, 1967), pp. 326–329. My analysis of stories also suggests that emotional factors are involved in these racial differences. However, the effect of environment on IQ should be carefully investigated in further use of this test.

28. Deutsch, *Ibid.,* p. 106.

29. There is no difference in picture scores by sex, controlling for class and race, but boys seem more likely to include features like arms and legs in the drawings and girls emphasize items like hair and eyebrows more than boys do. These characteristics are related to sex-role norms. Because of recent stress on the problems of the lower-class black male, it is interesting that a sex difference does not appear for black children. This should be investigated further with a larger sample.

30. These social class results on story categories may of course be contaminated

by class-related verbal skills; however, some of the working-class and ADC five-year-old children did tell long and elaborate stories. In these stories, themes such as powerlessness appeared more frequently and lively daily descriptions less often than they did in the middle-class productions. But the relationship between verbal skills, social class, and story content should be carefully investigated in further use of this test.

31. Paul Mussen, "Differences between the TAT Responses of Negro and White Boys," *Journal of Consulting Psychology,* 17 (1953), 373–376. David Palermo, "Racial Comparisons and Additional Normative Data on the Children's Manifest Anxiety Scale," *Child Development,* 30 (1959), 53–57.

32. See Rainwater, "Crucible of Identity: The Negro Lower-Class Family," *Daedalus,* Winter 1966, pp. 172–216. Also, Elliot LieBow, *Tally's Corner* (Boston, 1967).

33. There is no clear class trend in this subsample on the "racial concept" part of self-esteem. The working class ranks slightly below the middle class in racial self-identification and slightly above in pro-Negro attitudes. In Chapter 6, we saw that self-identification and attitudes were related in a complex fashion not only to class but also to sex, contact, and other factors. Because of the small size of the Negro subsample in each social class, it is not possible to control for all these other relevant effects simultaneously. Yet in the complete sample we saw that, holding these other factors constant, racial self-identification and attitudes were related to class in the predicted direction.

8   Actual Playmate Choice in a
Desegregated Setting

1. Harold and Nancy Stevenson, "Social Interaction in an Interracial Nursery School," *Genetic Psychology Monographs,* 61 (1960), 37–75.

2. Mary Ellen Goodman, *Race Awareness in Young Children* (New York, 1964), pp. 311–313.

3. Paul Mussen, "Reliability and Validity of Horowitz Faces Test," *Journal of Abnormal and Social Psychology,* 45 (1950), 504–506.

4. Joan H. Criswell, "A Sociometric Study of Race Cleavage in the Classroom," *Archives of Psychology,* 1939, No. 235.

5. Joseph Rosner, "When White Children Are in the Minority," *Journal of Educational Sociology,* 28 (October 1954), 69–72.

6. Bernard Kutner, Carol Wilkins, and Penny Yarrow, "Verbal Attitudes and

Overt Behavior Involving Racial Prejudice," *Journal of Abnormal and Social Psychology,* 47 (July 1952), 649–652. R. T. LaPiere, "Attitudes v. Actions," *Social Forces* 13 (December 1934), 230–237.

7. Robin Williams, *Strangers Next Door,* (Englewood Cliffs, N.J., 1964), pp. 143–222.

8. On the attitude index, 1=high and 2=low white doll choice. The percentage of actual white playmates selected ranged from 0 to 100 for each child. Therefore, a positive correlation means that the higher the white doll choice, the lower the white playmate choice. The actual correlations are: School A: Negroes (−.05); whites (+.02); School B: whites (+.87); Negroes (−.34). The correlation for School B Negroes is not statistically significant.

9. Evelyn Helgerson, "The Relative Significance of Race, Sex, and Facial Expression in Choice of Playmate by the Pre-school Child," *Journal of Negro Education,* 12 (1943), 612–622.

10. Children's names are all fictional.

11. Gordon Allport suggests that the full support of authority figures for integration is one of the important conditions under which contact leads to attitude change. See *Nature of Prejudice* (New York, 1958), p. 267.

9   Implications for Theory

1. Gordon Allport, *The Nature of Prejudice* (Garden City, N.Y., 1958), pp. 292–295.

2. Because of the recent stress on black pride, many black children now or in the future may not have this type of reaction. The pre-generalized phase will still exist, but the content of these incipient attitudes will be reversed: the Negro youngster will have vague positive feelings about brown.

3. Thomas Pettigrew, *Profile of the Negro American* (Princeton, N.J., 1964), pp. 3–5.

4. Alexis deTocqueville, *American Institutions and Their Influence* (New York, 1851), p. 338.

5. Abram Kardiner and Lionel Ovesey, *The Mark of Oppression* (New York, 1962), p. 297.

6. *Ibid.,* p. 304.

7. Franklin Frazier, *Black Bourgeoisie* (New York, 1962), p. 176.

8. *Ibid.,* p. 141.

9. William Grier and Price Cobbs, *Black Rage* (New York, 1968), pp. 198–199.

10. *Ibid.,* p. 38.

11. Erik Erikson, "The Concept of Identity in Race Relations: Notes and Queries," *Daedalus,* Winter 1966, p. 155.

12. Ralph Ellison, *Shadow and Act* (New York, 1966), pp. 301, p. 119.

13. Robert Coles, "It's the Same But Its Different," *Daedalus,* Fall 1965, pp. 1114, 1122.

14. Stokely Carmichael and Charles Hamilton, *Black Power: The Politics of Liberation in America* (New York, 1967), pp. 31, 37. Similar passages are found in the works of Eldridge Cleaver and Malcolm X.

15. Eldridge Cleaver, *Soul on Ice* (New York, 1968), pp. 206–207.

16. Martin Grossack, "Group Belongingness among Negroes," *Mental Health and Segregation,* ed. Martin Grossack (New York, 1963), pp. 18–33.

17. Pettigrew, *Profile of the Negro American,* p. 27.

18. Robert Johnson, "Negro Reactions to Minority Group Status," *American Minorities,* ed. Milton Barron (New York, 1957). Johnson's continua are hostility/friendliness to whites; self-hatred/race pride; lassitude/militance; avoidance/whiteward mobility; insulation/integration.

19. Donald Noel, "Group Identification among Negroes: an Empirical Analysis," *Journal of Social Issues,* 20 (April 1964), 71–84. Gary Marx, *Protest and Prejudice* (New York, 1967) pp. 90, 199.

20. William McCord, John Howard, Bernard Friedberg, and Edwin Harwood, *Life Styles in the Black Ghetto* (New York, 1969). The life styles they describe are the stoic, the defeated, the exploiter, the achiever, the rebel without a cause, the activist, and the revolutionary.

21. Allison Davis and John Dollard, *Children of Bondage* (New York, 1940). Viola Bernard, "Psychoanalysis and Members of Minority Groups," *Journal of the American Psychoanalytic Association* 2 (1953), 256–267. John Rohrer and Munro Edmundson, in their follow-up to the Davis and Dollard study, also give secondary importance to group identity in the formation of ego structure. Family and socialization patterns are given primary importance in the development of personality, and racial self-concept is considered to be more or less determined by the particular family constellations described. See Rohrer and Edmundson, *The Eighth Generation Grows Up* (New York, 1960).

22. Margaret Brenman, "Urban Lower Class Negro Girls," in *Mental Health and Segregation,* p. 90. Robert Kleiner and Seymour Parker, "Status Position, Mobility, and Ethnic Identification of the Negro," *Journal of Social Issues* 20 (April 1964), 85–102.

23. Elliot LieBow, *Tally's Corner* (Boston, 1967). David Schultz, *Coming up Black* (Englewood Cliffs, N.J., 1969). Daniel Moynihan, *The Negro Family: The Case for National Action* (Washington, D.C., 1965).

24. Kardiner and Ovesey, *Mark of Oppression,* p. 119.

25. Martin Grossack, Donald Noel, Kurt Lewin, and Erik Erikson, among others, also suggest that these two dimensions are related.

26. Everett Stonequist, *Marginal Man* (New York, 1937), p. 8.

27. St. Clair Drake, "The Social and Economic Status of the Negro in the U.S.," *Daedalus,* Fall 1965, pp. 781–782.

28. Thomas Pettigrew, "Social Evaluation Theory: Convergences and Applications," *Nebraska Symposium on Motivation,* 15 (1967), 277.

29. As a result of these factors, the middle-class parent may also put pressure on his children to be a living refutation of Negro stereotypes; this is one means by which his racial attitudes may be transmitted to the child. See Kenneth Clark, *Prejudice and Your Child* (Boston, 1963), p. 114.

30. Pettigrew, *Profile of the Negro American,* p. 22.

31. Pettigrew, "Social Evaluation Theory," pp. 274–302.

32. See, for instance, Gary Marx, *Protest and Prejudice* and William Brink and Louis Harris, *The Negro Revolution in America* (New York, 1964).

33. Marx, *Protest and Prejudice,* and Brink and Harris, *Negro Revolution.*

34. The working-class and lower-class distinctions used in this discussion do not correspond exactly to the working-class and ADC division by which I have analyzed my data. In this chapter my distinction is based on the Miller and Reissman criteria of steady occupational income and family stability: the working class has these attitudes and the lower-class does not. See S. M. Miller and Frank Reissman, *Social Class and Social Policy* (New York, 1968), pp. 35–51. The ADC group is one key segment of the lower class and is most subject to the pressures to be described shortly. However, that group of unskilled laborers who have low and irregular incomes and family instability also are in the "lower-class" category described here. I have had to include this segment in the working-class group because I was unable to acquire the necessary data on income and family patterns with which to divide the sample into more refined categories than purely occupational ones. This probably reduces class differences in the results.

35. Drake, "Social and Economic Status," p. 778.

36. Morton Beiser, "Poverty, Social Disintegration, and Personality," *Journal of Social Issues,* 21 (January 1965), 56–78.

37. LieBow, *Tally's Corner.*

38. *Trends in Social and Economic Conditions in Metropolitan Areas, Current Population Reports,* 27 (February 1969), 13–15.

39. Roger Burton and John Whiting, "The Absent Father: Effects on the Developing Child," paper read at American Psychological Association Convention in Chicago, September 1960.

40. Roy D'Andrade, *Father Absence and Cross-Sex Identification,* unpub. diss., Harvard University, 1962.

41. Pettigrew, *Profile of the Negro American,* p. 20.

42. Daniel Moynihan, *The Negro Family: Case for National Action.*

43. David Schultz, *Coming up Black.* Elliot LieBow, *Tally's Corner.*

44. Schultz, *Coming up Black,* p. 41.

45. *Ibid.,* p. 175.

46. Lee Rainwater, "Crucible of Identity: The Negro Lower-Class Family," *Daedalus,* Winter 1966, pp. 203–204.

47. Andrew Billingsley, *Black Families in White America* (Englewood Cliffs, N.J., 1968), p. 33. Also Hylan Lewis, "Child Rearing among Low Income Families," *Poverty in America,* ed. Ferman, Kornbluh, and Haber (Ann Arbor, Mich., 1968), pp. 433–443, and Schultz, *Coming up Black.*

48. McCord, *Life Styles in the Black Ghetto,* p. 55.

49. Rainwater, "Crucible of Identity," p. 205.

50. Erikson suggests that it is often easier to derive a sense of identity by total identification with what one is least supposed to be rather than to struggle for a sense of reality in acceptable roles which are unattainable. See Erikson, *Identity: Youth and Crisis* (New York, 1968), p. 176. LieBow's interpretation of black lower-class street-corner men comes close to this "negative identity" description. This, of course, raises the issue of whether these behavior patterns are to be interpreted as a "lower-class cultural tradition" or as a reaction to failure. Probably some part of both is involved. See Ulf Hannerz, "The Roots of Black Manhood," *Trans-action,* 6 (October 1969), 12–21.

51. David Ausubel, "Ego Development among Segregated Negro Children," in *Mental Health and Segregation,* pp. 33–40.

52. Robert Coles, *Children of Crisis* (Boston, 1966), p. 323.

53. For instance, a hostile contact situation might have either negative or positive effects on self-concept. The latter outcome might depend on such factors as the presence of supportive black groups and/or the motivation to remain in the contact situation in order to create institutional change.

10 Implications for Research

1. "Say it Loud — I'm Black and I'm Proud," by James Brown, Golo Publishing Co., used by permission of the publisher.

2. Steven Asher and Vernon Allen, "Racial Preference and Social Comparison Processes," *Journal of Social Issues,* 25 (1969), 157–165.

3. Mary Ellen Goodman, *Race Awareness in Young Children* (New York, 1964).

4. For white children, however, my results are lower than Goodman's on amount of in-group preference. This discrepancy is probably due to the fact that my sample includes more low-awareness white children (segregated youngsters and three-year-olds).

5. Goodman, *Race Awareness,* p. 87.

6. Trager has also found ambivalence toward whites among Negro children, but her subjects were slightly older than those in my sample.

7. Angus Campbell and Howard Schuman, "Racial Attitudes in Fifteen American Cities," *Supplemental Studies for the National Advisory Commission on Civil Disorders* (Washington, D.C., 1968), p. 16. Also see Brink and Harris, *The Negro Revolution* (New York, 1964).

8. Campbell and Schuman, "Racial Attitudes," p. 19.

9. Helen Trager and Marion Radke, "Children's Perception of Social Roles of Negroes and Whites," *Journal of Psychology,* 29 (1950), 3–33. Robert Coles, *Children of Crisis* (Boston, 1967). Trager's study shows that among white children, there is a tendency for perception that blacks are in subordinate roles and hostile attitudes toward blacks to appear together.

10. William McCord, John Howard, Bernard Friedberg, and Edwin Harwood, *Life Styles in the Black Ghetto* (New York, 1969), p. 88.

11. Campbell and Schuman, "Racial Attitudes," p. 17.

12. This conclusion assumes that today's high school and college students will not become significantly more conservative within the next several years, and it also assumes that black pride will continue to grow in the black community. The projection of current trends is, of course, risky, since unforeseen events can alter the direction of racial change.

13. Andrew Billingsley, *Black Families in White America* (Englewood Cliffs, N. J., 1968), pp. 11–13. The Campbell and Schuman data confirm this statement. See "Racial Attitudes," p. 50.

14. By lower class I mean what Miller and Reissman call the "unstable poor."

Individuals in this group either have an irregular income or are on welfare; in addition they are characterized by familial instability. See Miller and Reissman, *Social Class and Social Policy* (New York, 1968), pp. 35–49. The criteria of security and source of income and familial stability are probably more valid than occupation alone for differentiating the "lower class" from the working class. Some unskilled laborers are closer to the semiskilled and skilled occupations in terms of their family and economic patterns and others are closer to the welfare group on these dimensions. I was unable to make this distinction between these two groups of unskilled laborers in my data because of lack of relevant information. I probably thus inadvertently classified some of the latter group of unskilled laborers' children as working class when they in fact were closer in life style to the welfare group.

15. Campbell and Schuman, "Racial Attitudes," p. 62.

16. John Harding, Marilyn Schwartzapel, and Erna Benjamin, "Declining Prejudice Among New York City School Children," unpublished ms.

17. Kenneth and Mamie Clark, "Racial Identification and Preference in Negro Children," *Readings in Social Psychology,* ed. Maccoby, Newcomb, and Hartley (New York, 1958), pp. 602–611.

18. One study does show that programs aimed at creating racial tolerance have some effect. See Helen Trager and Marion Yarrow, *They Learn What They Live* (New York, 1952).

19. W. Stephenson, *Studies of Behavior: The Q-Sort Technique and Its Methodology* (Chicago, 1953).

11 Implications for Public Policy

1. Clark's *Prejudice and Your Child* is a summary and revision of the manuscript which was prepared for the Mid-Century White House Conference.

2. The Clarks find that southern children have greater brown preference than do northern youngsters. Clark's interpretation of this evidence, based on the children's actual comments and reactions during the test, is somewhat similar to my interpretation of the ADC results in terms of negative identity. The Clarks' northern sample exhibited more reactions of evasion to the questions. This may be due to the fact that the northern youngsters have more opportunity for social comparison with whites, which may have complex effects on attitudes and self-esteem. See Pettigrew, "Social Evaluation Theory: Convergences and Applications," *Nebraska Symposium on Motivation,* 15 (1967), 241–318.

3. Part Three of *Prejudice and Your Child* contains not only the relevant legal documents but also an important discussion of the part played by social science and by Clark himself in the 1954 Supreme Court decisions. I have based my conclusions in this section on these documents and the revised version of the White House manuscript; the original version of the manuscript is unavailable.

4. Clairette Armstrong and A. James Gregor, "Integrated Schools and Negro Character Development," *Psychiatry*, 27 (1964), 69–72.

5. Steven Asher and Vernon Allen, "Racial Preference and Social Comparison Processes," *Journal of Social Issues*, 25 (1969), 157–166.

6. It is important to note that there is no statistically significant difference in self-identification between Negro children in desegregated schools that are less than 50 percent black and those that are more than 50 percent black.

7. *Racial Isolation in the Public Schools*, U.S. Commission on Civil Rights (Washington, D.C., 1967), pp. 157–158.

8. See, for instance, Gordon Allport, *Nature of Prejudice* (New York, 1958), pp. 250–270, and Robin Williams, *Strangers Next Door* (Englewood Cliffs, N.J., 1964), pp. 143–222.

9. Mark Chesler, Simon Wittes, and Norma Radin, "What Happens When Northern Schools Desegregate?", *American Education*, June 1968, pp. 2–4.

10. James Teele, Ellen Jackson, and Clara Mayo, "Family Experiences in Operation Exodus," Community Mental Health Journal Monograph no. 3 (New York, 1967).

11. James Coleman et al., *Equality of Educational Opportunity* (Washington, D.C., 1966), p. 332. The achievement test scores of Negro children in classes with a white majority also show positive effects of interracial schooling in the early grades. The quality of integration is not controlled in these findings.

12. I stress again that the ADC black youngsters deserve particularly careful investigation, because this is the only group of black children who may be negatively affected by "desegregation."

13. This, of course, is true at any age level, as several studies have demonstrated. See, for instance, Chesler, Radin, and Wittes, "What Happens When Northern Schools Desegregate?"

14. Martin Deutsch, *The Disadvantaged Child* (New York, 1967), p. 291.

15. The use of nonprofessional aides drawn from the children's neighborhood is one way of providing a more balanced perspective in a classroom with lower-class children.

16. It is interesting that although many of the other factors listed in this

section were virtually ignored, brown dolls were available in most of the desegregated classrooms.

17. The United States Civil Rights' Commission's re-analysis of the Coleman data is not totally applicable to preschool-age children, but it does at least demonstrate that lower-class children may be benefited by contact with middle-class children in terms of scholastic achievement. (The possibility of positive effects on cognitive development of black children may make integration important even if a middle-class white, lower-class black preschool classroom results; but in this case, special attention must be paid to creating a setting conducive to positive attitude development.) These data suggest that class heterogeneity within each race may well be the most preferable alternative in a preschool situation; however, the effects of race and class composition on attitudes as well as on cognitive development must be carefully studied for this age group.

18. Deutsch, *The Disadvantaged Child.* He argues that early cognitive training helps obviate the low personal self-esteem which is created by academic failure in the early grades.

19. Angus Campbell and Howard Schuman, "Racial Attitudes in Fifteen American Cities," *Supplemental Studies for the National Advisory Commission on Civil Disorders* (Washington, D.C., 1968), pp. 1–68.

20. Stokely Carmichael and Charles V. Hamilton, *Black Power: the Politics of Liberation in America* (New York, 1967), p. 37.

21. Pettigrew, "Social Evaluation Theory."

22. Campbell and Schuman, "Racial Attitudes," pp. 19–21.

Bibliography

Adorno, T. W., Else Frenkel-Brunswik, Daniel J. Levinson, and R. Nevitt Sanford. *The Authoritarian Personality.* New York: Harper Brothers, 1950.

Allport, Gordon. *The Nature of Prejudice.* Garden City, N.Y.: Doubleday Anchor Books, 1958.

Ammons, R. B. "Reactions in a Projective Doll Play Interview of White Males Two to Six Years Old to Differences in Skin Color and Facial Features," *Journal of Genetic Psychology,* 76 (1950), 323–341.

Armstrong, Clairette, and A. James Gregor. "Integrated Schools and Negro Character Development," *Psychiatry,* 27 (February 1964), 69–72.

Asher, Steven, and Vernon Allen. "Racial Preference and Social Comparison Processes," *Journal of Social Issues,* 25 (1969), 157–166.

Ausubel, David. "Ego Development among Segregated Negro Children." In *Mental Health and Segregation.* Ed. Martin Grossack. New York: Springer Publishing Company, 1963, pp. 33–40.

Axline, Virginia. "Play Therapy and Race Conflict in Young Children," *Journal of Abnormal and Social Psychology,* 43 (1948), 300–310.

Babchuk, N., and Paul McDaniel. "Negro Conceptions of White People in a Northeastern City," *Phylon,* 21 (1960), 7–19.

Baldwin, James. "Letter from a Region in My Mind," *New Yorker,* Nov. 17, 1962, pp. 59–144.

Baughman, Earl, and Grant Dahlstrom. *Negro and White Children: A Psychological Study in the Rural South.* New York: Academic Press, 1968.

Bayton, James A. "The Racial Stereotypes of Negro College Students," *Journal of Abnormal and Social Psychology,* 36 (January 1941), 97–103.

Beiser, Morton. "Poverty, Social Disintegration, and Personality," *Journal of Social Issues,* 21 (January 1965), 56–78.

Bernard, Viola. "Psychoanalysis and Members of Minority Groups," *Journal of the American Psychoanalytic Association,* 2 (1953), 256–267.

Billingsley, Andrew. *Black Families in White America.* Englewood Cliffs, N.J.: Prentice-Hall, 1968.

Bird, Charles, Elio Monachesi, and Harvey Burdick. "Infiltration and the Attitudes of White and Negro Parents and Children," *Journal of Abnormal and Social Psychology,* 47 (July 1952), 688–699.

———— "Studies of Group Tensions: III. The Effect of Parental Discouragement of Play Activities upon the Attitudes of White Children toward Negroes," *Child Development,* 23 (December 1952), 295–306.

Blake, Robert, and Wayne Dennis. "Development of Stereotypes Concerning the

Negro," *Journal of Abnormal and Social Psychology,* 38 (1943), 525–531.

Bodwin, R. F., and M. Bruck. "The Adaptation and Validation of the Draw-A-Person Test as a Measure of Self-Concept," *Journal of Clinical Psychology,* 16 (1960), 427–429.

Brenman, Margaret. "Urban Lower Class Negro Girls." In *Mental Health and Segregation.* Ed. Martin Grossack. New York: Springer Publishing Company, 1963, pp. 83–108.

Brink, William, and Louis Harris. *Black and White.* New York: Simon and Schuster, 1967.

—— *The Negro Revolution in America.* New York: Simon and Schuster, 1964.

Brody, Eugene. "Color and Identity Conflict in Young Boys: Observations of Negro Mothers and Sons in Urban Baltimore," *Psychiatry,* 2 (May 1963), 188–201.

Brown, Claude. *Manchild in the Promised Land.* New York: Macmillan, 1965.

Burgess, Elaine. "Poverty and Dependency: Some Selected Characteristics," *Journal of Social Issues,* 21 (January 1965), 83–85.

Burton, Roger, and John Whiting. "The Absent Father. Effects on the Developing Child." Paper read at the Annual Meeting of the American Psychological Association in Chicago, September 1960.

Campbell, Angus, and Howard Schuman. "Racial Attitudes in Fifteen American Cities." In *Supplemental Studies for the National Advisory Commission on Civil Disorders.* Washington, D.C.: U.S. Government Printing Office, 1968, pp. 1–68.

Carmichael, Stokely, and Charles V. Hamilton. *Black Power: The Politics of Liberation in America.* New York: Vintage Books, 1967.

Chesler, Mark, Simon Wittes, and Norma Radin. "What Happens When Northern Schools Desegregate?," *American Education,* June 1968, pp. 2–4.

Children of Cardozo Tell It Like It Is. Cambridge, Mass.: Education Development Center, 1968.

Cleaver, Eldridge. *Soul on Ice.* New York: McGraw-Hill, 1968.

Clark, Kenneth. *Prejudice and Your Child.* Boston: Beacon Press, 1955; 2nd ed. enl., 1963.

—— and Mamie Clark. "The Development of Consciousness of Self and the Emergence of Racial Identity in Negro Preschool Children," *Journal of Social Psychology,* 10 (1939), 591–599.

—— "Emotional Factors in Racial Identification and Preference in Negro Children." In *Mental Health and Segregation.* Ed. Martin Grossack. New York:

Springer Publishing Company, 1963, pp. 53–63.

———— "Racial Identification and Preference in Negro Children." In *Readings in Social Psychology.* Ed. Eleanore Maccoby, T. Newcomb, and E. Hartley. New York: Henry Holt and Company, 1958, pp. 602–611.

———— "Segregation as a Factor in the Racial Identification of Negro Pre-School Children," *Journal of Experimental Education,* 8 (1939), 161–163.

———— "Skin Color as a Factor in Racial Identification of Negro Pre-school Children," *Journal of Social Psychology,* 11 (1940), 159–169.

Coleman, James S., Ernest Campbell, Carol Hobson, James McPartland, Alexander Mood, Frederic Weinfeld, and Robert York. *Equality of Educational Opportunity.* Washington, D.C.: U.S. Government Printing Office, 1966.

Coles, Robert. *Children of Crisis.* Boston: Little, Brown, 1967.

———— "It's the Same but It's Different," *Daedalus,* Fall 1965, pp. 1107–1132.

Criswell, Joan H. "A Sociometric Study of Race Cleavage in the Classroom," *Archives of Psychology,* 1939, no. 235.

Dai, Bingham. "Problems of Personality Development among Negro Children." In *Personality in Nature, Society, and Culture.* Ed. C. Kluckhohn, H. Murray, and D. Schneider. New York: Alfred A. Knopf, 1959, pp. 545–566.

D'Andrade, Roy. "Father Absence and Cross-Sex Identification," unpub. diss., Harvard University, 1962.

Davis, Allison, and John Dollard. *Children of Bondage.* New York: Harper and Row, 1940.

Dennis, Wayne. *Group Values through Children's Drawings.* New York: John Wiley and Sons, 1966.

Deutsch, Martin, and associates. *The Disadvantaged Child.* New York: Basic Books, 1967.

———— "Minority Group and Class Status as Related to Social and Personality Factors in Scholastic Achievement." In *Mental Health and Segregation.* Ed. Martin Grossack. New York: Springer Publishing Company, 1963, pp. 64–75.

———— "Social Influences in Negro-White Intelligence Differences," *Journal of Social Issues,* 20 (April 1964), 24–35.

Dollard, John. *Caste and Class in a Southern Town.* New York: Doubleday, 1937.

Drake, St. Clair. "Social and Economic Status of the Negro in the U.S.," *Daedalus,* Fall 1965, pp. 771–814.

———— and Horace Cayton. *Black Metropolis,* vols. I and II. New York: Harper and Row, 1962.

Dreger, R., and Kent Miller. "Comparative Psychological Studies of Negroes and

Whites in the United States," *Psychological Bulletin,* 57 (1960), 361–402.

Ellison, Ralph. *Shadow and Act.* New York: New American Library, 1966.

Erikson, Erik. *Childhood and Society.* New York: Norton, 1963.

———— "The Concept of Identity in Race Relations: Notes and Queries," *Daedalus,* Winter 1966, pp. 145–171.

———— *Identity: Youth and Crisis.* New York: Norton, 1968.

———— "Memorandum on Identity and Negro Youth," *Journal of Social Issues,* 20 (October 1964), 29–42.

Evans, Mary C., and Isidor Chein. "The Movie-Story Game: A Projective Test of Interracial Attitudes for Use with Negro and White Children." Paper read at 56th Annual Meeting of the American Psychological Association in Boston, Sept. 8, 1948.

Fanon, Frantz. *Black Skin, White Masks.* New York: Grove Press, 1967.

Frazier, E. Franklin. *Black Bourgeoisie.* New York: Collier Books, 1962.

Freeman, Don. *Corduroy.* New York: Viking Press, 1968.

Frenkel-Brunswik, Else. "A Study of Prejudice in Children," *Human Relations,* 1 (1948), 295–306.

Gesell, Arnold, and Frances Ilg. *The Child from Five to Ten.* New York: Harper Brothers, 1946.

Giddings, Franklin Henry. *Principles of Sociology.* New York: Macmillan Company, 1896.

Goodenough, F. L. *Measurement of Intelligence by Drawings.* Yonkers, N.Y.: World Book Company, 1926.

Goodman, Mary Ellen. "Evidence Concerning the Genesis of Interracial Attitudes," *American Anthropologist,* 48 (1946), 624–630.

———— *Race Awareness in Young Children.* Cambridge, Mass.: Addison-Wesley Press, 1952; 2nd ed. enl., New York: Collier Books, 1964.

Greenwald, H. J., and D. B. Oppenheim. "Reported Magnitude of Self-Misidentification among Negro Children – Artifact?" *Journal of Personality and Social Psychology,* 8 (1968), 49–52.

Grier, William, and Price Cobbs. *Black Rage.* New York: Basic Books, 1968.

Grossack, Martin. "Group Belongingness among Negroes." In *Mental Health and Segregation.* Ed. Martin Grossack. New York: Springer Publishing Company, 1963, pp. 18–33.

Hannerz, Ulf. "The Roots of Black Manhood," *Transaction,* 6 (October 1969), 12–21.

Harding, John, Marilyn Schwartzapel, and Erna Benjamin. "Declining Prejudice among New York City School Children." MS.

Harris, Dale. *Children's Drawings as Measures of Intellectual Maturity.* New York: Harcourt, Brace, and World, 1963.

Helgerson, Evelyn. "The Relative Significance of Race, Sex, and Facial Expression in Choice of Playmates by the Preschool Child," *Journal of Negro Education,* 12 (1943), 617–622.

Horowitz, Eugene. "The Development of Attitude toward the Negro," *Archives of Psychology,* 28 (1936), no. 194.

_____ and Ruth Horowitz. "Development of Social Attitudes in Children," *Sociometry,* 1 (1938), 301–338.

Horowitz, Ruth. "Racial Aspects of Self-Identification in Nursery School Children," *Journal of Psychology,* 7 (1939), 91–99.

Johnson, Robert. "Negro Reactions to Minority Group Status." In *American Minorities.* Ed. Milton Barron. New York: Alfred A. Knopf, 1957, pp. 192–214.

Kagan, Jerome, and Howard Moss. *Birth to Maturity.* New York: John Wiley and Sons, 1962.

Kardiner, Abram, and Lionel Ovesey. *The Mark of Oppression.* New York: Meridian Books, 1962.

Katz, Irwin. "Review of Evidence Relating to the Effects of Desegregation on the Performance of Negroes," *American Psychologist,* 19 (1964), 381–399.

_____ Thomas Henchey, and Harvey Allen. "Effects of Race of Tester, Approval-Disapproval and Need on Negro Children's Learning," *Journal of Personality and Social Psychology,* 8 (1968), 38–42.

_____ James Robinson, Edgar Epps, and Patricia Waly, "The Influence of Race of the Experimenter and Instructions upon the Expression of Hostility by Negro Boys," *Journal of Social Issues,* 20 (April 1964), 54–59.

Keats, Ezra Jack. *The Snowy Day.* New York: Viking Press, 1962.

Keller, Suzanne. "Social World of the Urban Slum Child," *American Journal of Orthopsychiatry,* 33 (1963), 823–831.

Kleiner, Robert, and Seymour Parker. "Status Position, Mobility, and Ethnic Identification of the Negro," *Journal of Social Issues,* 20 (April 1964), 85–102.

Koch, Helen. "The Social Distance between Certain Racial, Nationality, and Skin Pigmentation Groups in Selected Populations of American School Children," *Journal of Genetic Psychology,* 68 (1946), 63–95.

Koppitz, Elizabeth. *Psychological Evaluation of Children's Human Figure Drawings.* New York: Grune and Stratton, 1968.

Krech, David, Richard Crutchfield, and Egerton Ballachey. *Individual in Society.* New York: McGraw-Hill, 1962.

Kutner, Bernard. "Patterns of Mental Functioning Associated with Prejudice in Children," *Psychological Monographs,* 72 (1958), no. 460.

—— Carol Wilkins, and Penny Yarrow. "Verbal Attitudes and Overt Behavior Involving Racial Prejudice," *Journal of Abnormal and Social Psychology,* 47 (1952), 649–652.

Landreth, Catherine, and Elizabeth Platt. "A Problem in Factorial Design: The Development of a Picture and Inset Test for Determining Young Children's Responses to Persons of Different Skin Colors," *Journal of Educational Psychology,* 42 (November 1951), 385–398.

—— and B. C. Johnson. "Young Children's Responses to a Picture and Inset Test Designed to Reveal Reactions to Persons of Different Skin Colors," *Child Development,* 24 (1953), 65–79.

La Piere, Richard. "Attitudes v. Actions," *Social Forces,* 13 (December 1934), 230–237.

Lasker, Bruno. *Race Attitudes in Children.* New York: Henry Holt and Company, 1929.

Levin, Harry, and Elinor Wardwell. "The Research Uses of Doll Play," *Psychological Bulletin,* 59 (January 1962), 27–56.

Lewin, Kurt. "Psycho-sociological Problems of a Minority Group," *Character and Personality,* 3 (1935), 175–187.

—— *Resolving Social Conflicts.* New York: Harper Brothers, 1948.

Lewis, Hylan. "Child Rearing among Low Income Families." In *Poverty in America.* Ed. Louis Ferman, Joyce Kornbluh, and Alan Haber. Ann Arbor, Mich.: University of Michigan Press, 1968, pp. 433–443.

LieBow, Elliot. *Tally's Corner.* Boston: Little, Brown, 1967.

McCord, William, John Howard, Bernard Friedberg, and Edwin Harwood. *Life Styles in the Black Ghetto.* New York: Norton, 1969.

McGovern, Ann. *Black Is Beautiful.* New York: Four Winds Press, 1969.

Machover, Karen. *Personality Projection in the Drawing of the Human Figure.* Springfield, Ill.: Charles C Thomas, 1949.

Malcolm X. *The Autobiography of Malcolm X.* New York: Grove Press, 1965.

Martin, Janet. *Red and Blue.* New York: Platt and Munk, 1965.

Marx, Gary. *Protest and Prejudice.* New York: Harper and Row, 1967.

Meltzer, H. "The Development of Children's Nationality Preferences, Concepts, and Attitudes," *Journal of Psychology,* 11 (1941), 343–358.

_____ "Nationality Preferences and Stereotypes of Colored Children," *Journal of Genetic Psychology,* 54 (1939), 403–424.

Miller, S. M., and Frank Reissman. *Social Class and Social Policy.* New York: Basic Books, 1968.

Morland, Kenneth. "Comparison of Racial Awareness in Northern and Southern Children," *American Journal of Orthopsychiatry,* 36 (1966), 22–32.

_____ "Racial Acceptance and Preference of Nursery School Children in a Southern City," *Merrill-Palmer Quarterly,* 8 (1962), 271–280.

_____ "Racial Recognition by Nursery School Children in Lynchburg, Virginia," *Social Forces,* 37 (December 1958), 132–137.

_____ "Racial Self-Identification: A Study of Nursery School Children," *American Catholic Sociological Review,* 24 (Fall 1963), 231–242.

Moynihan, Daniel. *The Negro Family: The Case for National Action.* Washington, D.C.: U.S. Government Printing Office, 1965.

Mussen, Paul H. "Differences between the TAT Responses of Negro and White Boys," *Journal of Consulting Psychology,* 17 (1953), 373–376.

_____ "The Reliability and Validity of the Horowitz Faces Test," *Journal of Abnormal and Social Psychology,* 45 (July 1950), 504–506.

_____ "Some Personality and Social Factors Related to Changes in Children's Attitudes towards Negroes," *Journal of Abnormal and Social Psychology,* 45 (July 1950), 423–441.

Myrdal, Gunnar. *An American Dilemma.* New York: Harper and Row, 1962.

Nixon, Richard M. "Text of Nixon's Address to the Nation Outlining His Proposals for Welfare Reform," *New York Times,* Aug. 9, 1969, p. 10.

Noel, Donald. "Group Identification among Negroes: An Empirical Analysis," *Journal of Social Issues,* 20 (April 1964), 71–84.

Osgood, C. E., G. Suci, and P. Tannebaum. *The Measurement of Meaning.* Urbana, Ill.: University of Illinois Press, 1957.

Palermo, David. "Racial Comparisons and Additional Normative Data on the Children's Manifest Anxiety Scale," *Child Development,* 30 (March 1959), 53–57.

Parsons, Talcott, and Edward Shils, eds. *Toward a General Theory of Action.* Cambridge, Mass.: Harvard University Press, 1951.

Pettigrew, Thomas. *Profile of the Negro American.* Princeton, N.J.: D. Van Nostrand, 1964.

———— "Social Evaluation Theory: Convergences and Applications," *Nebraska Symposium on Motivation,* 15 (1967), 241–311.

———— Michael Ross, David Armor, and Howard Freeman. "Color Gradation and Attitudes among Middle-Income Negroes," *American Sociological Review,* 31 (1966), 365–374.

Porter, Judith D. R. *Racial Concept Formation in Pre-school Age Children.* unpub. M.A. diss., Cornell University, 1963.

Racial Isolation in the Public Schools, vol. I. U.S. Commission on Civil Rights. Washington, D.C.: U.S. Government Printing Office, 1967.

Radke, Marion, Jean Sutherland, and Pearl Rosenberg. "Racial Attitudes of Children," *Sociometry,* 13 (1950), 154–171.

Rainwater, Lee. "Crucible of Identity: The Negro Lower Class Family," *Daedalus,* Winter 1966, pp. 172–216.

Reiss, Albert J., Otis Dudley Duncan, Paul K. Hatt, and Cecil C. North. *Occupations and Social Status.* New York: Free Press, 1961.

Report of the National Advisory Commission on Civil Disorders. New York: Dutton and Co., 1968.

Rohrer, John, and Munro Edmundson. *The Eighth Generation Grows Up.* New York: Harper Torchbooks, 1964.

Rosner, Joseph. "When White Children Are in the Minority," *Journal of Educational Sociology,* 28 (October 1954), 69–72.

Schultz, David. *Coming up Black.* Englewood Cliffs, N.J.: Prentice-Hall, 1969.

Schwartz, Mildred. *Trends in White Attitudes toward Negroes.* Chicago: National Opinion Research Center, 1967.

Simpson, George, and Milton Yinger. *Racial and Cultural Minorities.* New York: Harper Brothers, 1958.

Smith, Lillian, *Killers of the Dream.* Garden City, N.Y.: Anchor Books, 1963.

Springer, Doris. "Awareness of Racial Differences by Preschool Children in Hawaii," *Genetic Psychology Monographs,* 41 (1950), 215–270.

Stevenson, Harold, and Edward Stewart. "A Developmental Study of Racial Awareness in Children," *Child Development,* 29 (September 1958), 399–409.

———— and Nancy R. Stevenson. "Social Interaction in an Interracial Nursery School," *Genetic Psychology Monographs,* 61 (1960), 37–75.

Stonequist, Everett. *The Marginal Man.* New York: Charles Scribner's Sons, 1937.

Teele, James, Ellen Jackson, and Clara Mayo. *Family Experiences in Operation Exodus: The Bussing of Negro Children.* Community Mental Health Journal

Monograph no. 3. New York: Behavioral Publications, 1967.

Tocqueville, Alexis de. *American Institutions and Their Influence.* New York: Barnes and Company, 1851.

Thomas, W. I. "The Psychology of Race Prejudice," *American Journal of Sociology,* 9 (March 1904), 593–611.

Thompson, Jane. "The Ability of Children of Different Grade Levels to Generalize on Sorting Tests," *Journal of Psychology,* 11 (1941), 119–126.

Trager, Helen, and Marion Radke. "Children's Perception of Social Roles of Negroes and Whites," *Journal of Psychology,* 29 (January 1950), 3–33.

―――― Marion Radke, and Hadassah Davis. "Social Perceptions and Attitudes of Children," *Genetic Psychology Monographs,* 40 (1949), 327–447.

―――― and Marion Radke Yarrow. *They Learn What They Live.* New York: Harper Brothers, 1952.

Trends in Social and Economic Conditions in Metropolitan Areas, Current Population Reports 27, February, 1969.

Trent, Richard D. "The Color of the Investigator as a Variable in Experimental Research with Negro Subjects," *Journal of Social Psychology,* 40 (1954), 281–287.

―――― "The Relation between Expressed Self-Acceptance and Expressed Attitudes towards Negroes and Whites among Negro Children," *Journal of Genetic Psychology,* 91 (1957), 25–31.

Vaughan, Graham. "Concept Formation and the Development of Ethnic Awareness," *Journal of Genetic Psychology,* 103 (1963), 93–103.

Wellman, Barry. "Social Identities in Black and White." Paper read at 19th Annual Meeting of the Society for the Study of Social Problems, San Francisco, August 1969.

Williams, Robin M. *Strangers Next Door.* Englewood Cliffs, N.J.: Prentice-Hall, 1964.

Winer, B. J. *Statistical Principles in Experimental Design.* New York: McGraw-Hill, 1962.

Wylie, Ruth. *The Self Concept.* Lincoln, Neb.: University of Nebraska Press, 1961.

Zeligs, Ruth. "Children's Intergroup Attitudes," *Journal of Genetic Psychology,* 72 (1948), 101–110.

―――― "Racial Attitudes of Children," *Sociology and Social Research,* 21 (1937), 361–371.